WILD & PRECIOUS

JESSE BURKE

Daylight

For Clover Lee, Poppy Dee & Honey Bee

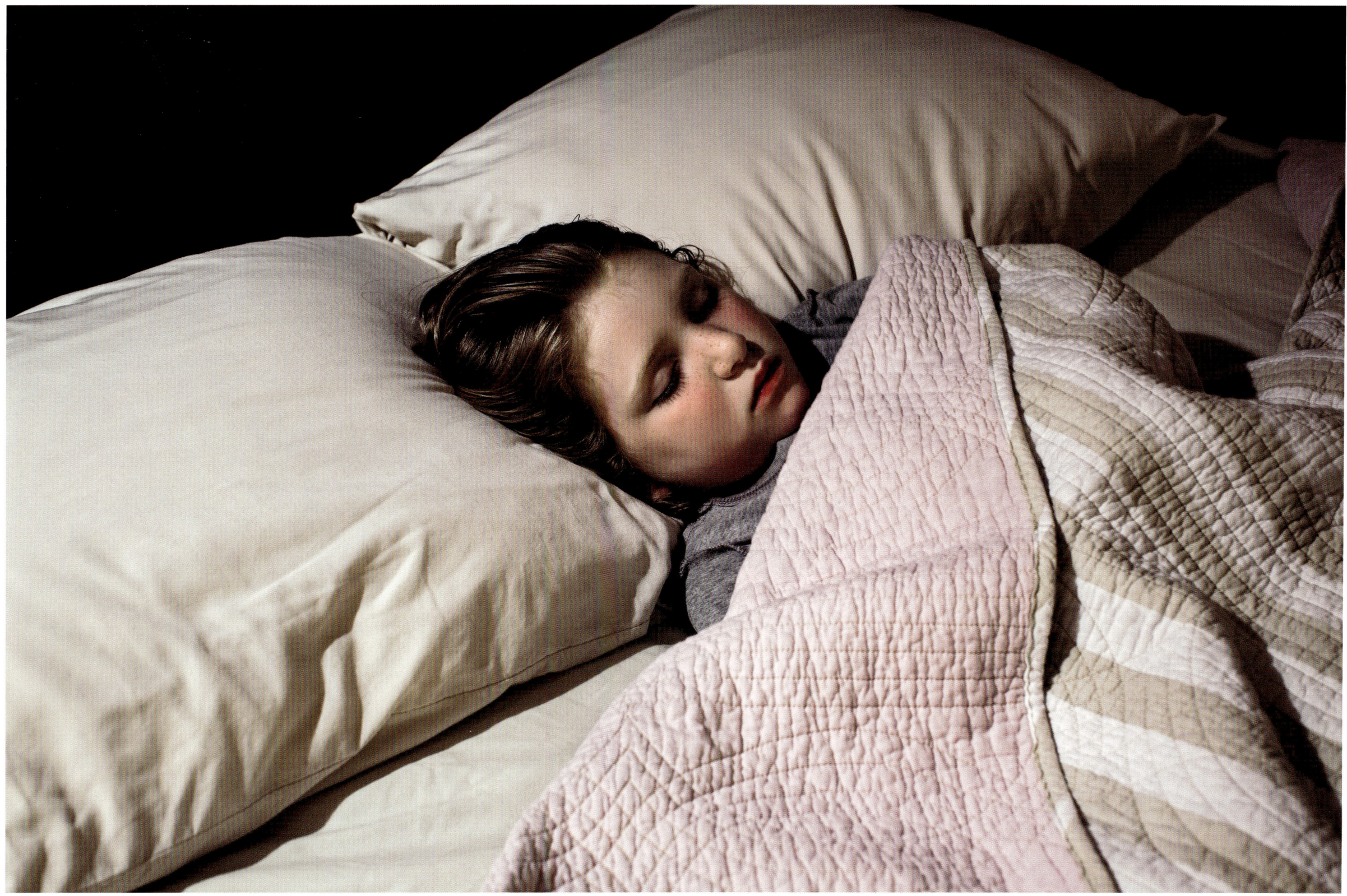

THE WOODS ARE BLANKETED IN BLACKNESS, A SUBTLE REMINDER OF HOW SMALL AND FRAGILE WE ARE. THE FIRE CRACKLES AS EMBERS FLOAT FROM THE FLAMES AND MIX WITH FIREFLIES AS THEY SPIRAL INTO THE SKY. I SIT HERE LISTENING TO THE CRICKETS SING YOU TO SLEEP AND WONDER IF YOU'RE DREAMING OF SALAMANDERS OR SUNSETS. WE'VE BEEN ROAMING ALL DAY AND LONG INTO THE NIGHT, OUT IN THE FERAL WOODS. WE COLLECTED MICA FLAKES ON THE SUMMIT OF MOUNT WASHINGTON AND WATCHED THE YELLOW-BELLIED SAPSUCKERS DRILL SHALLOW ROWS OF SAPWELLS. YOU ARE TIRED AND DIRTY, YET RADIANT. MY HEART SWELLS.

THERE ARE SO MANY THINGS I WANT TO TEACH YOU. I WANT YOU TO KNOW WHICH LEAVES BELONG TO WHICH TREES, WHAT THE BUMPS OF A TOAD FEEL LIKE, THE SWEET SMELL AND TASTE OF WILD HONEYSUCKLES. I WANT YOU TO TRUST THE NIGHT AIR, TO NOT BE AFRAID OF SPIDERS, TO KNOW THINGS THAT I DON'T, THINGS I WAS NEVER TAUGHT. I WANT YOU TO FEEL AT HOME IN THE WILD.

MY MIND IS FULL OF MOVING IMAGES: YOU RUNNING DOWN TO THE SEA AS THE GULLS LAUGH OVERHEAD, YOU COLLECTING SPINDLY STRIPS OF BIRCH BARK AND DOWNY STRIPED TURKEY FEATHERS, YOU AND ME QUIETLY BRUSHING OUR TEETH ALONGSIDE ONE ANOTHER BENEATH THE HUM OF THE GREEN FLUORESCENT LIGHT IN OUR MOTEL BATHROOM, YOU DUCKING IN AND OUT OF THE MASSIVE DRIFT LOGS AS SUNBEAMS CUT THROUGH THE DENSE FOG BEHIND YOU, AND YOU IN THE BACKSEAT WITH YOUR CHIN UP AND EYES TIGHTLY CLOSED, SINGING ALONG TO JOHNNY CASH WHILE THE MOUNTAIN WIND RIPS THROUGH YOUR HAIR.

EACH DAY IS A NEW ADVENTURE THAT WE ENTER AS IF UPON A STAGE. EVERY DAY YOU ARE BIGGER AND BRAVER. I KNOW I CAN'T ASK YOU TO STAY SMALL, TO STAY INNOCENT. NATURE WILL RUN ITS COURSE. YOU WILL CHANGE AND GROW. YOU'LL SHED THE VELVET CLOAK OF CHILDHOOD LIKE FLOWERS IN THEIR FINAL BLOOM BEFORE THE COLD OF WINTER ARRIVES. THE METAMORPHOSIS IS BEAUTIFUL TO WATCH, BUT HEARTBREAKING. OH, SWEET CHILD, I BEG YOU TO BE WILD, BUT STAY PRECIOUS.

SLEEP WELL, MY LOVE. THE FIRE CALLS ME.

I LOVE YOU TO THE MOON AND BACK.

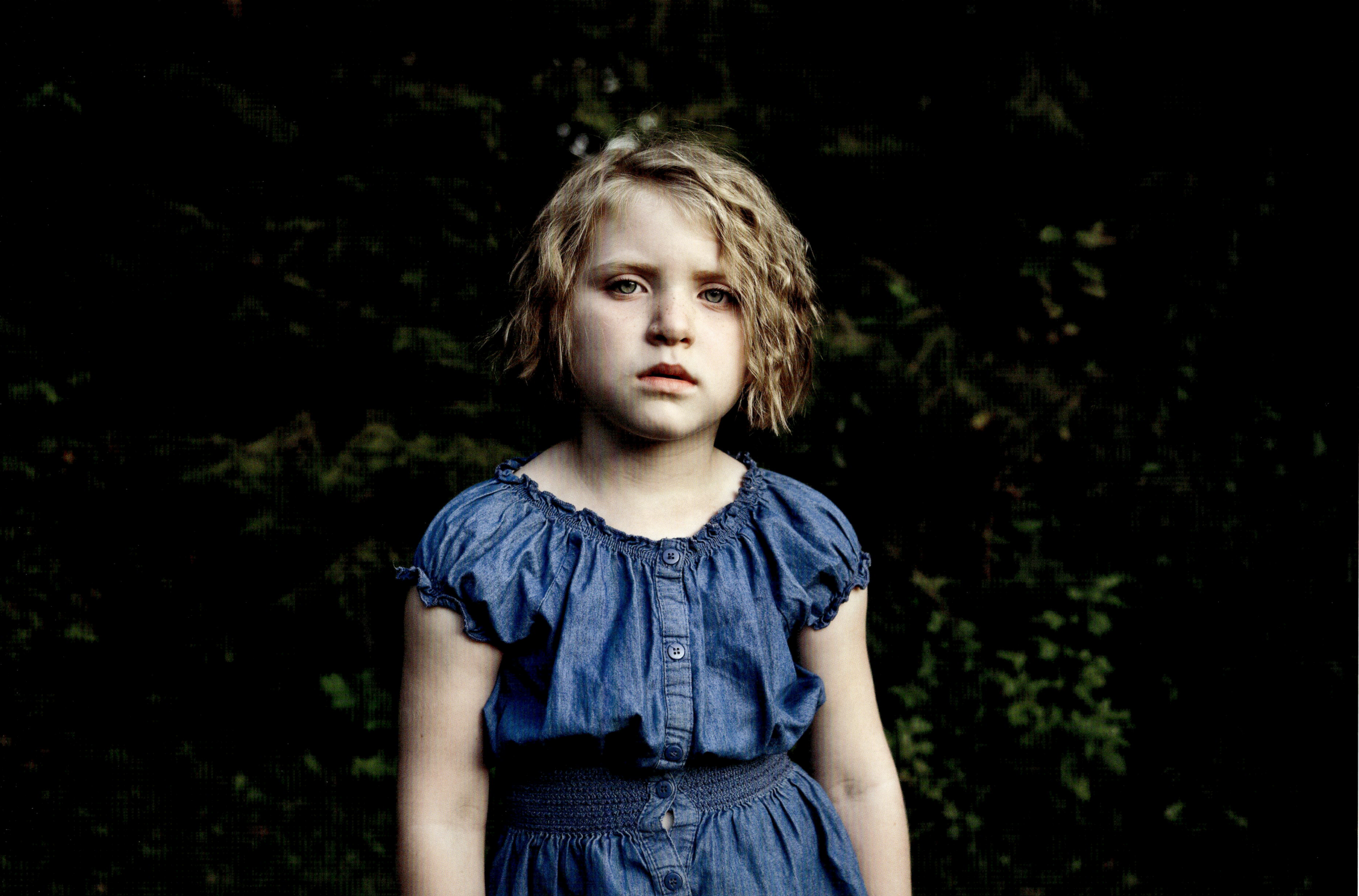

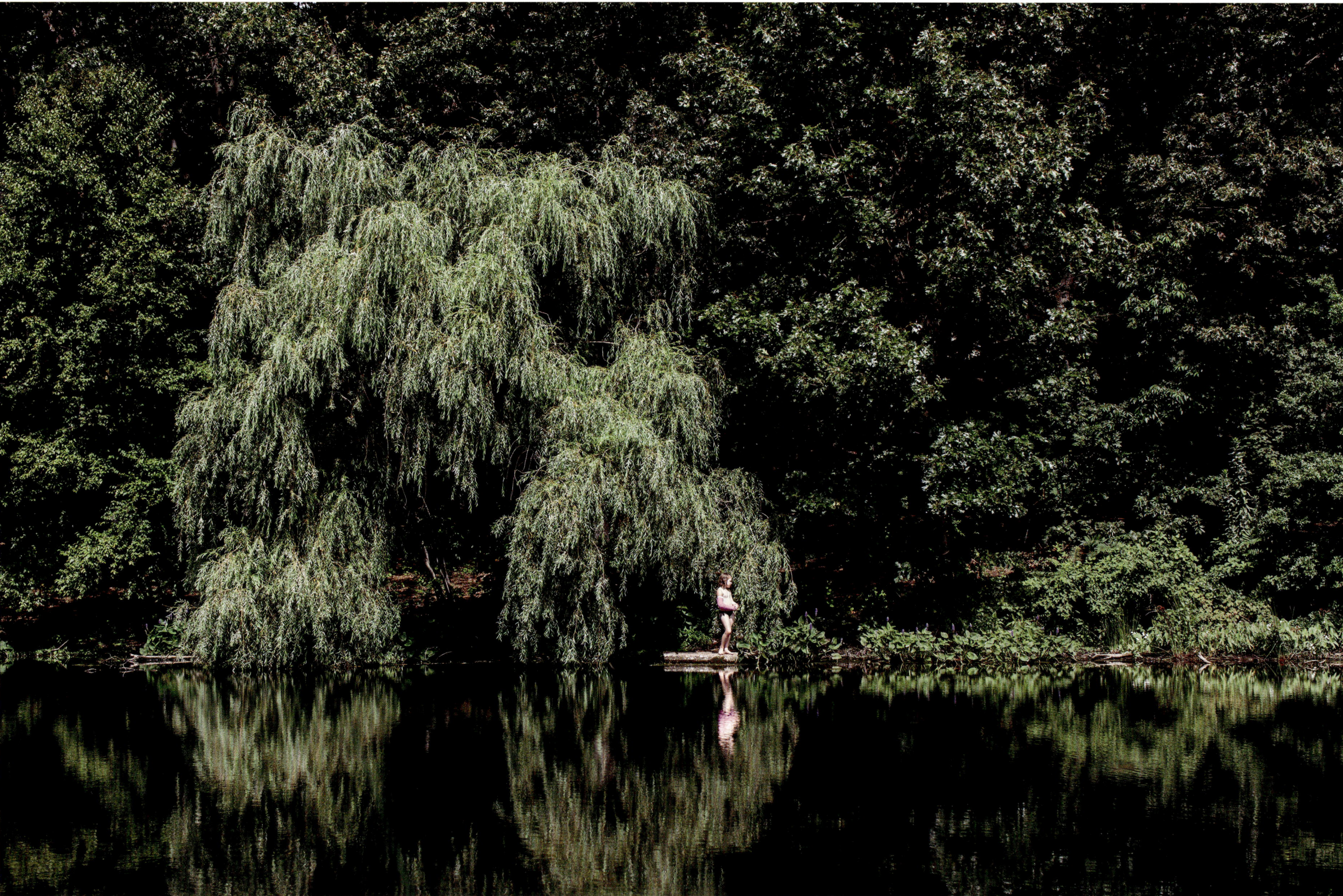

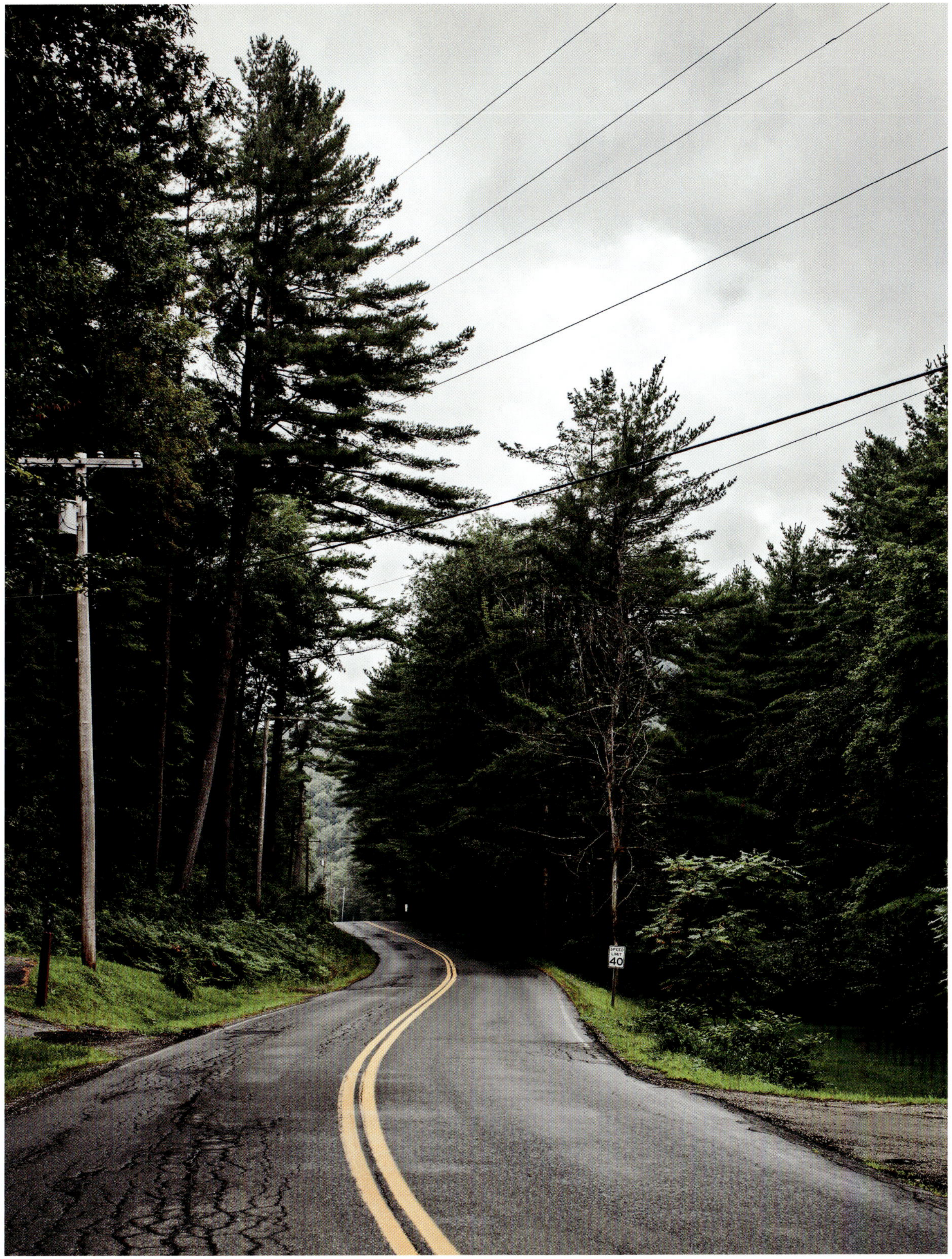

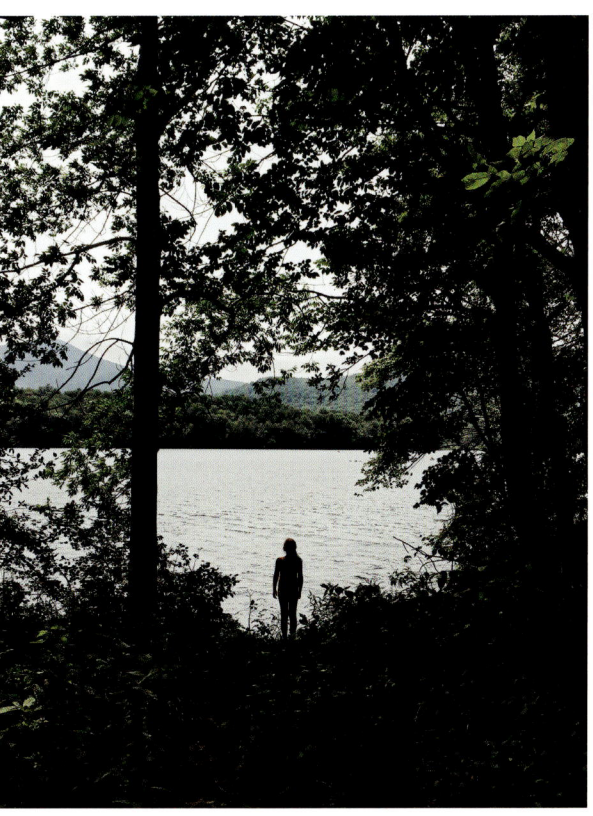

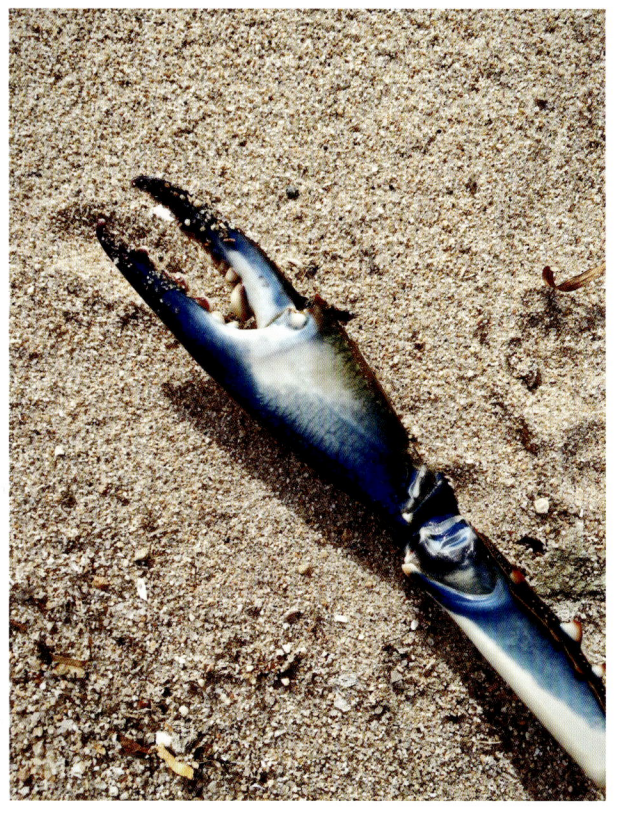
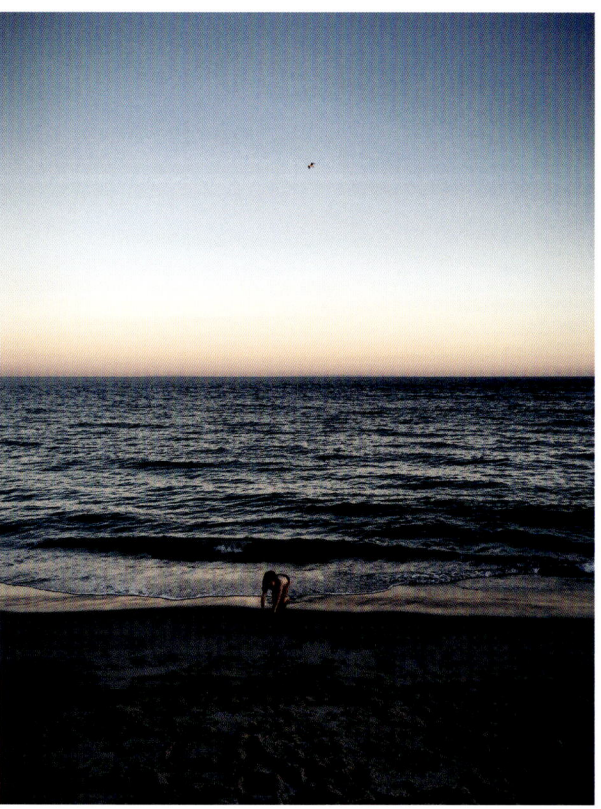

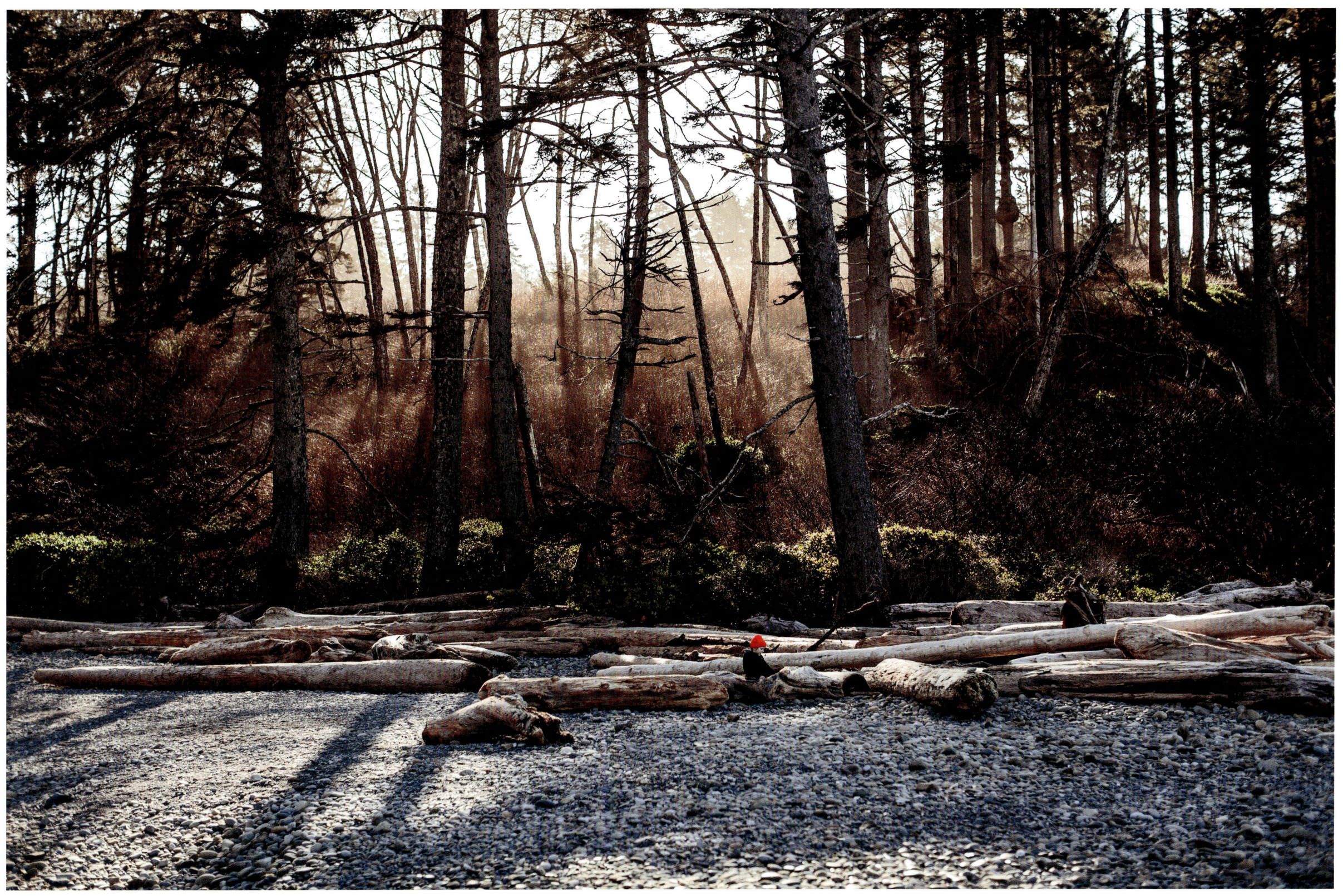

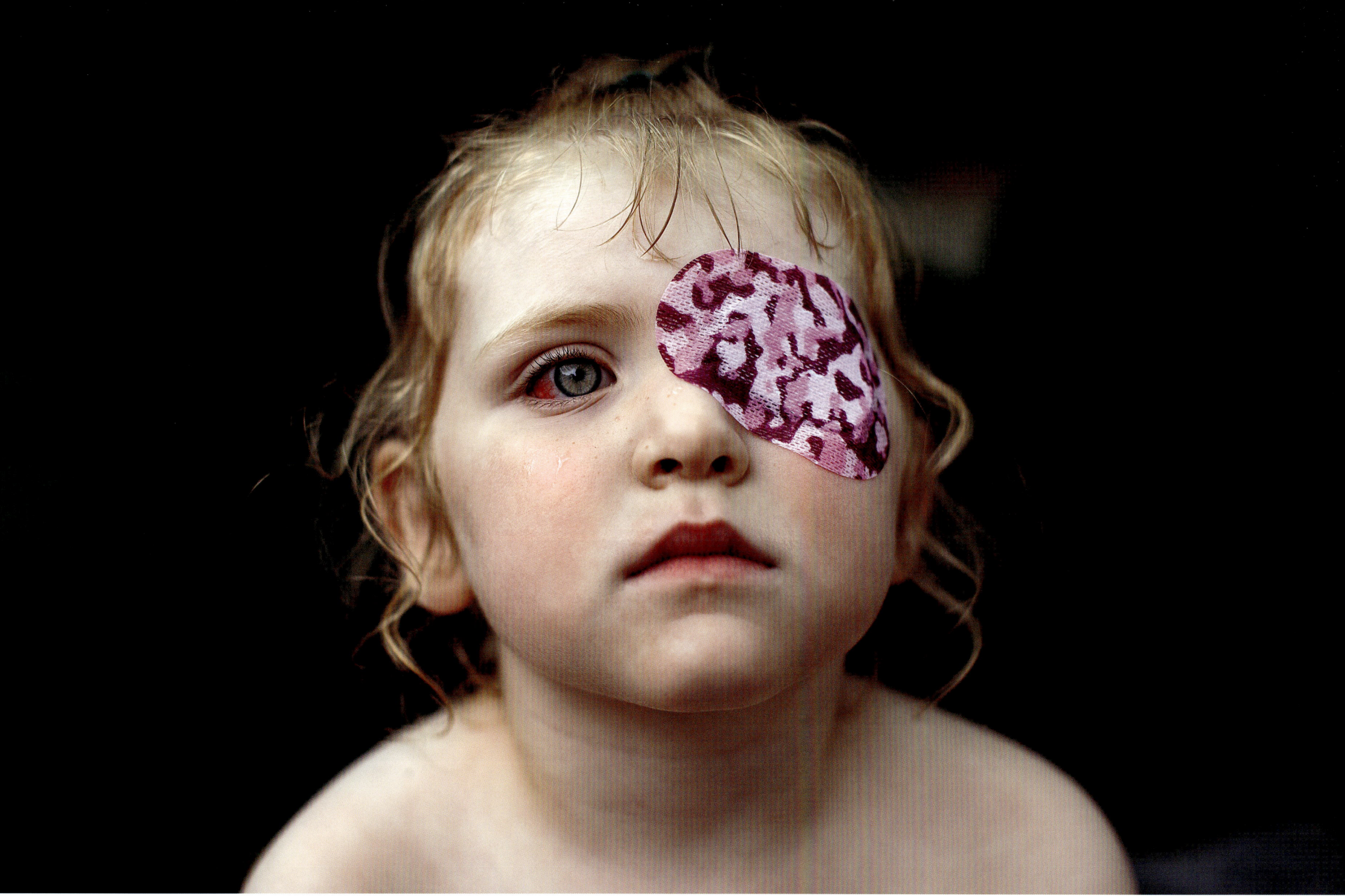

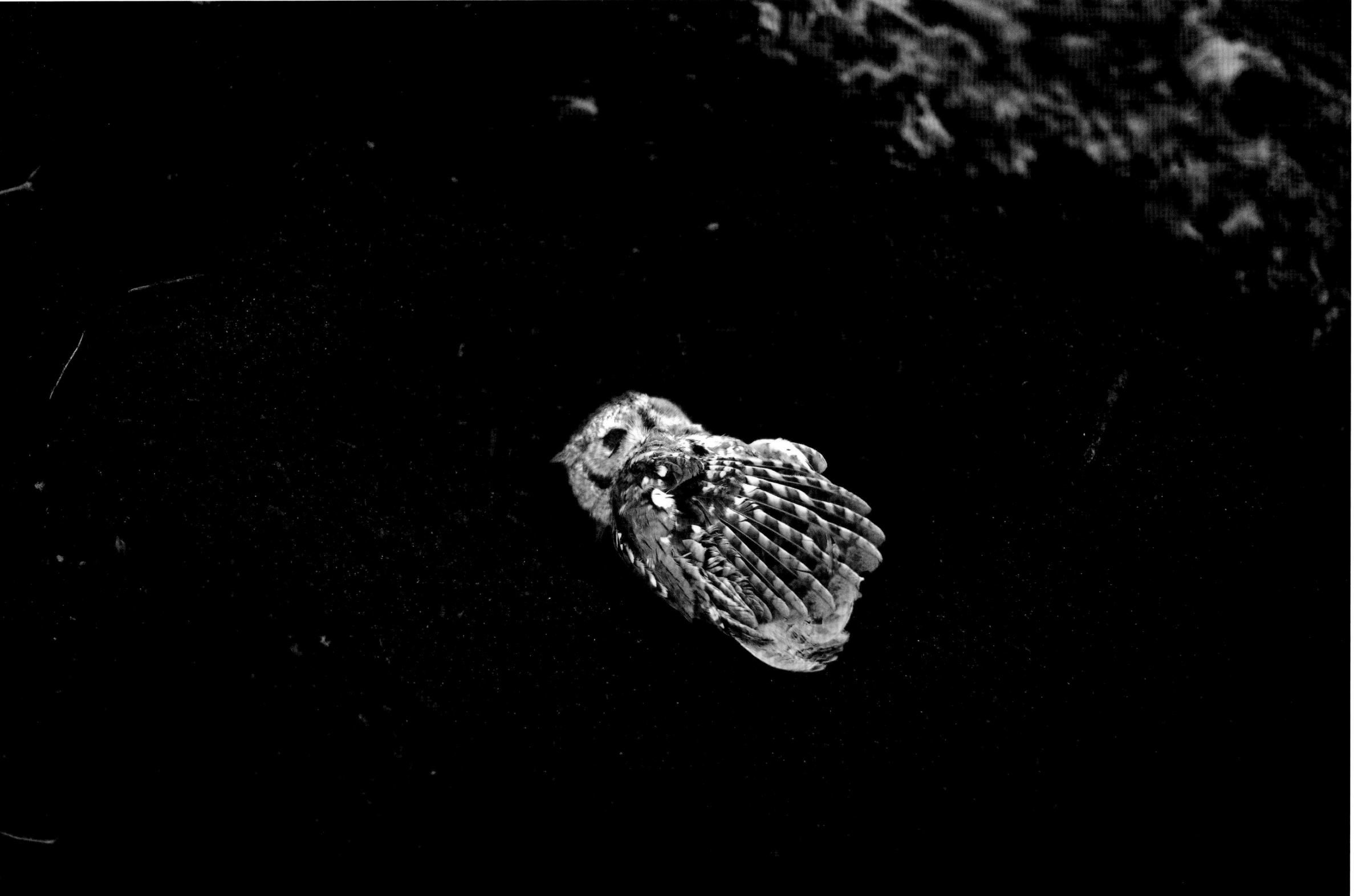

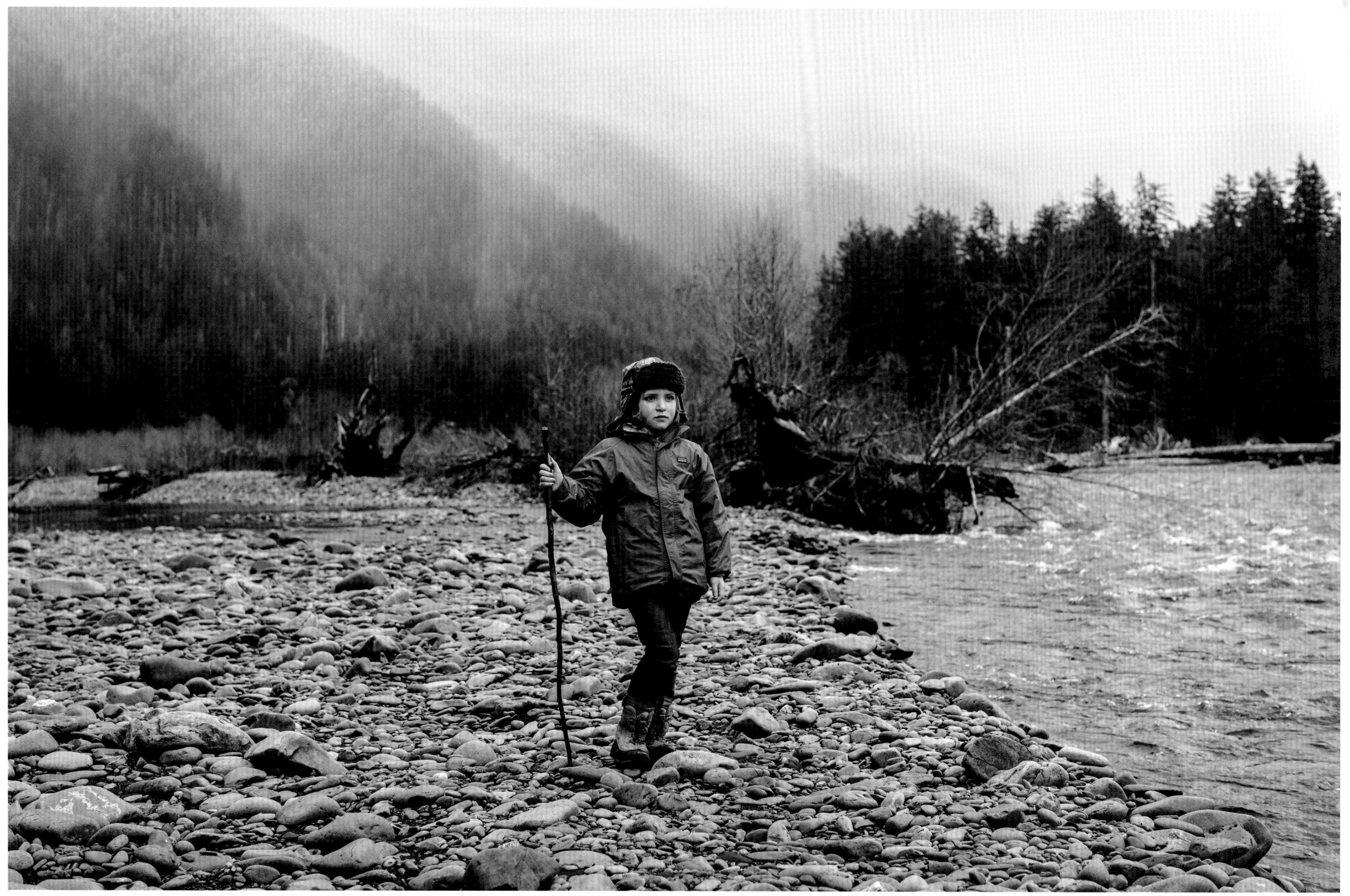

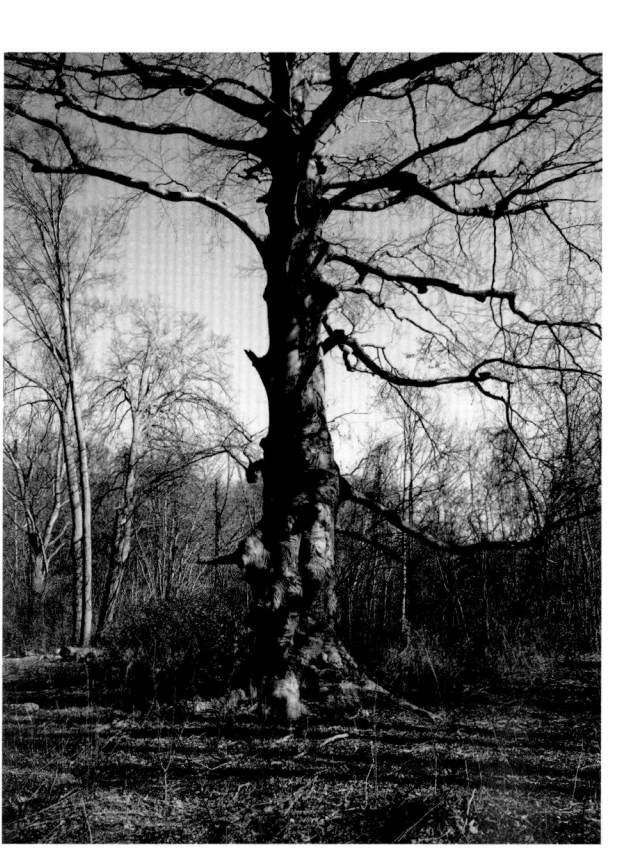

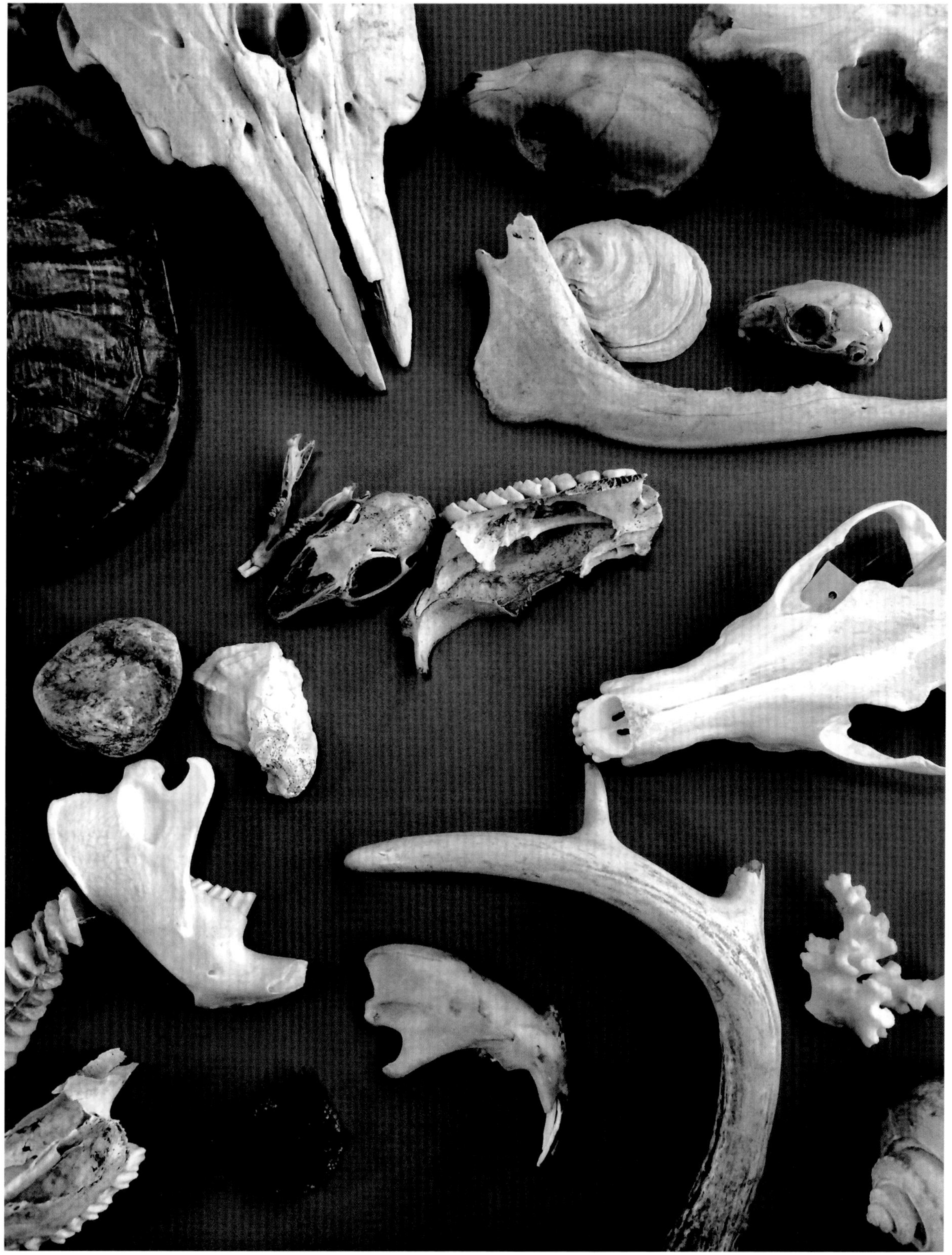

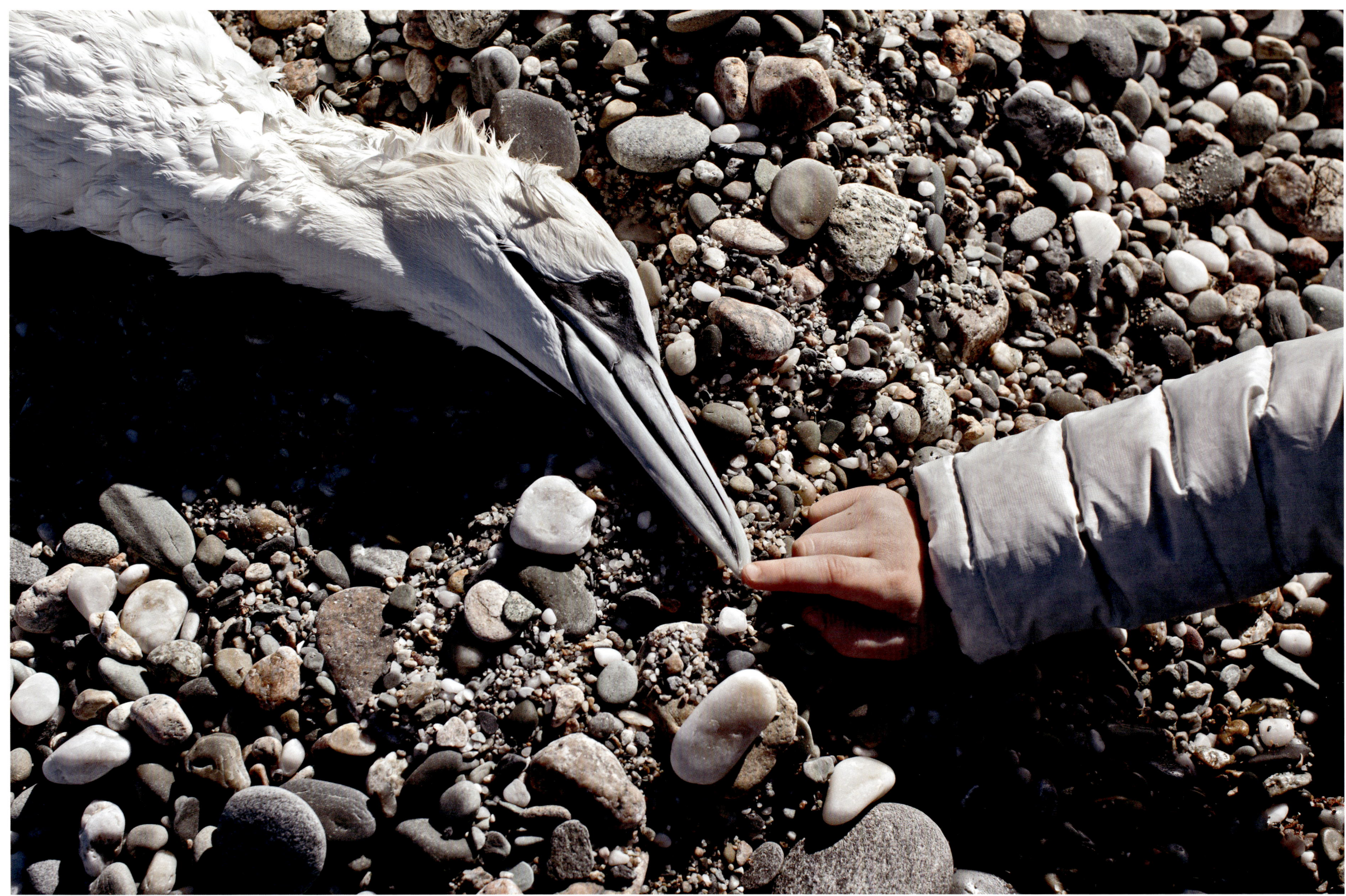

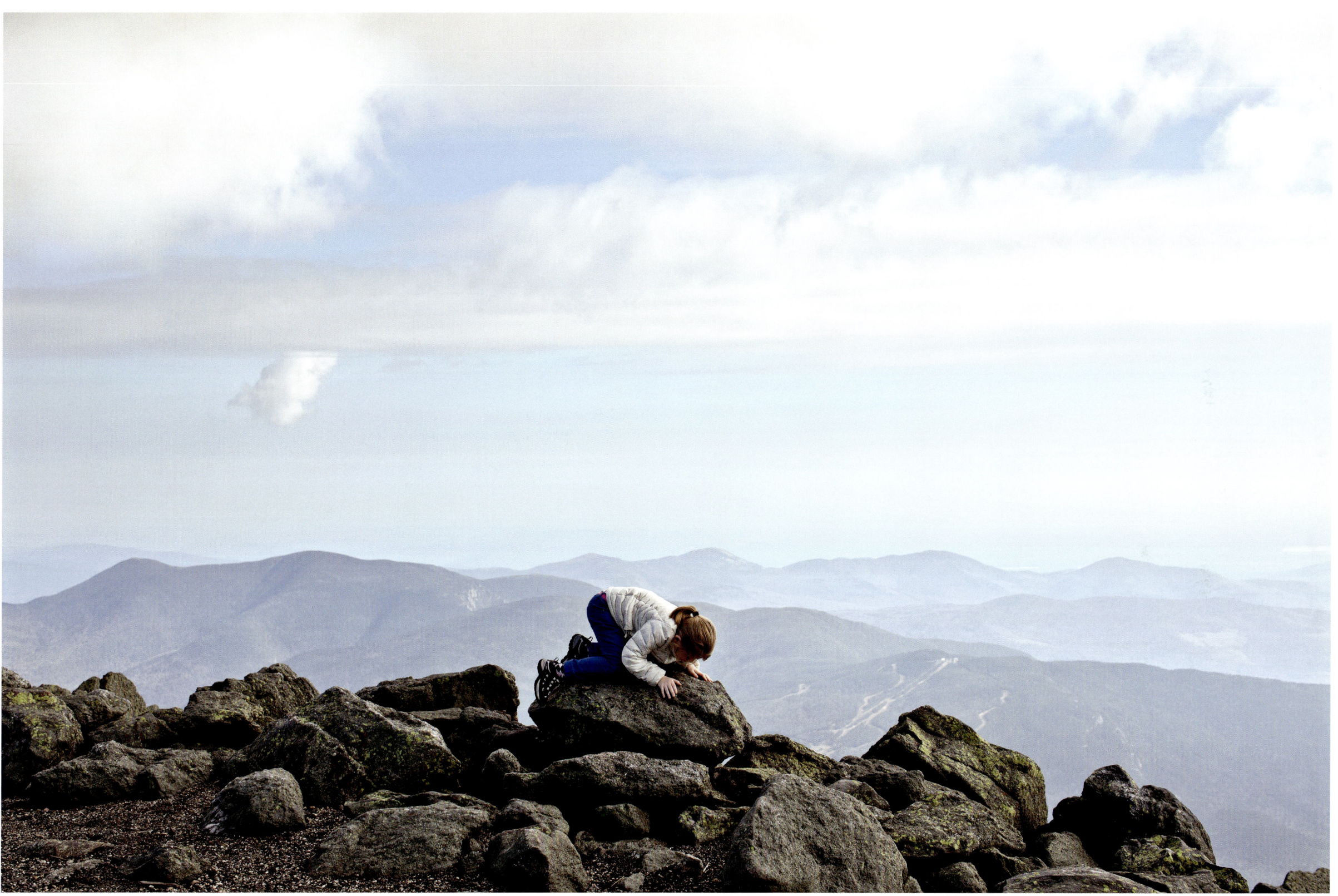

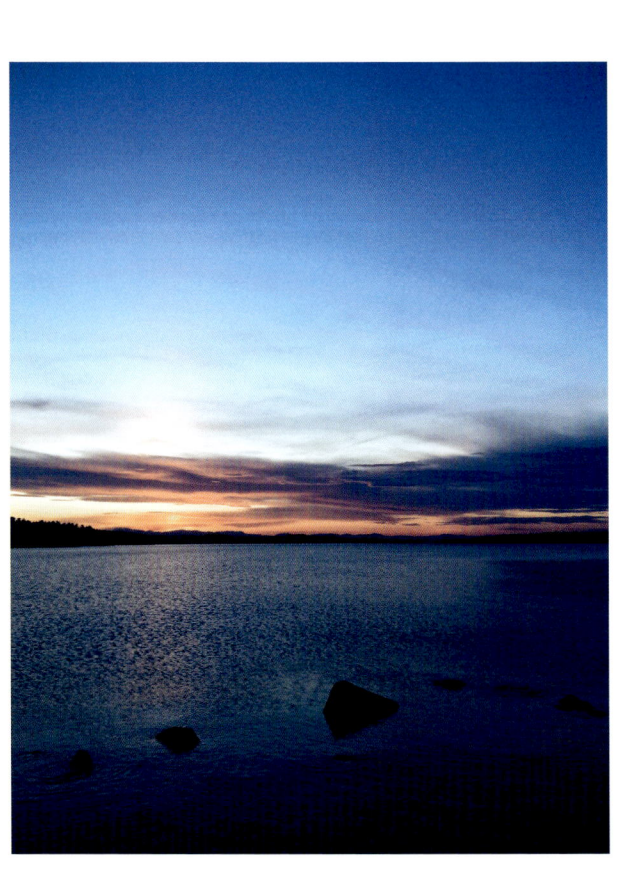

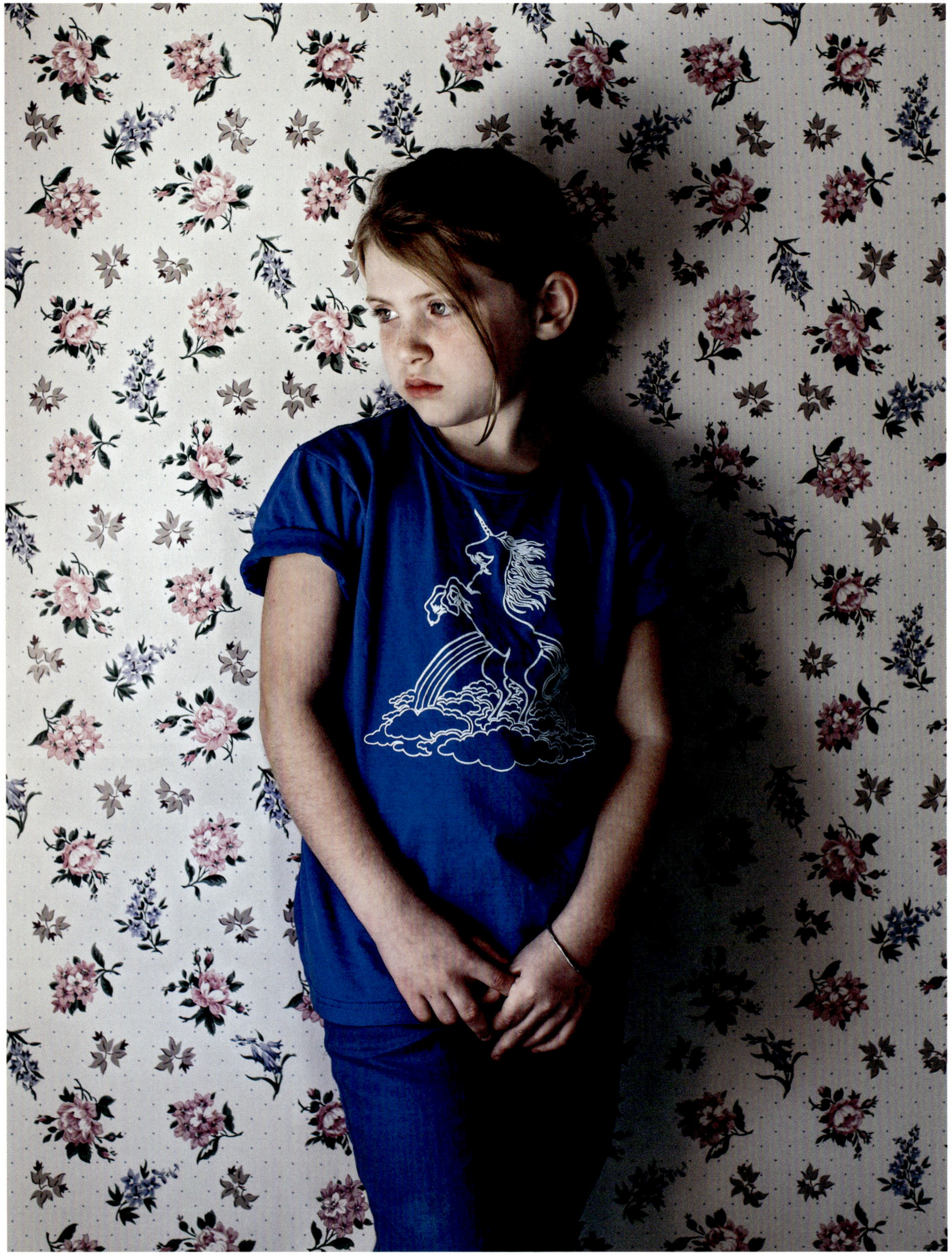

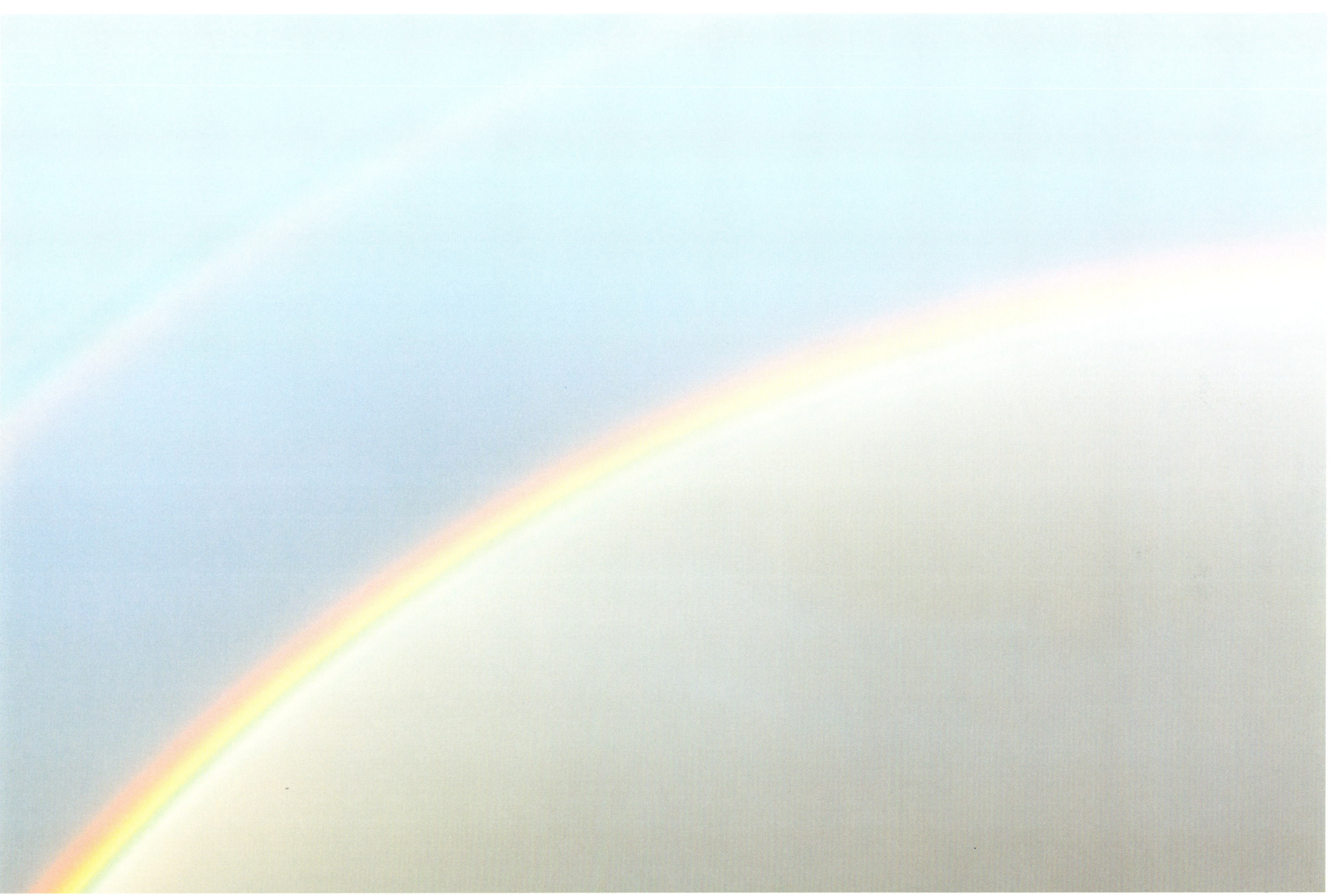

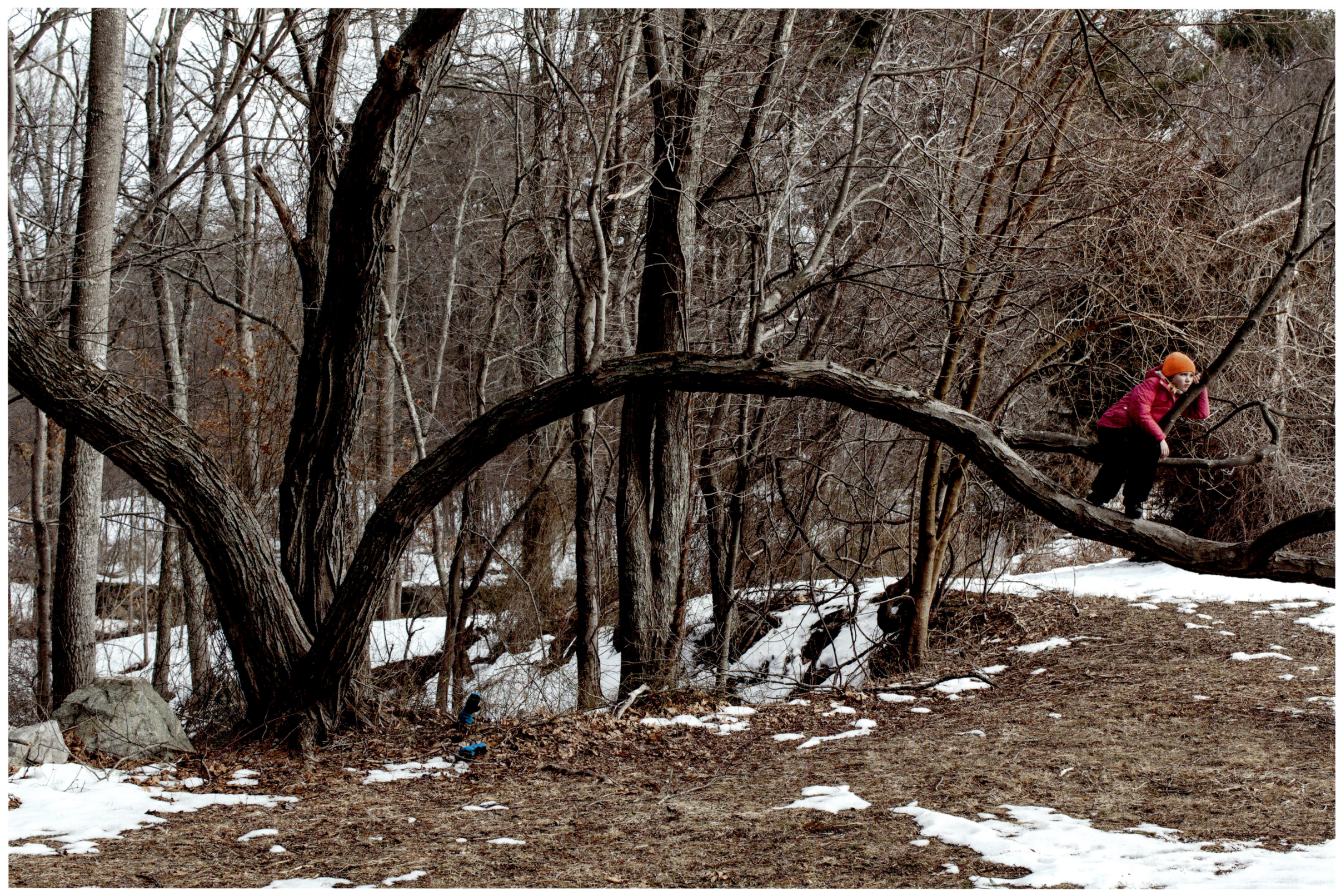

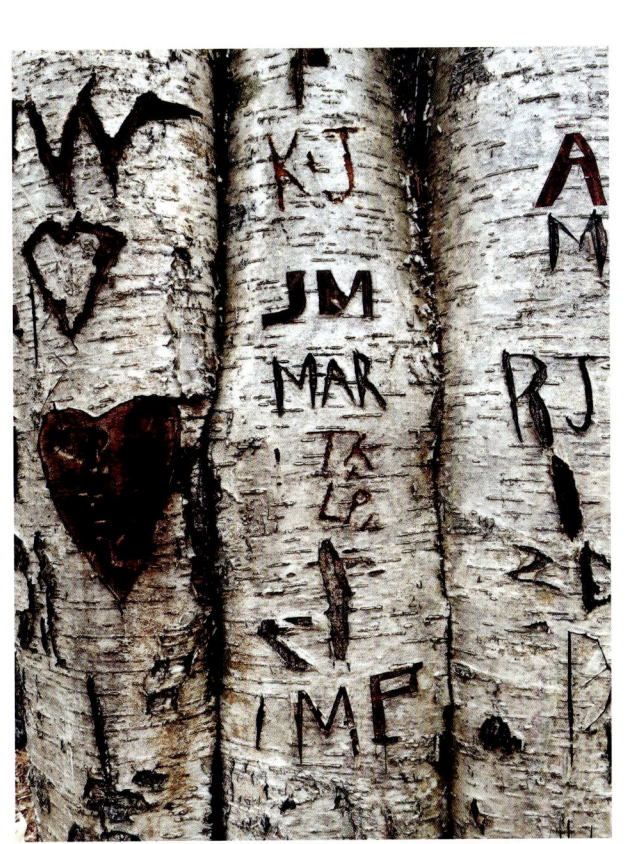

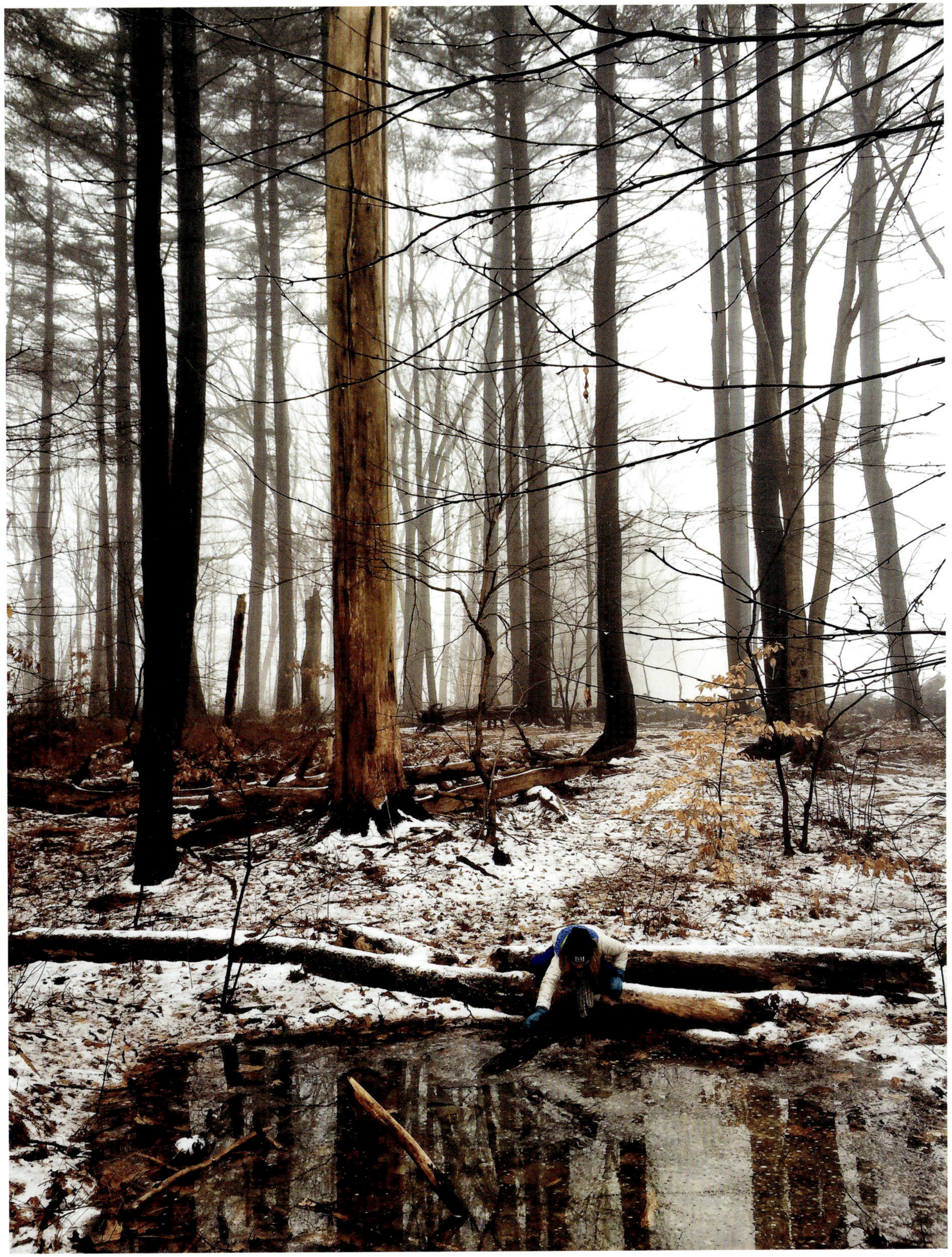

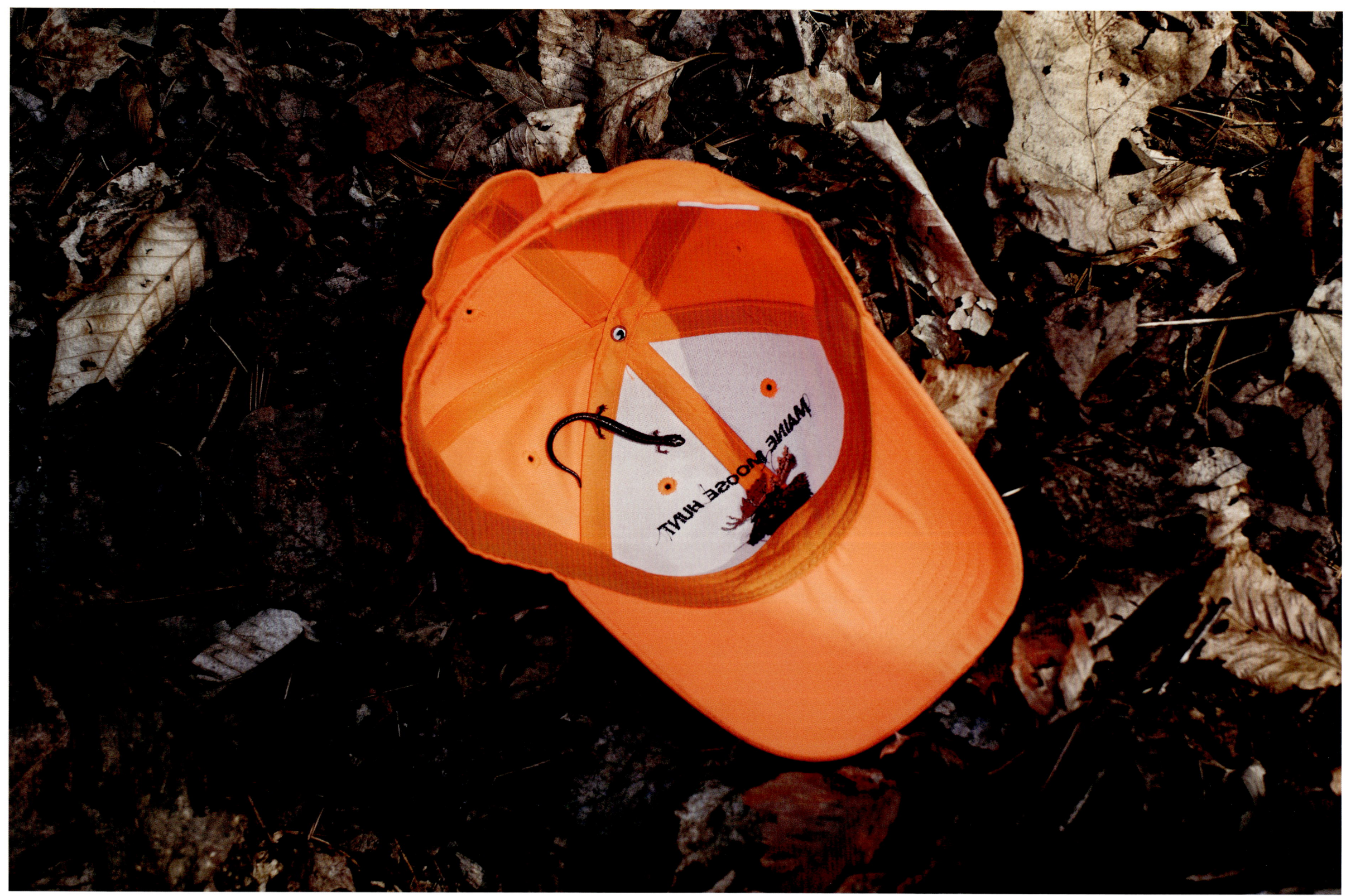

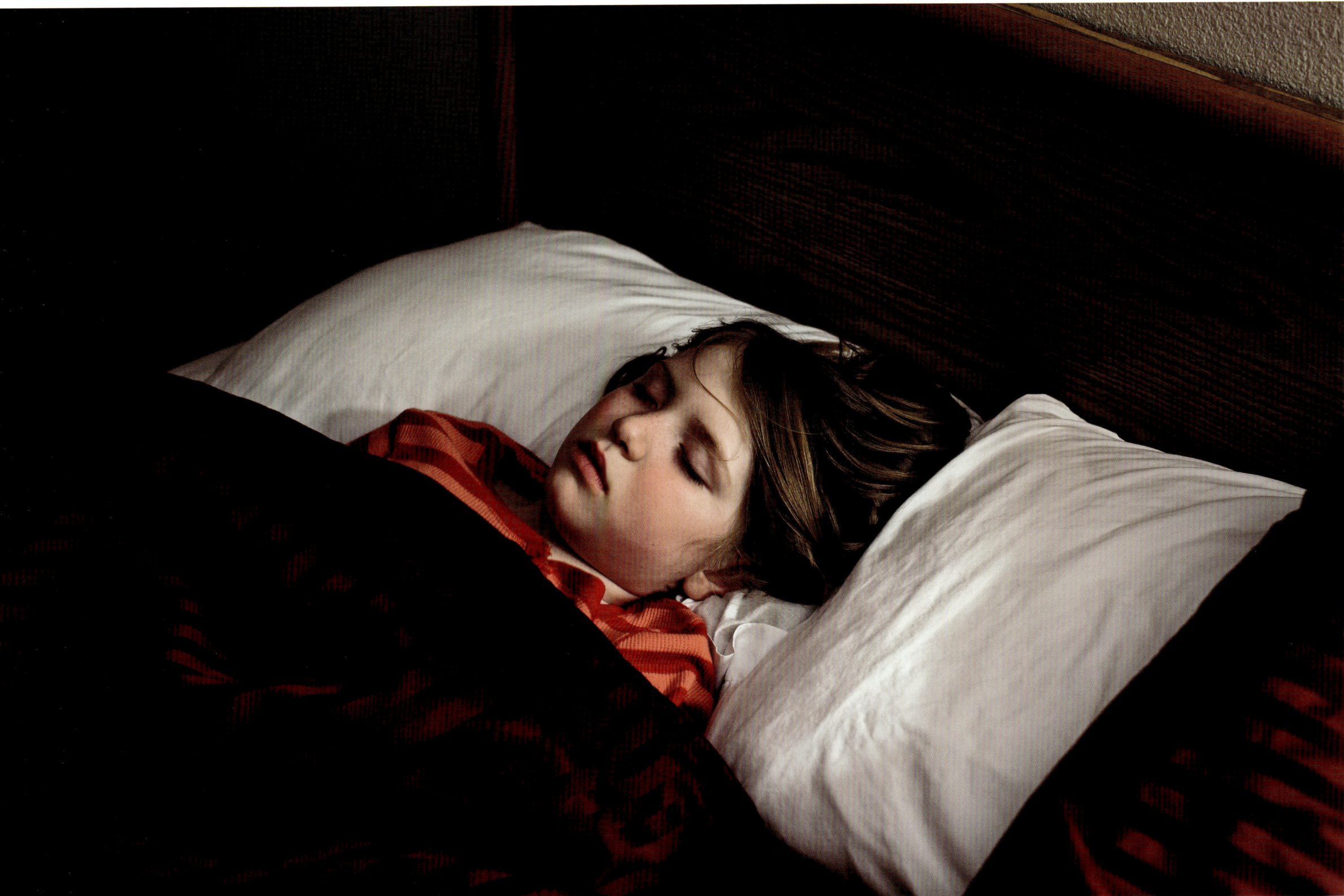

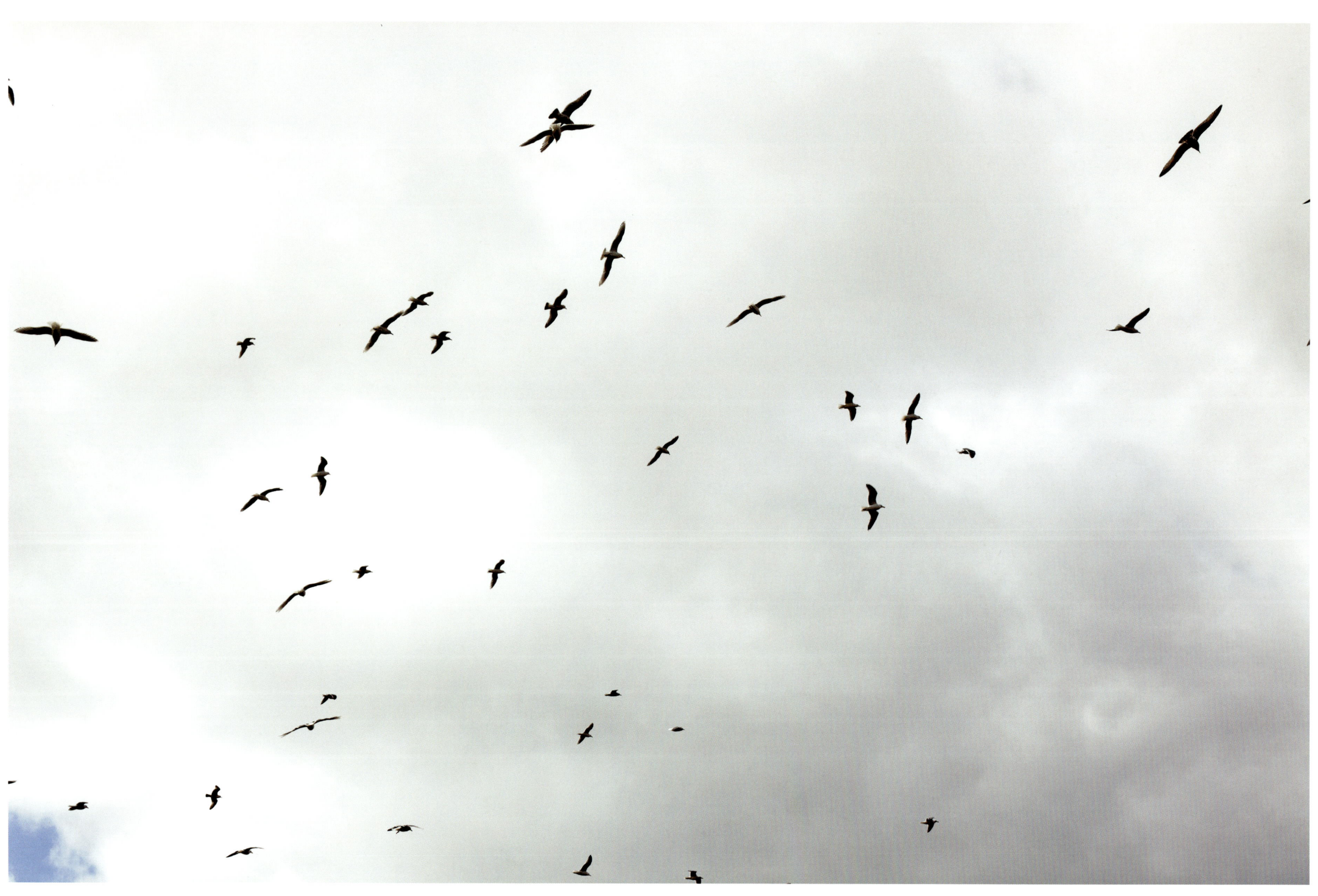

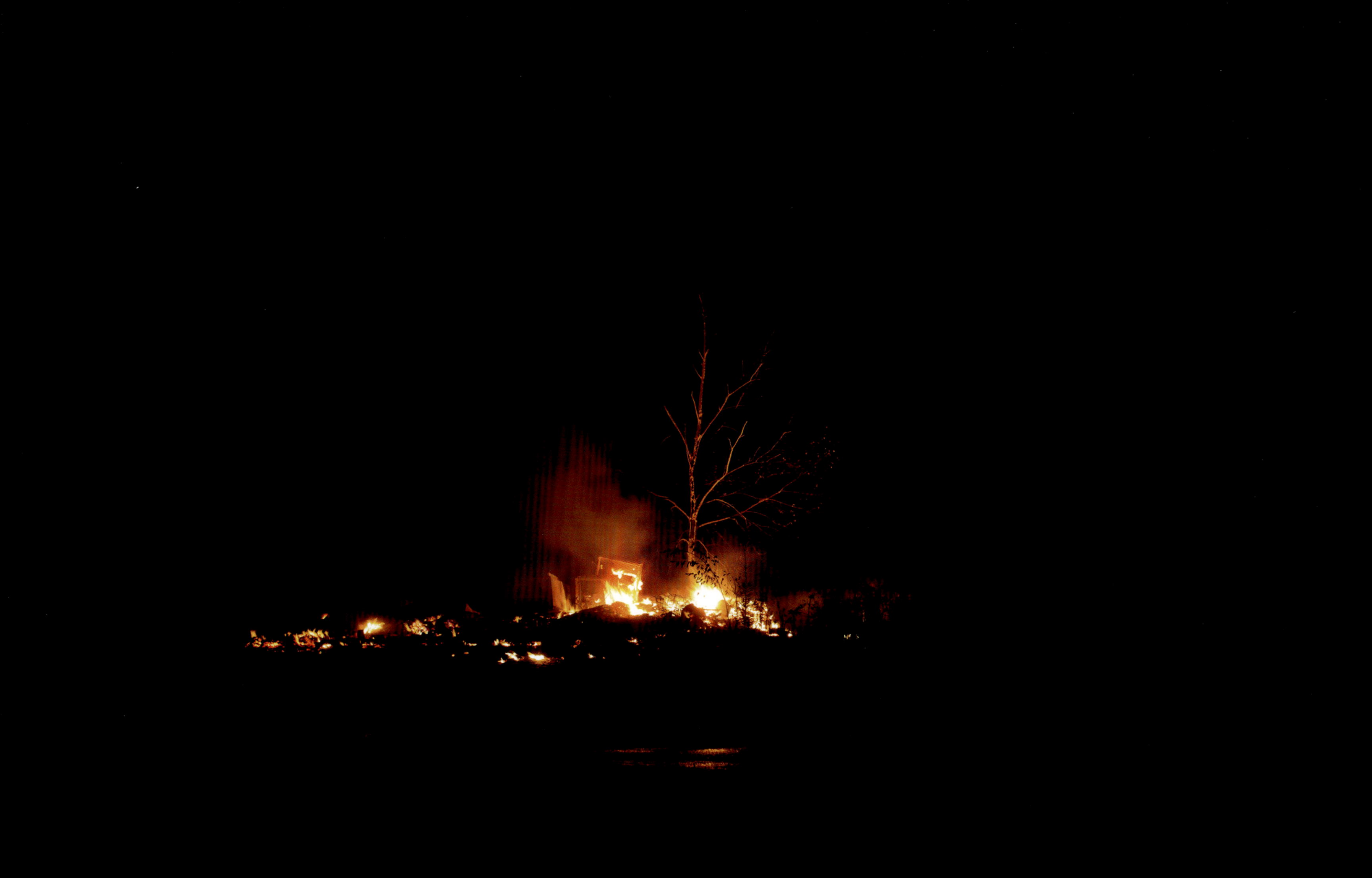

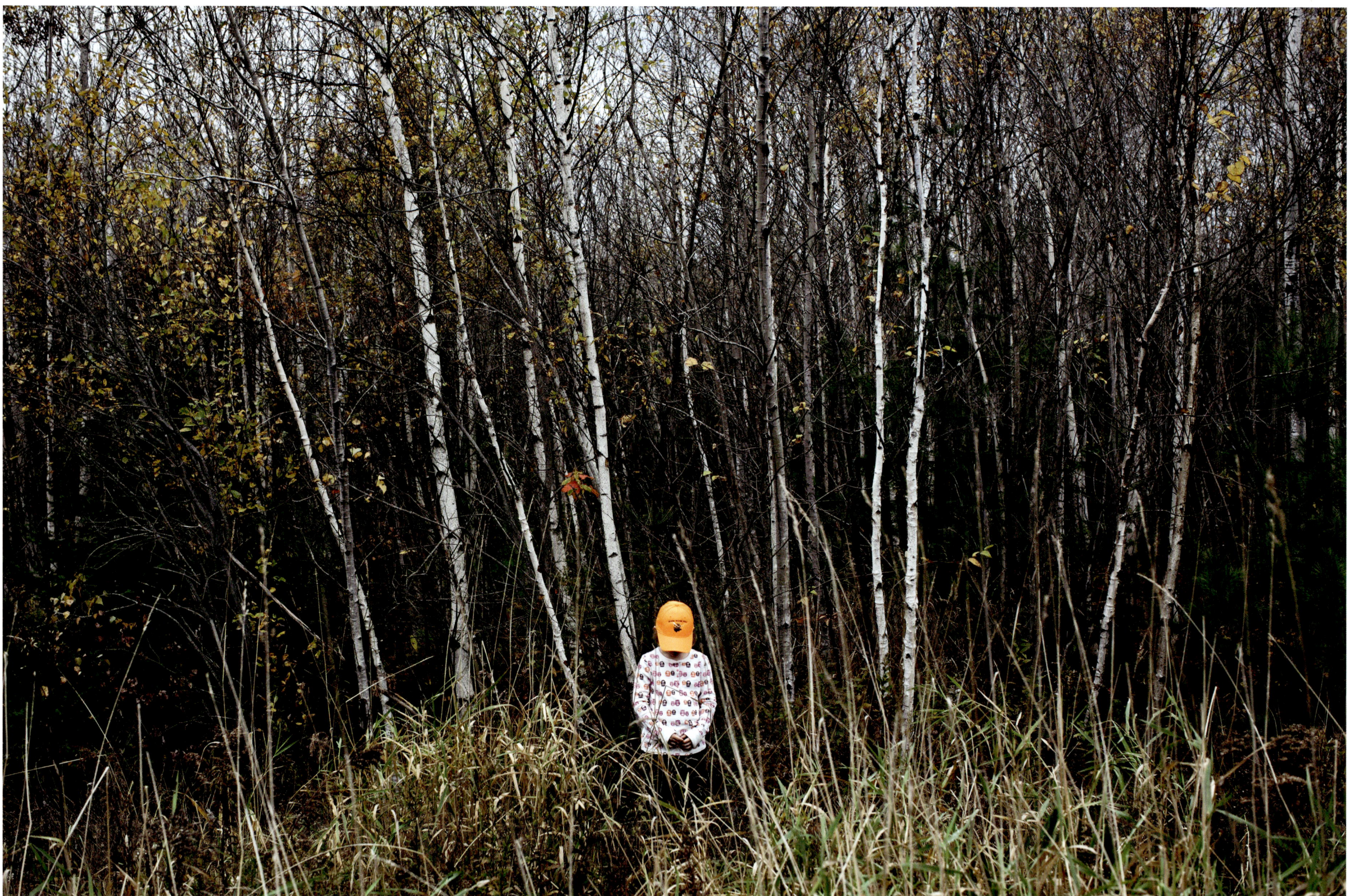

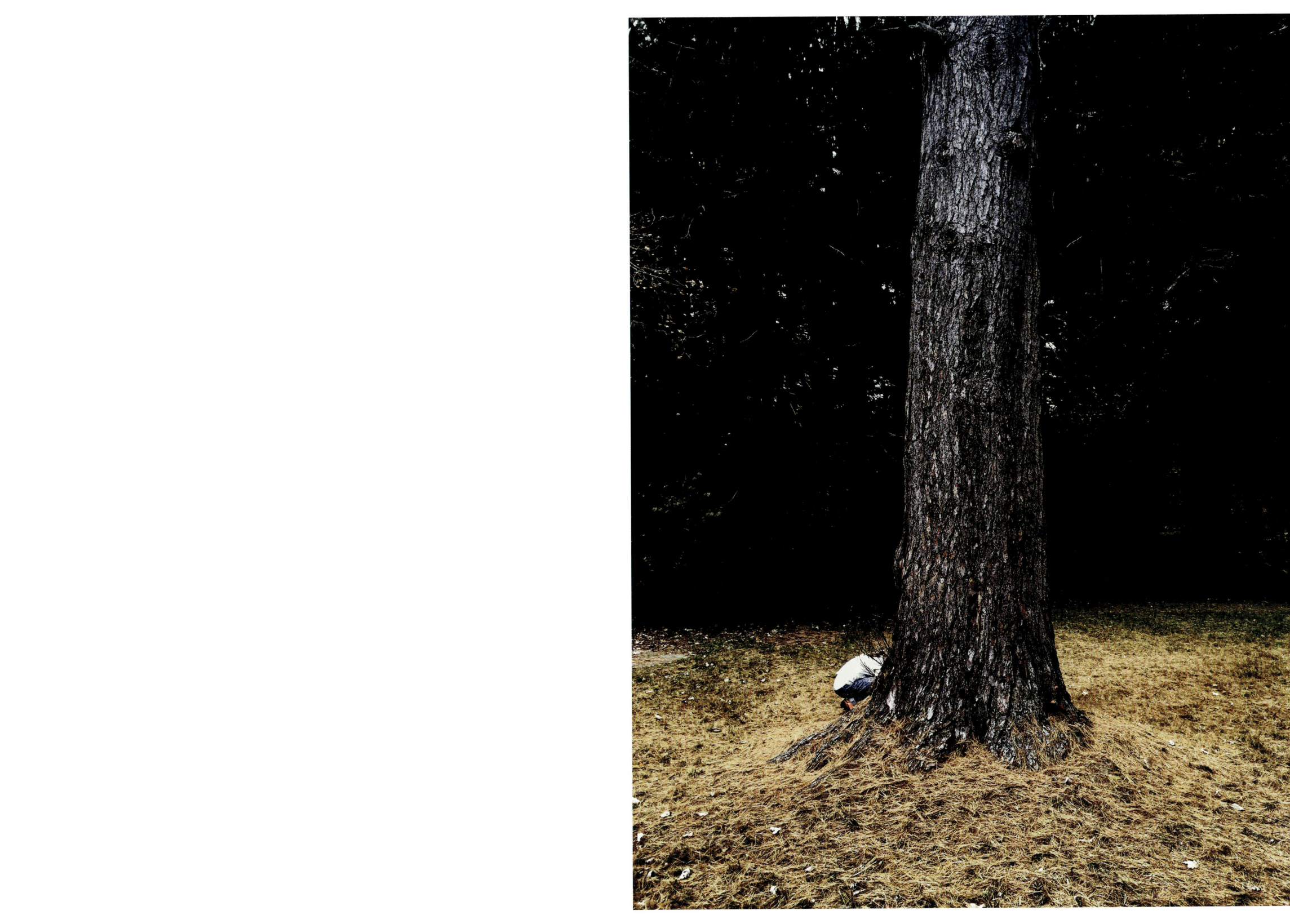

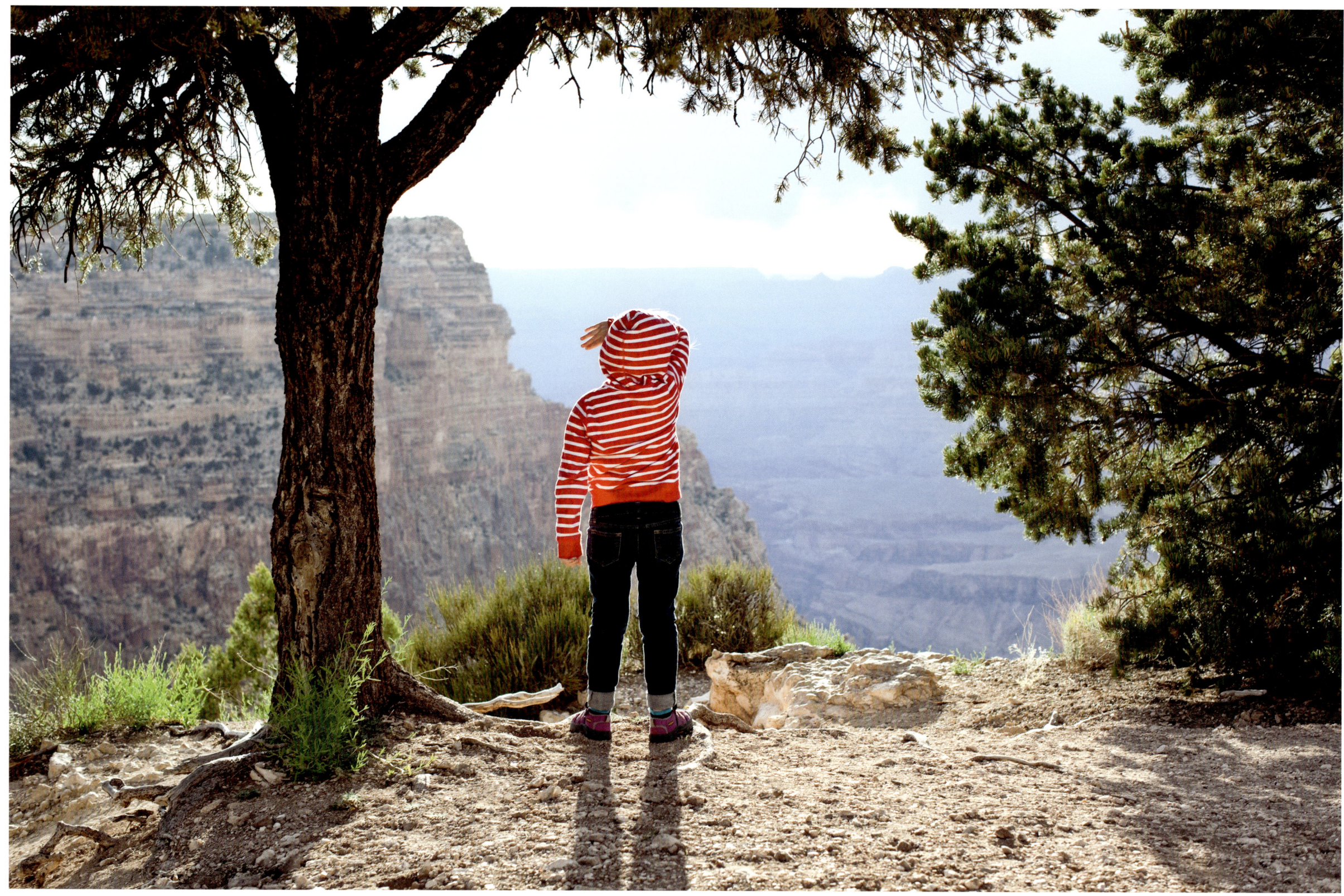

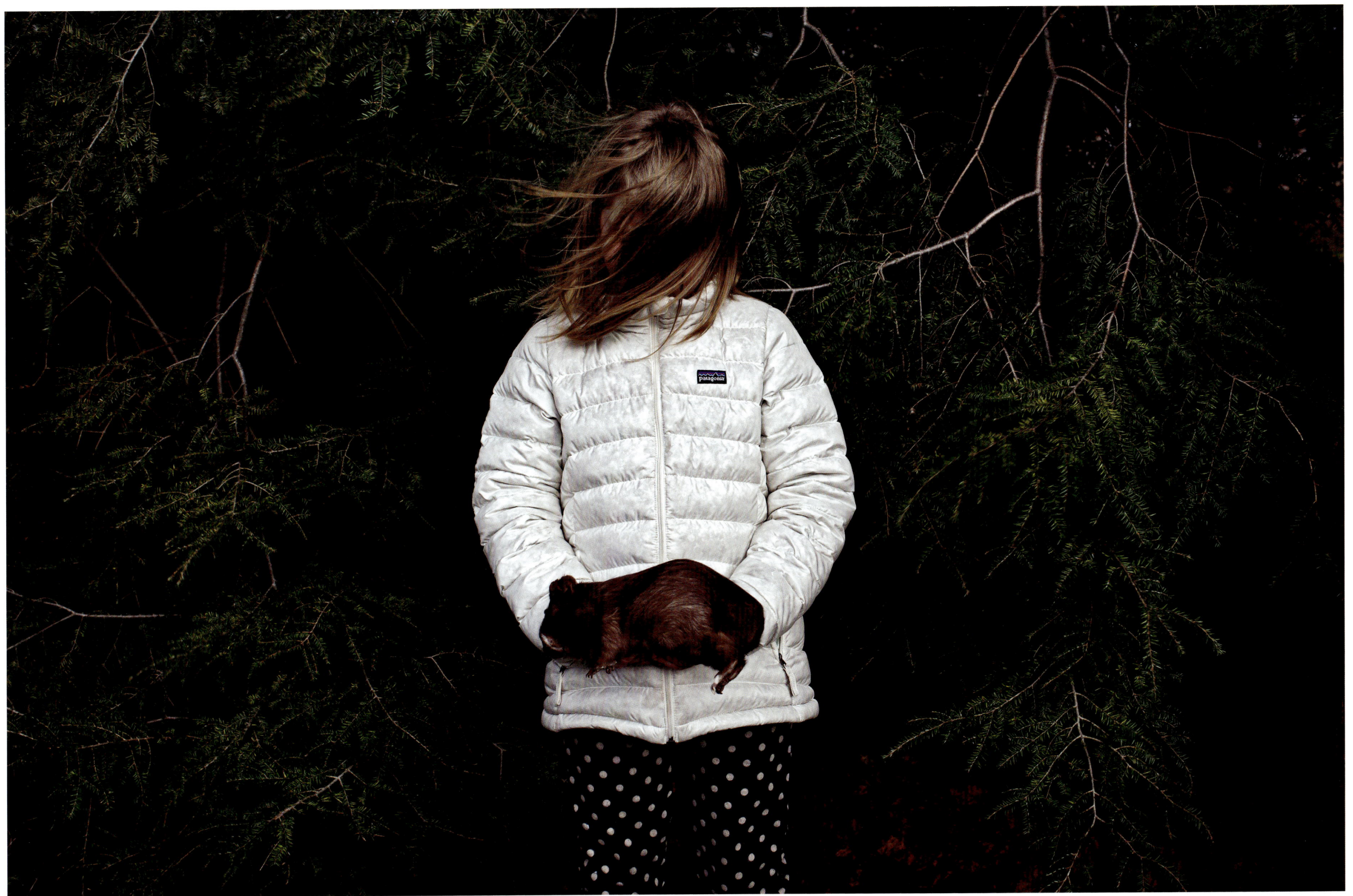

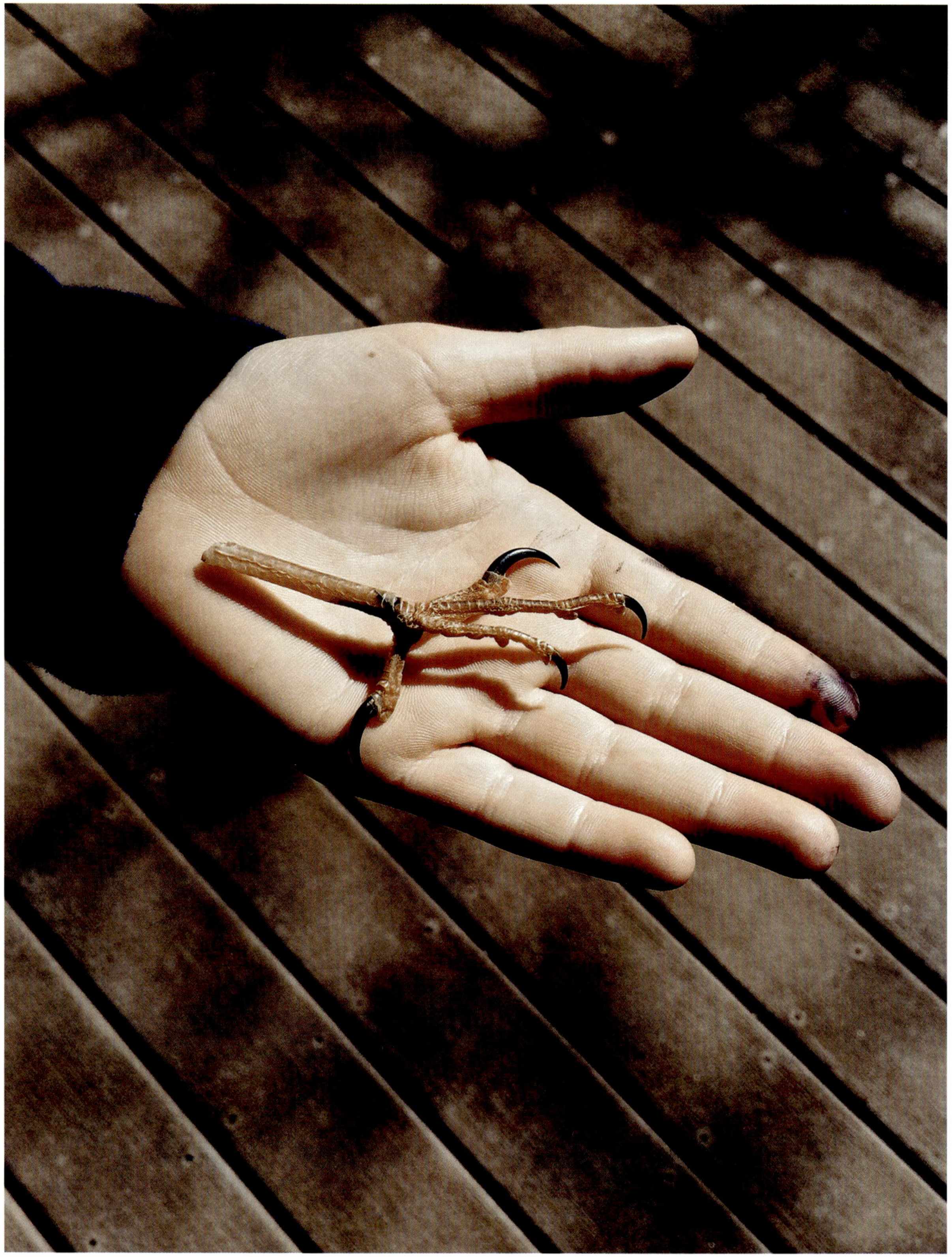

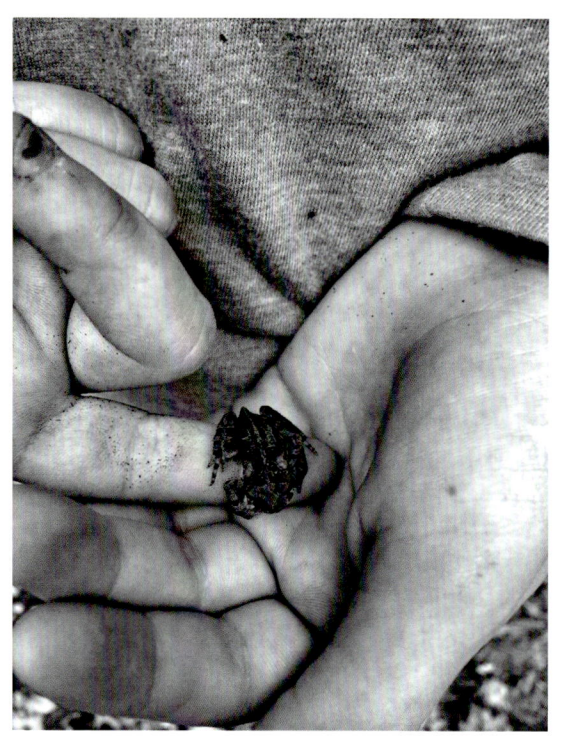
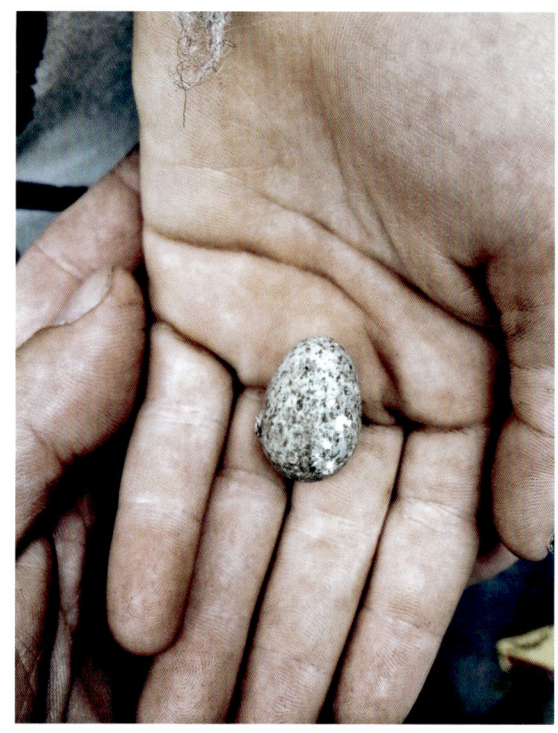

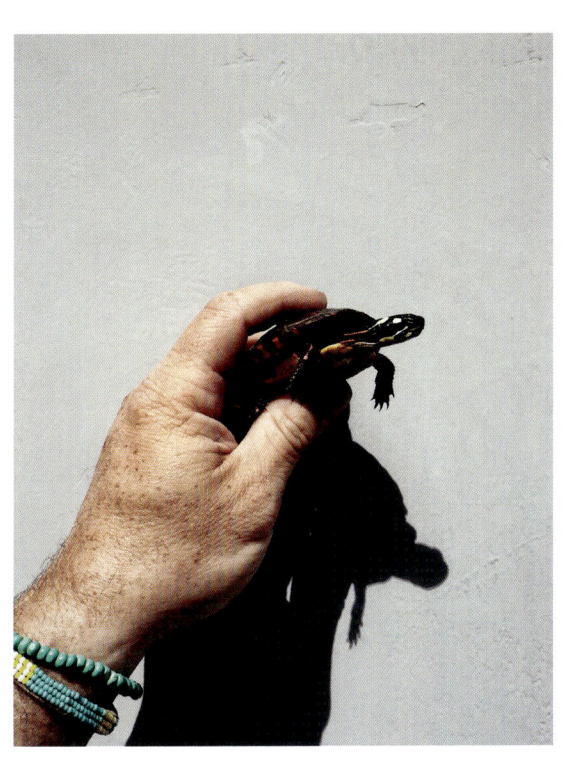
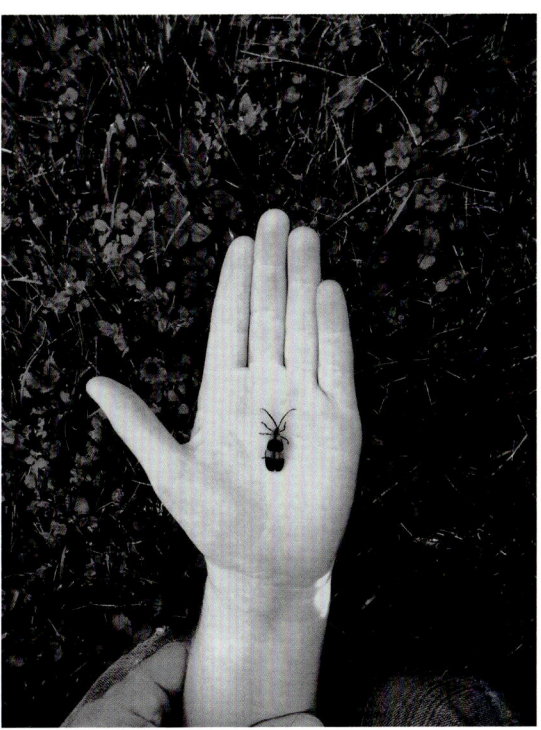

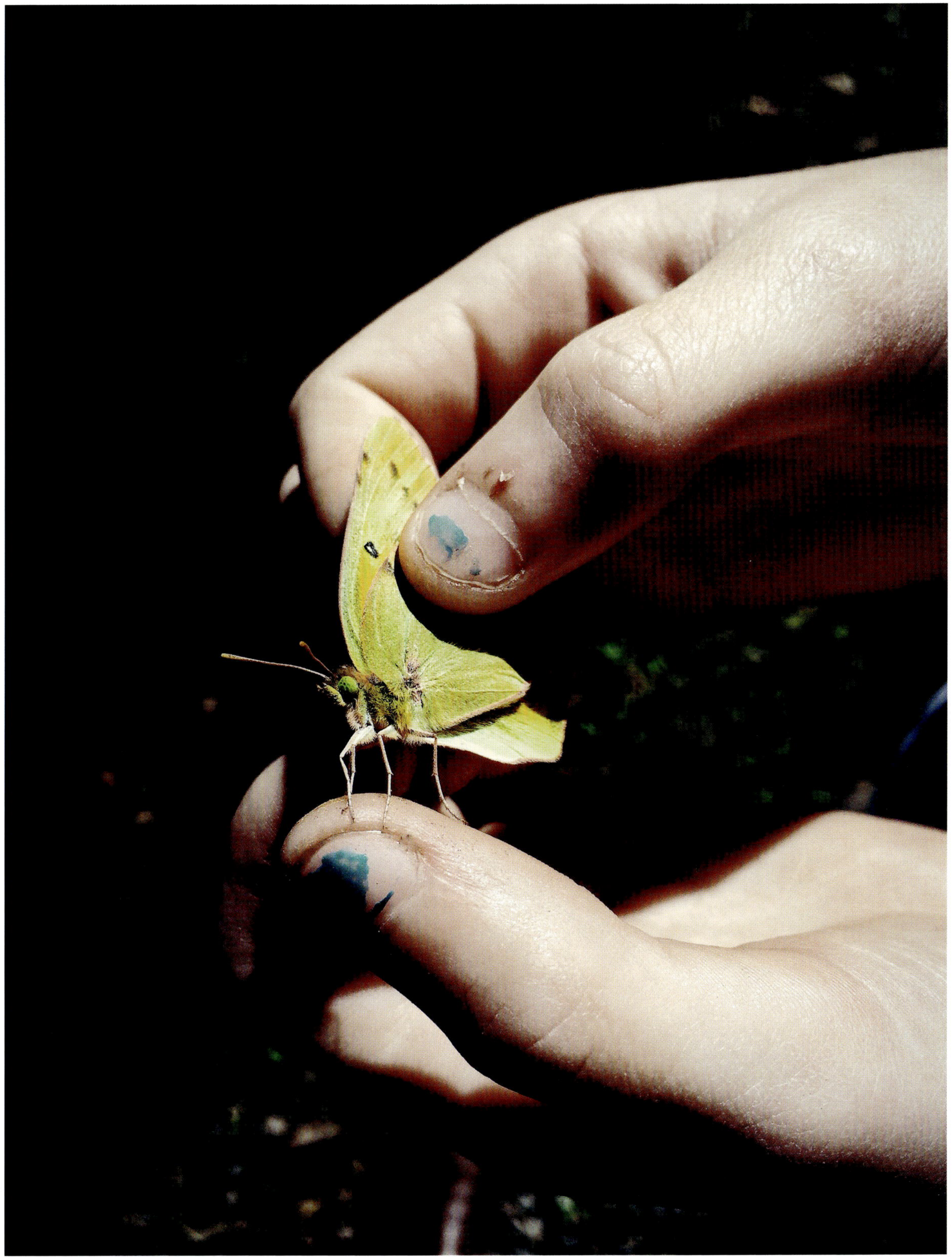

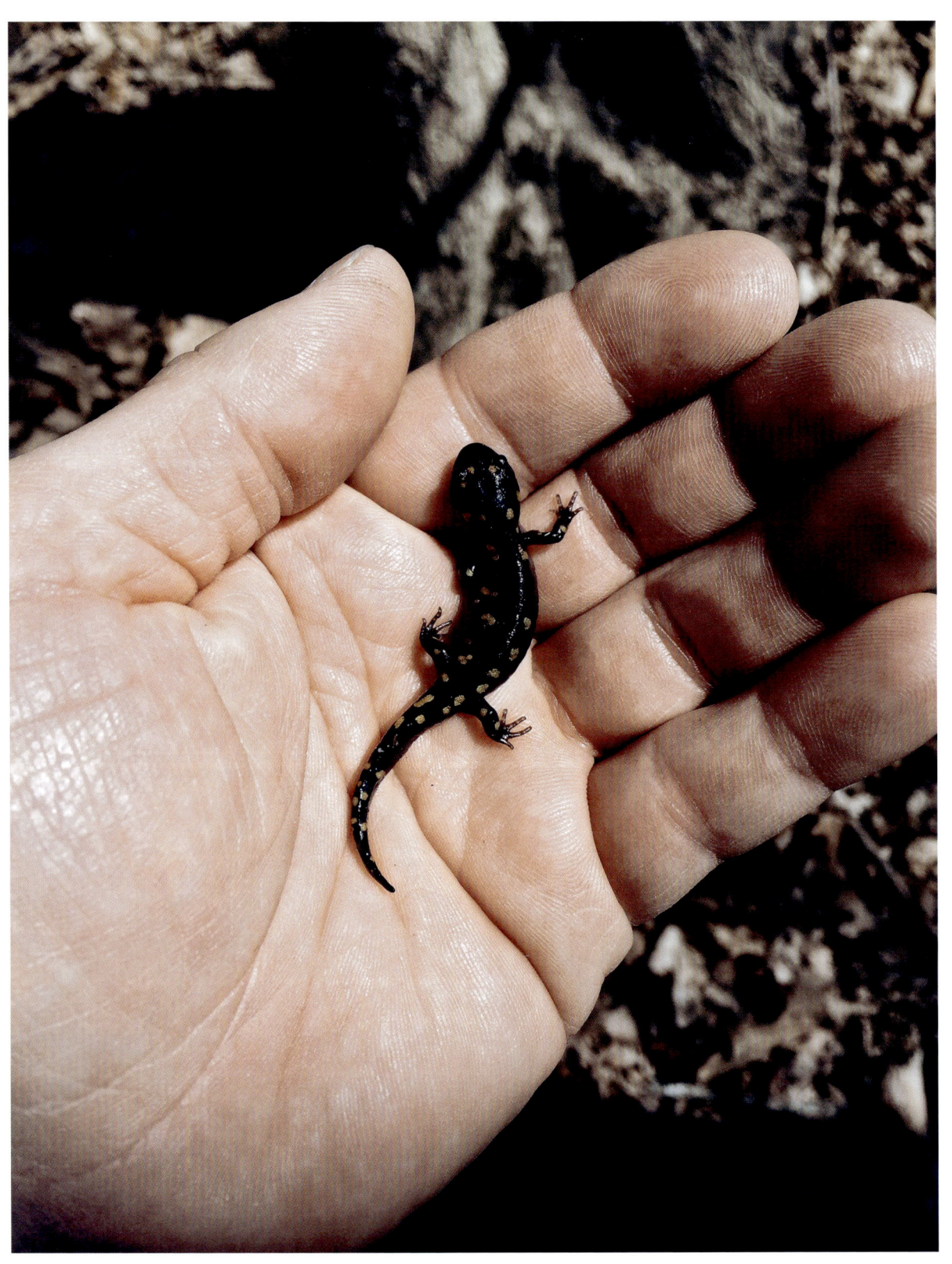

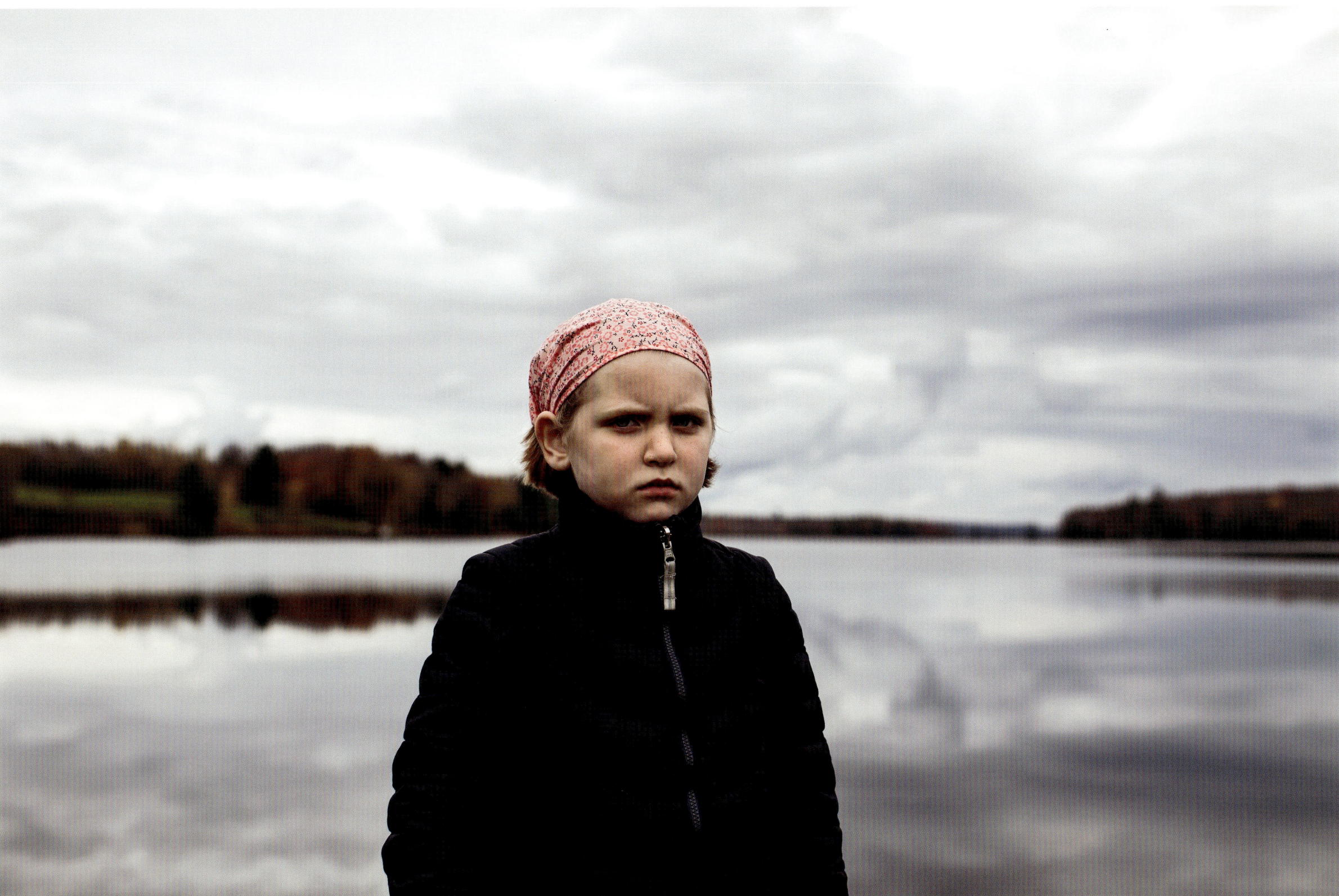

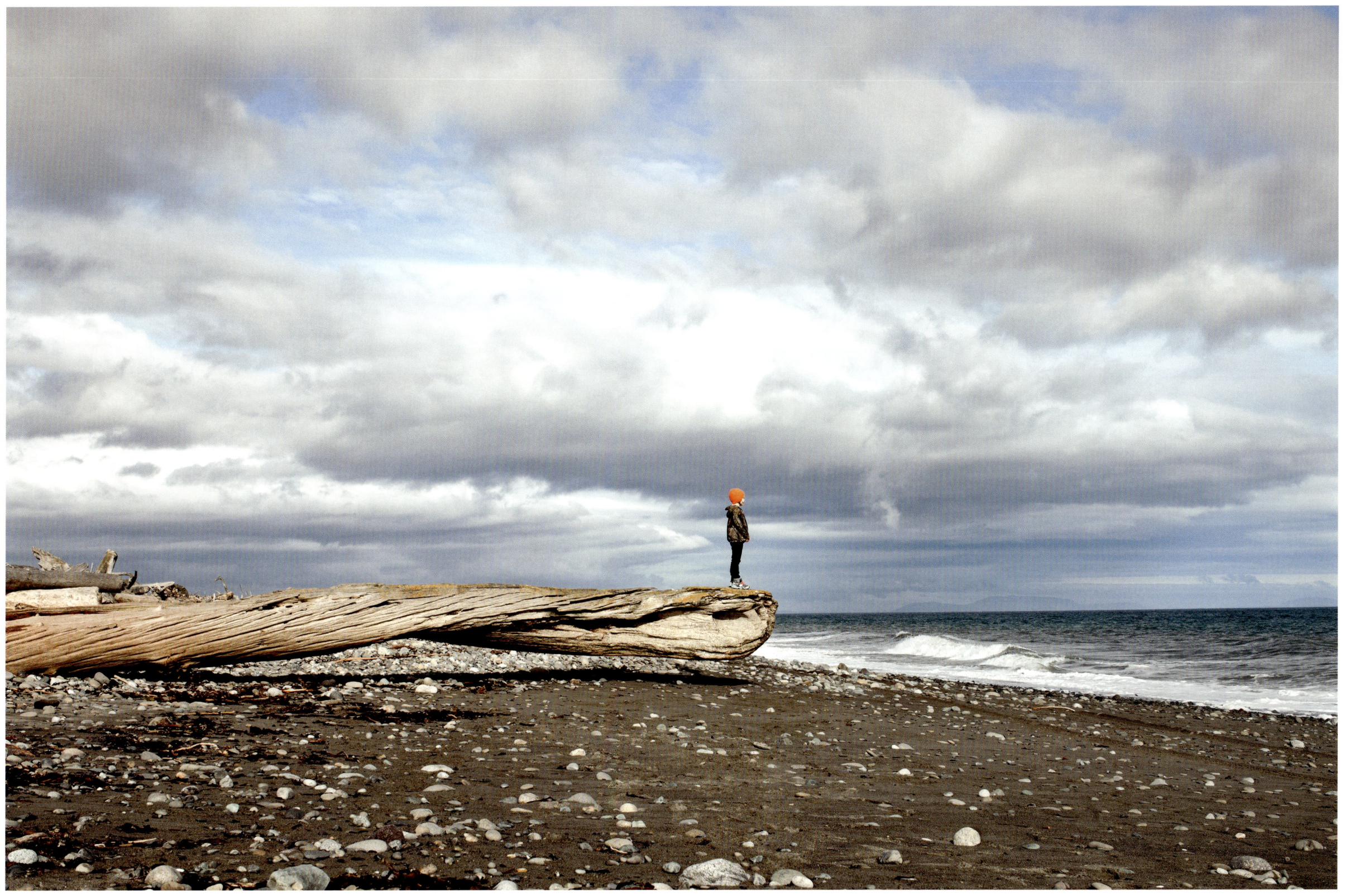

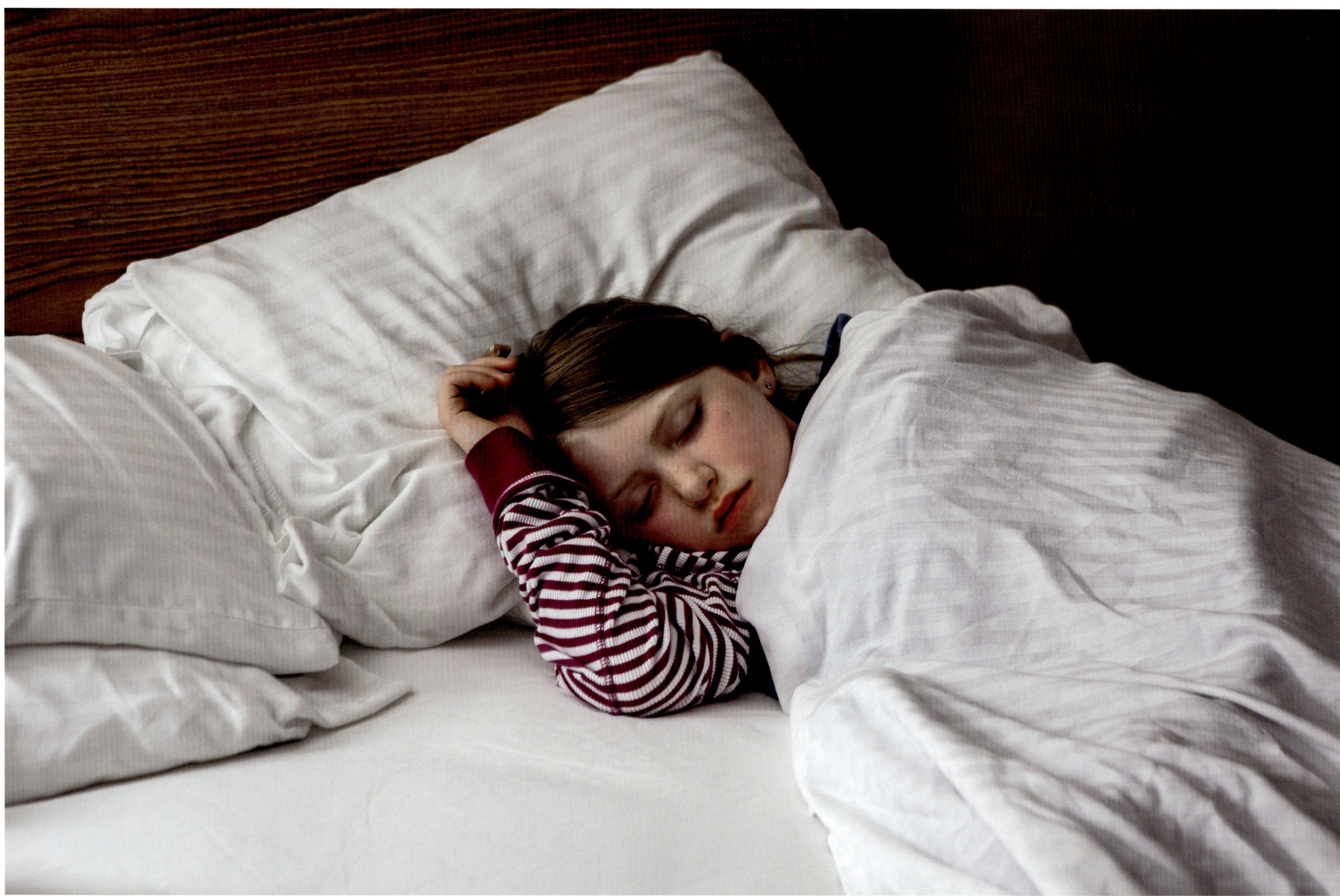

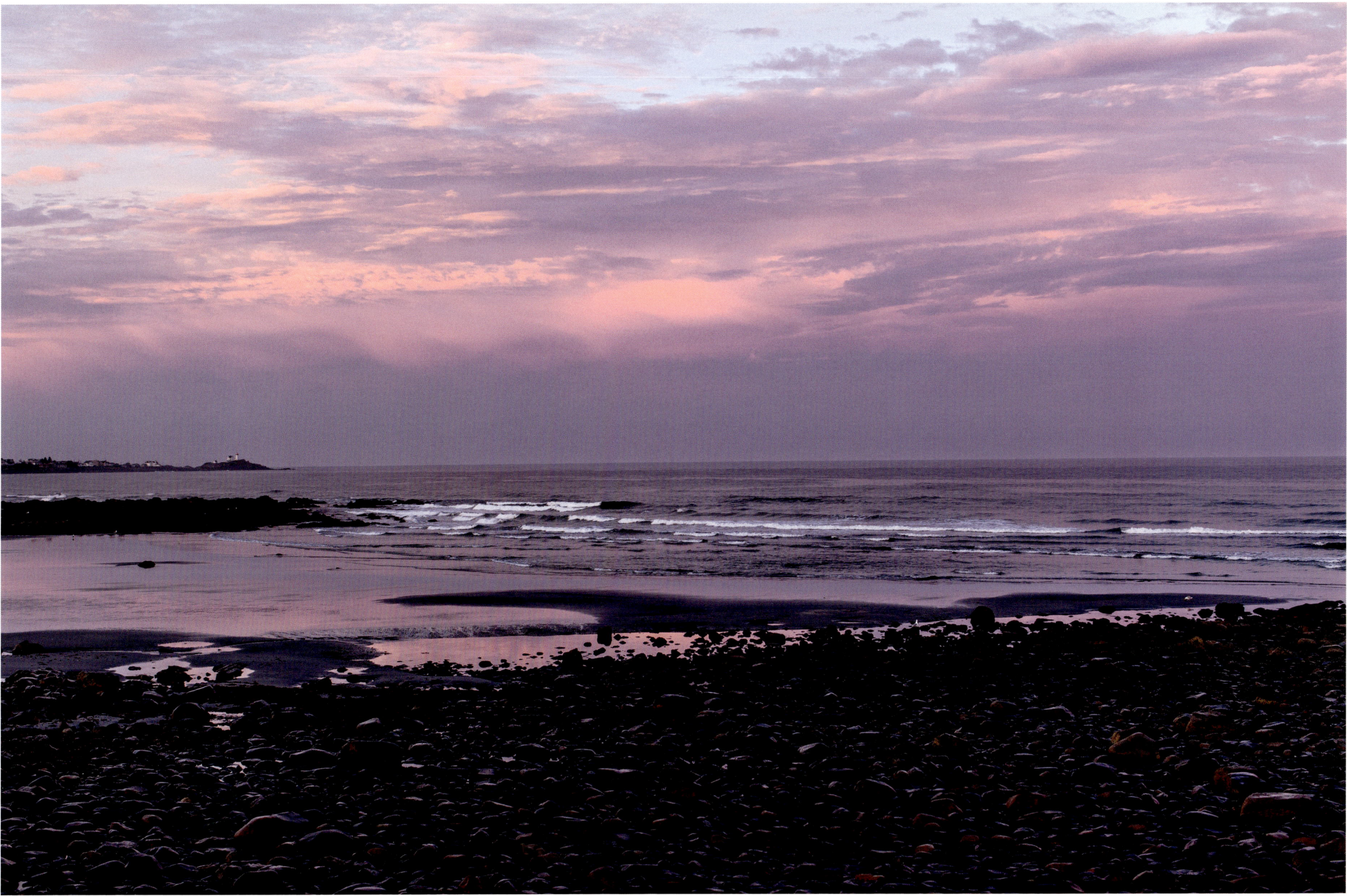

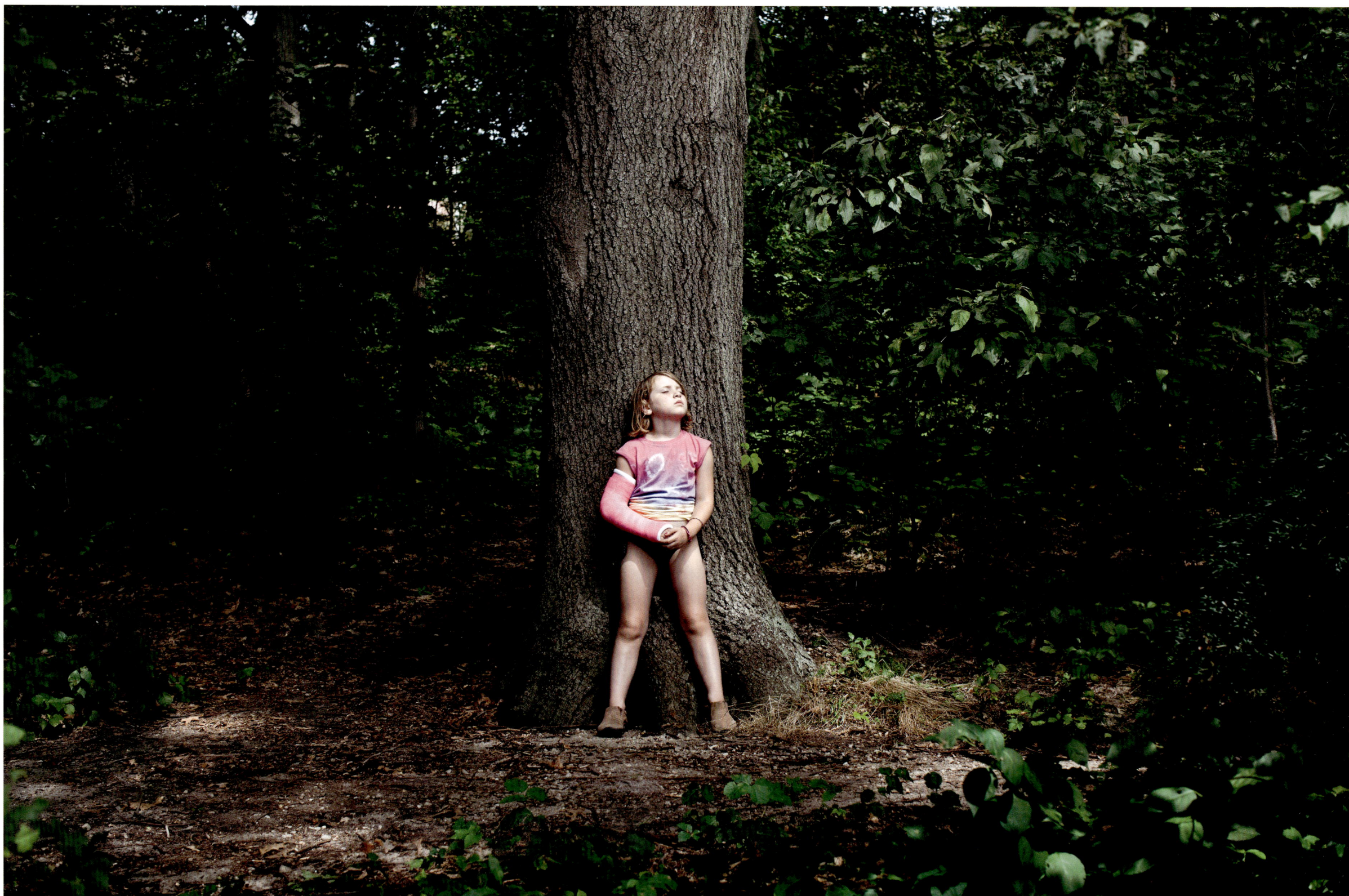

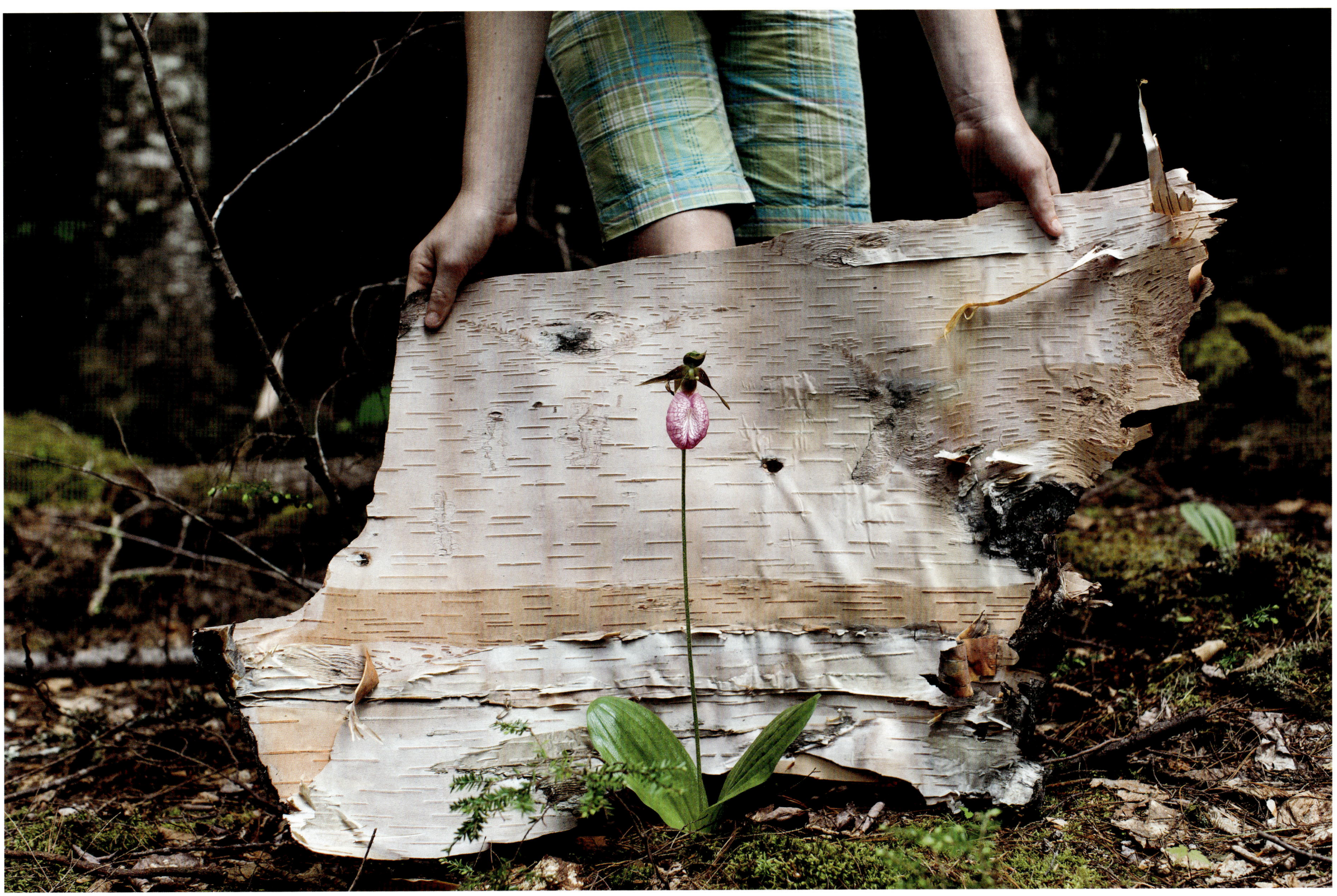

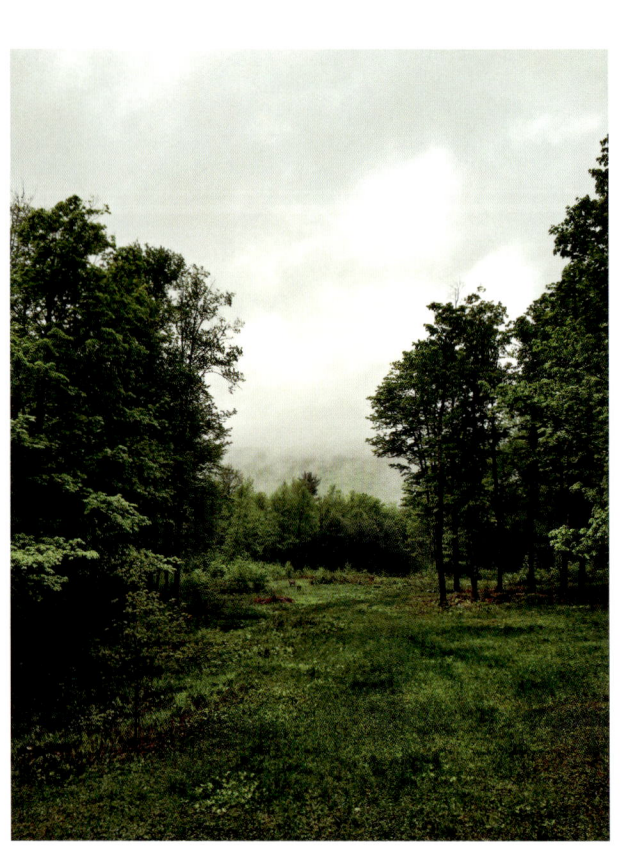

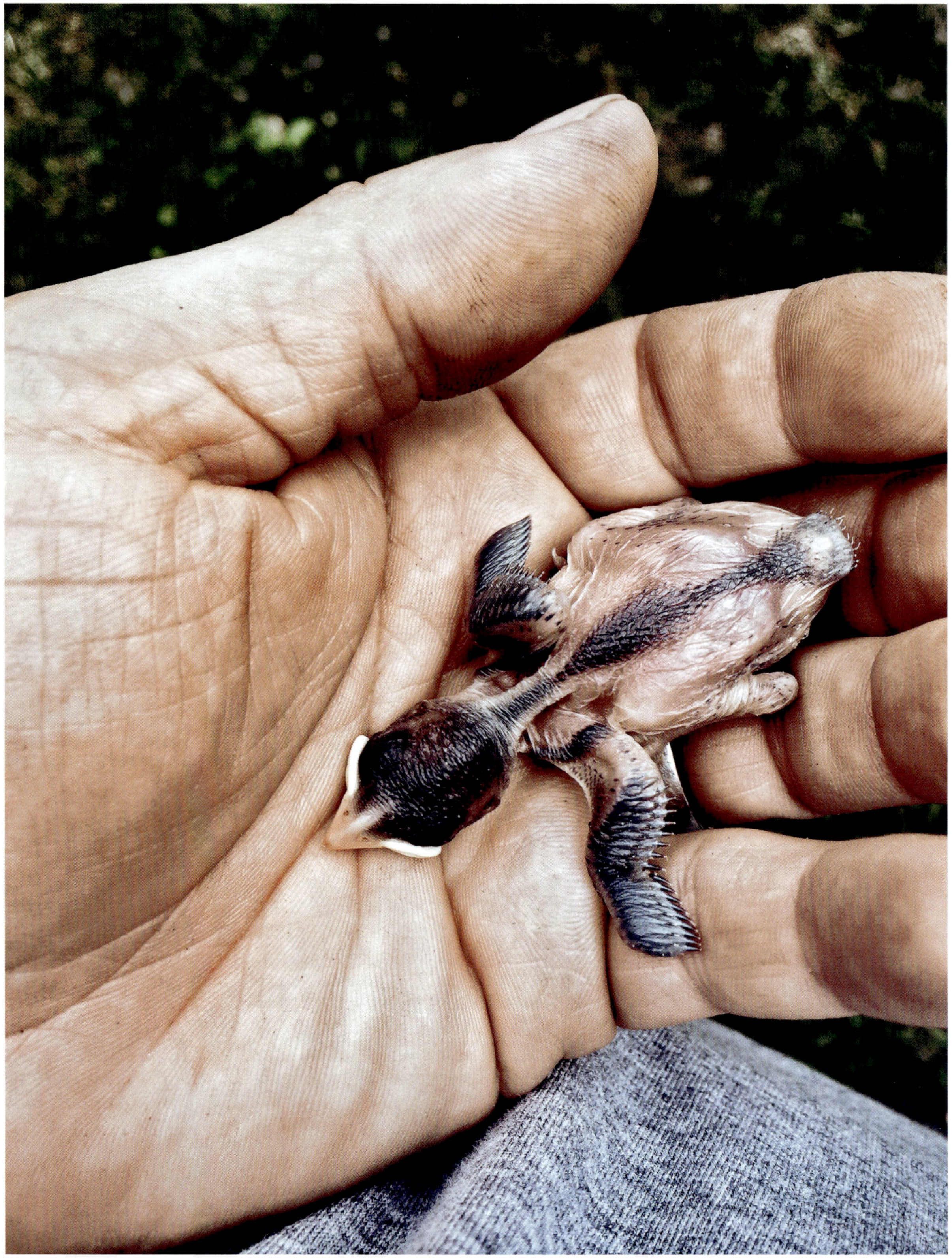

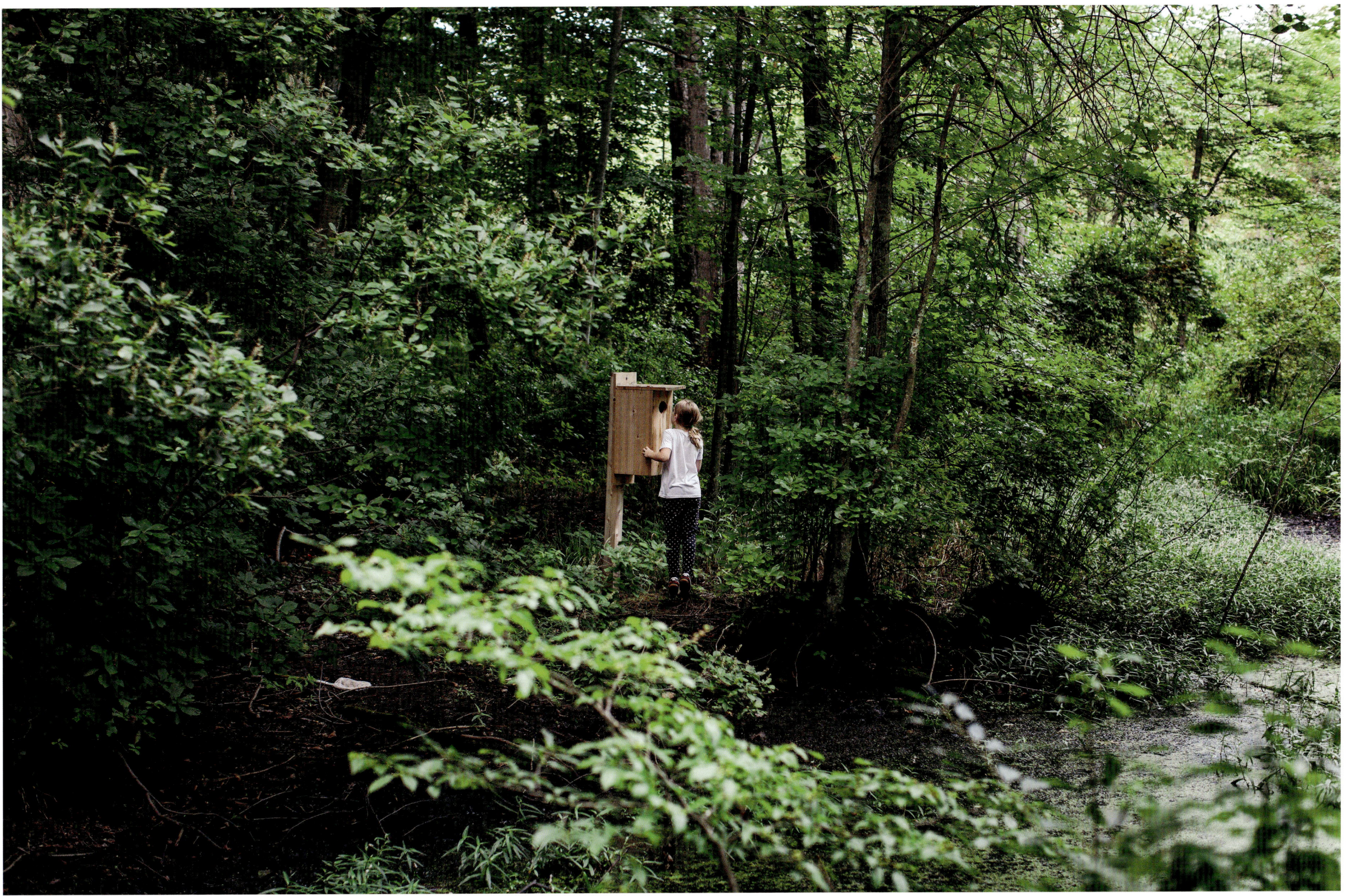

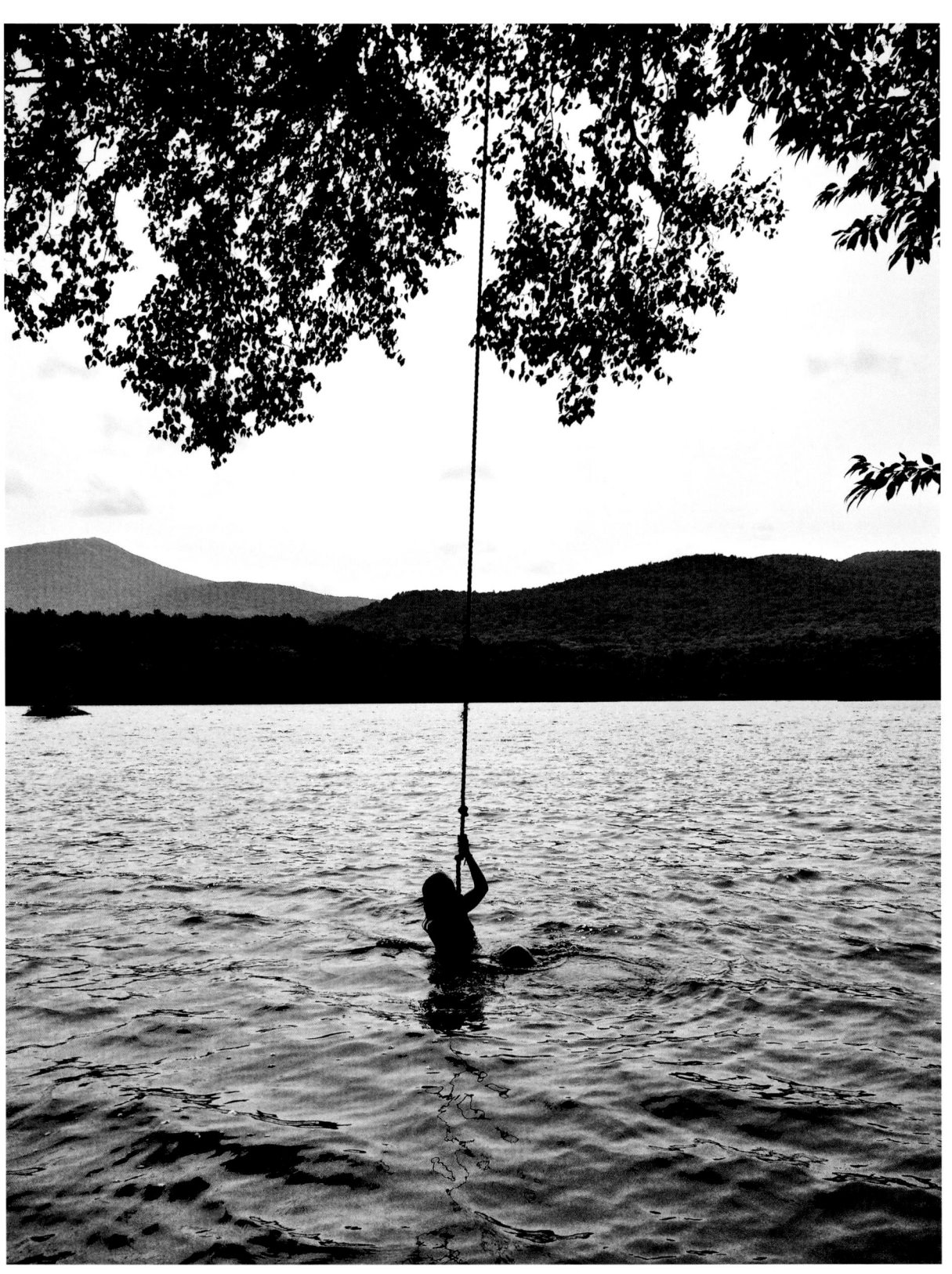

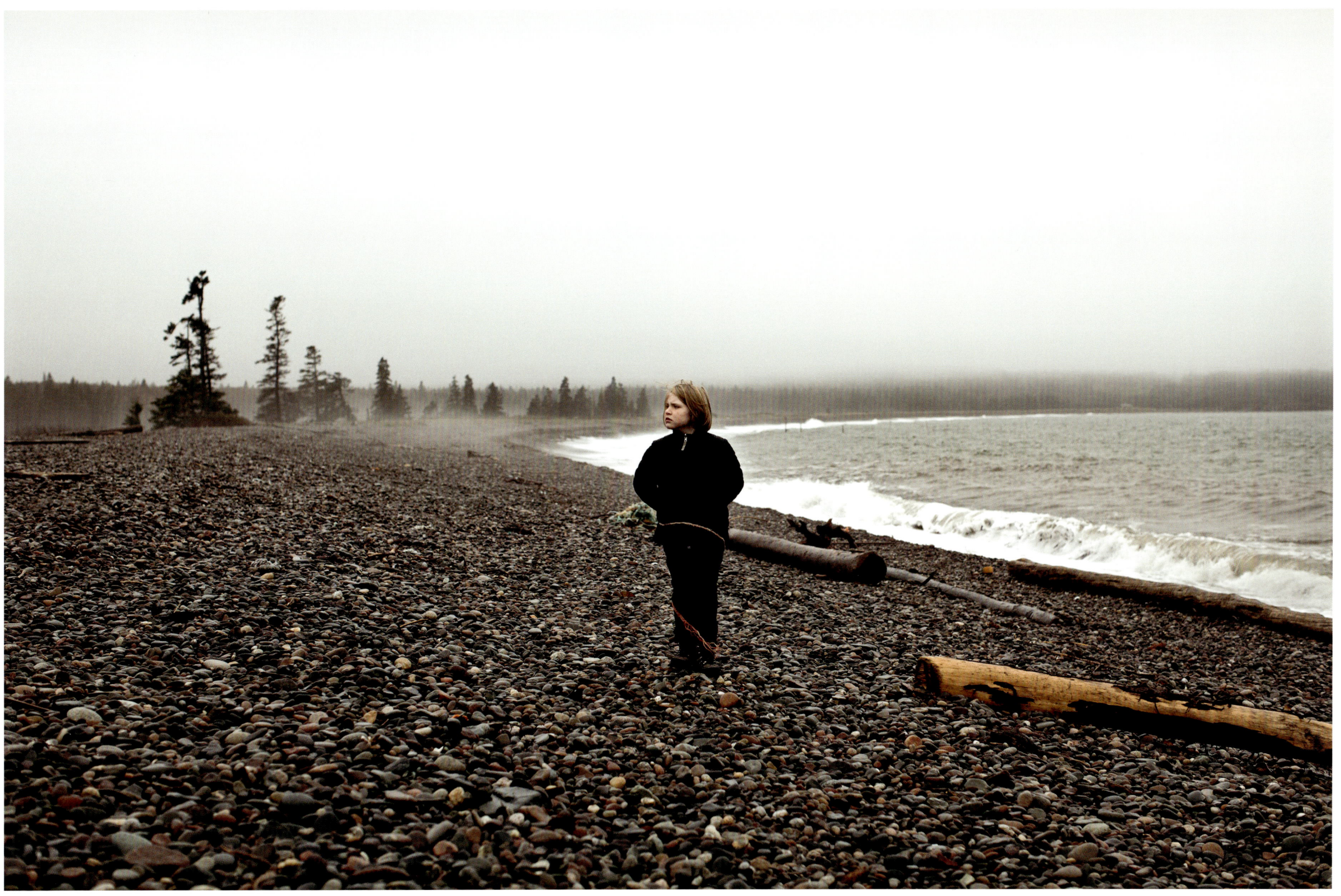

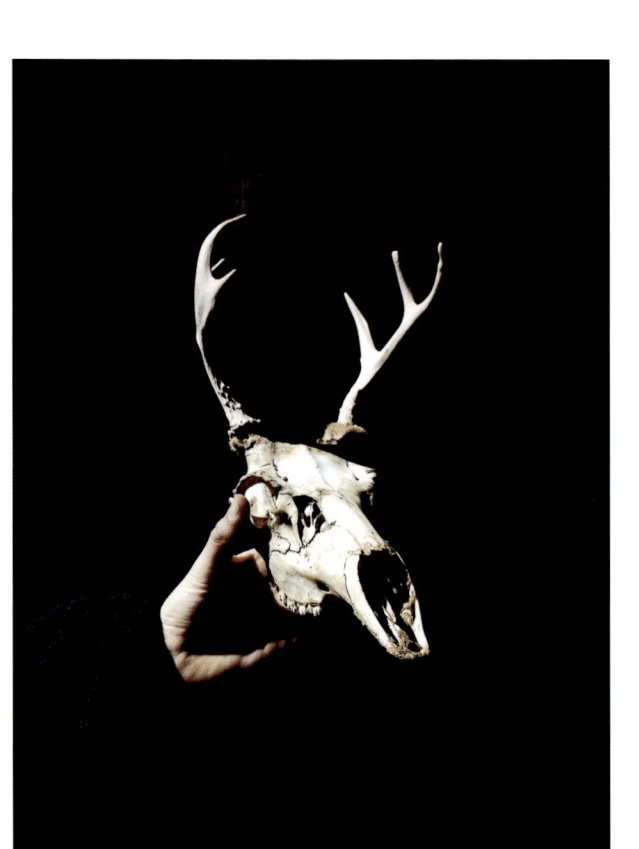

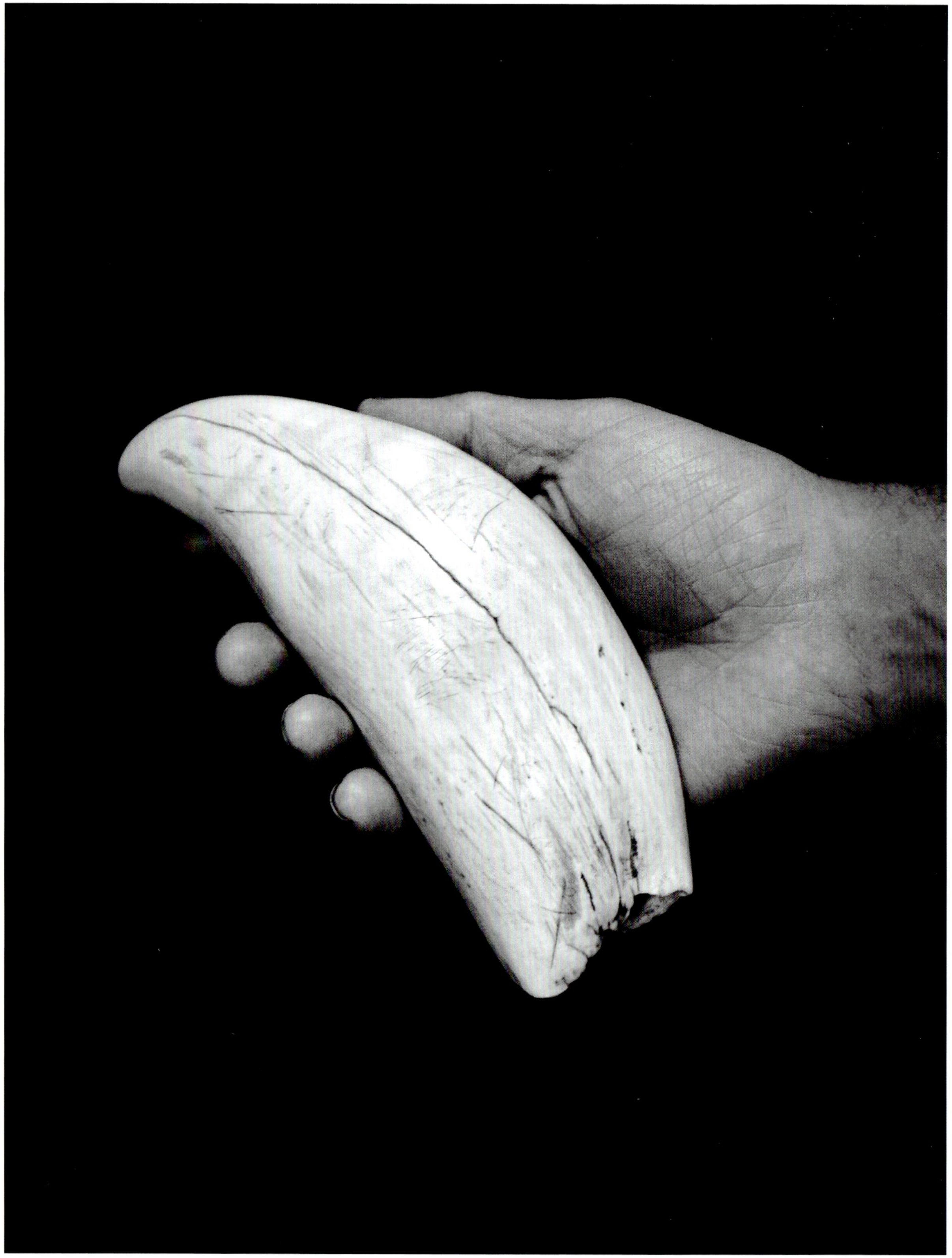

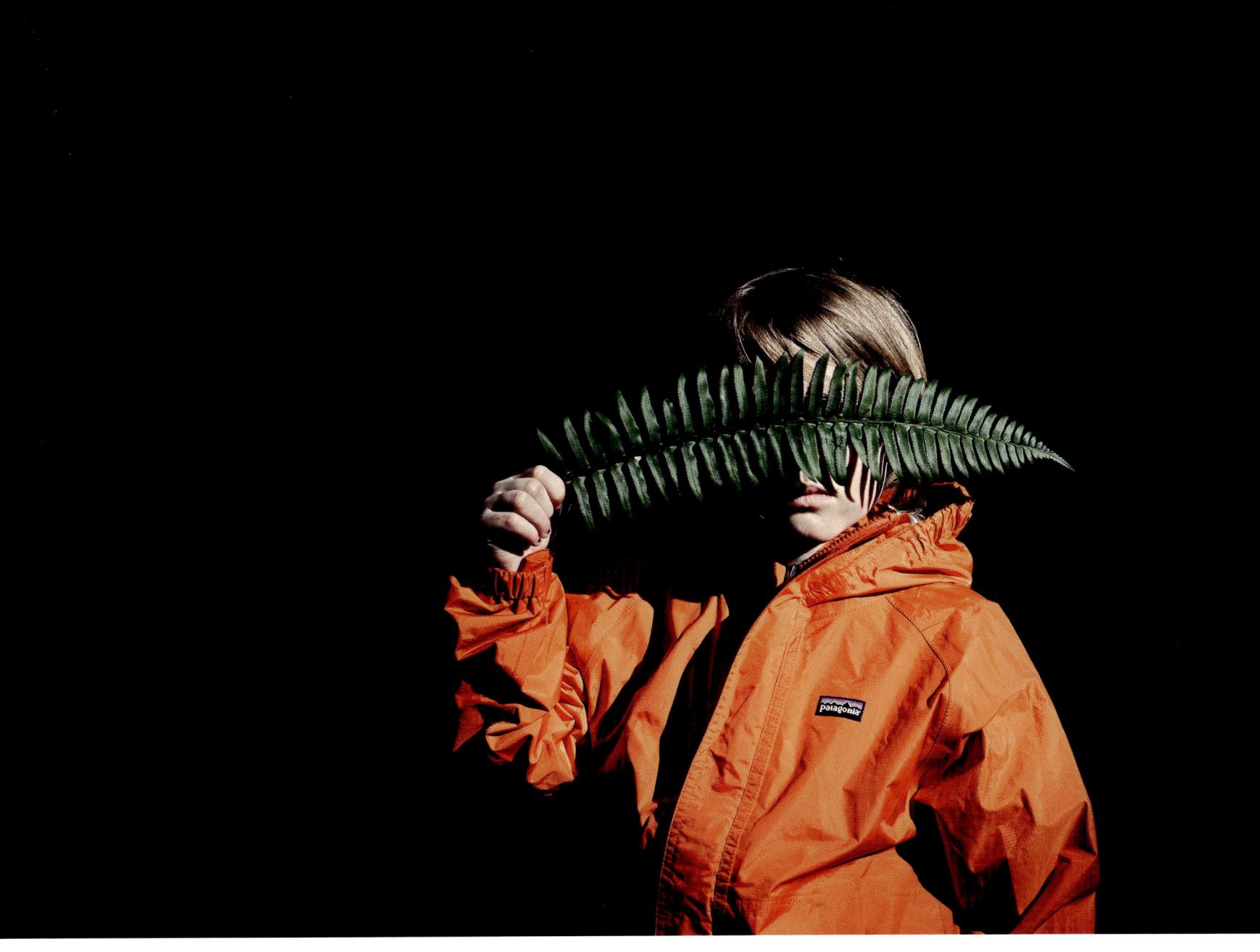

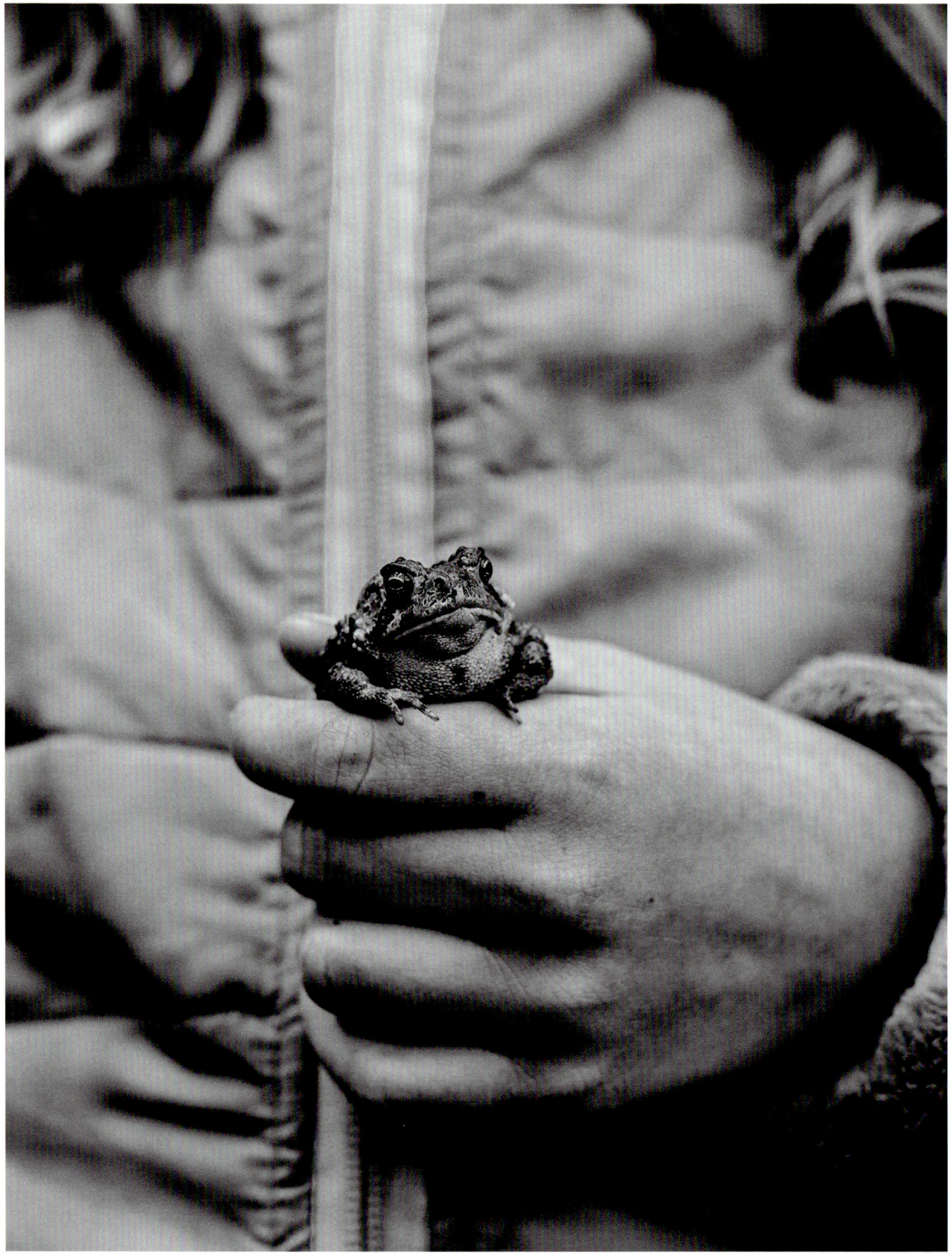

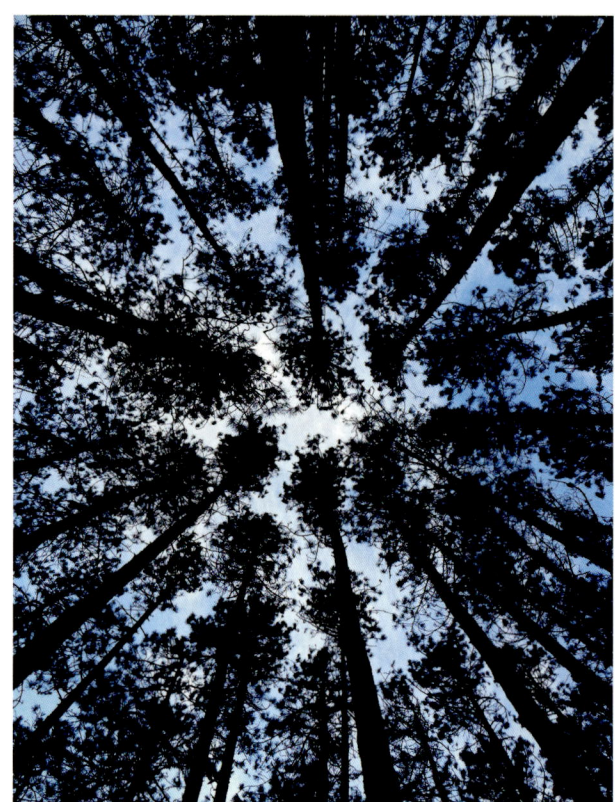

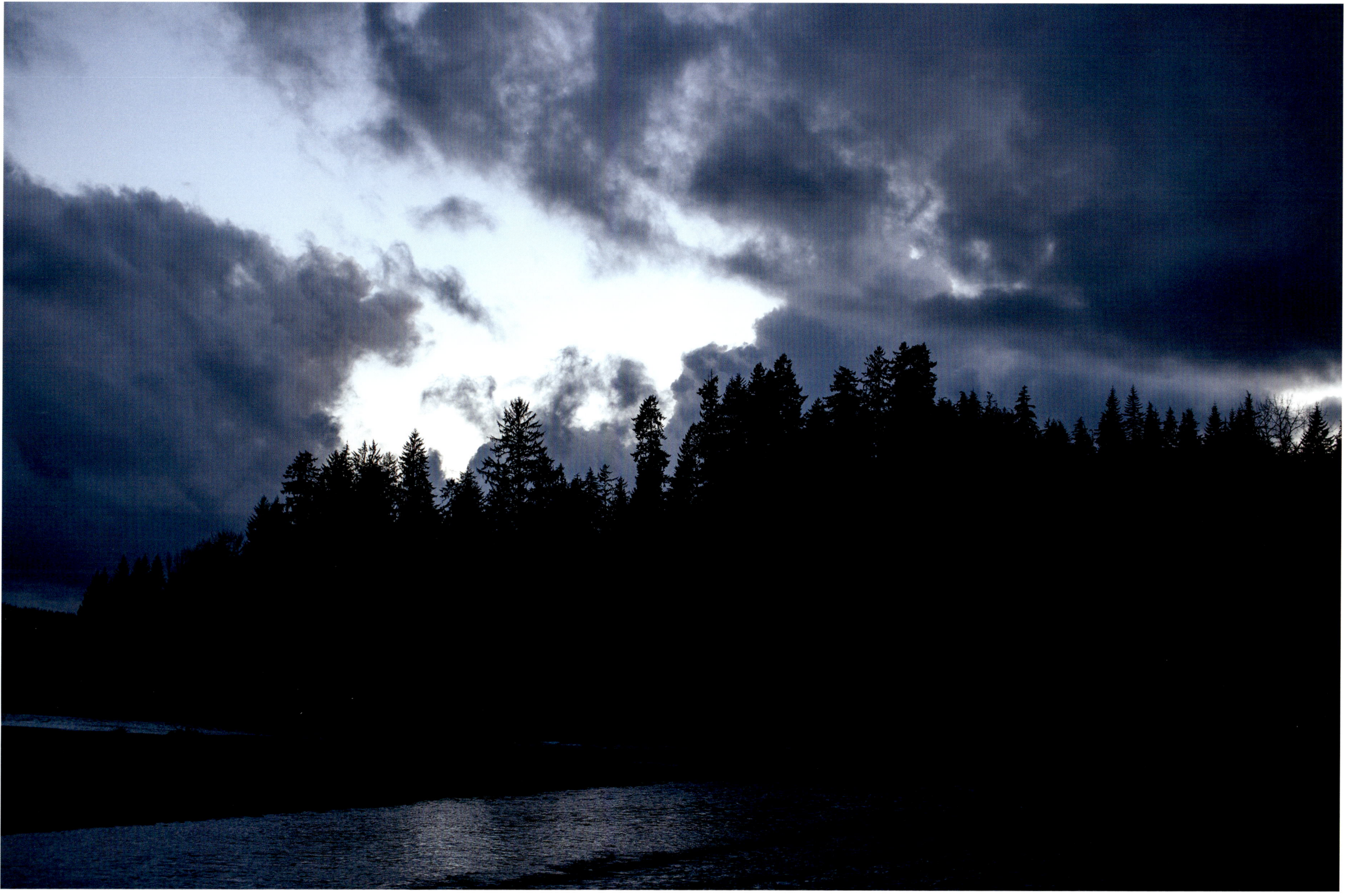

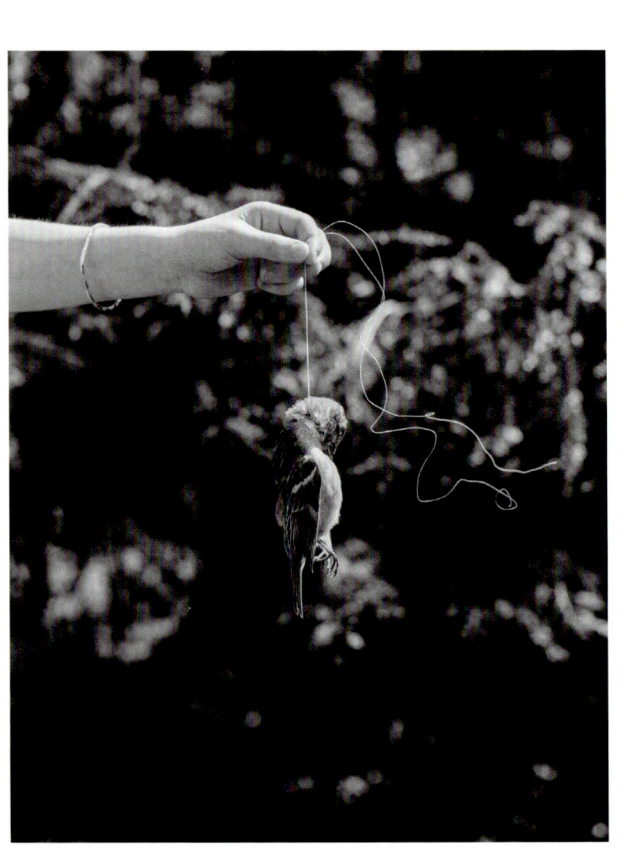

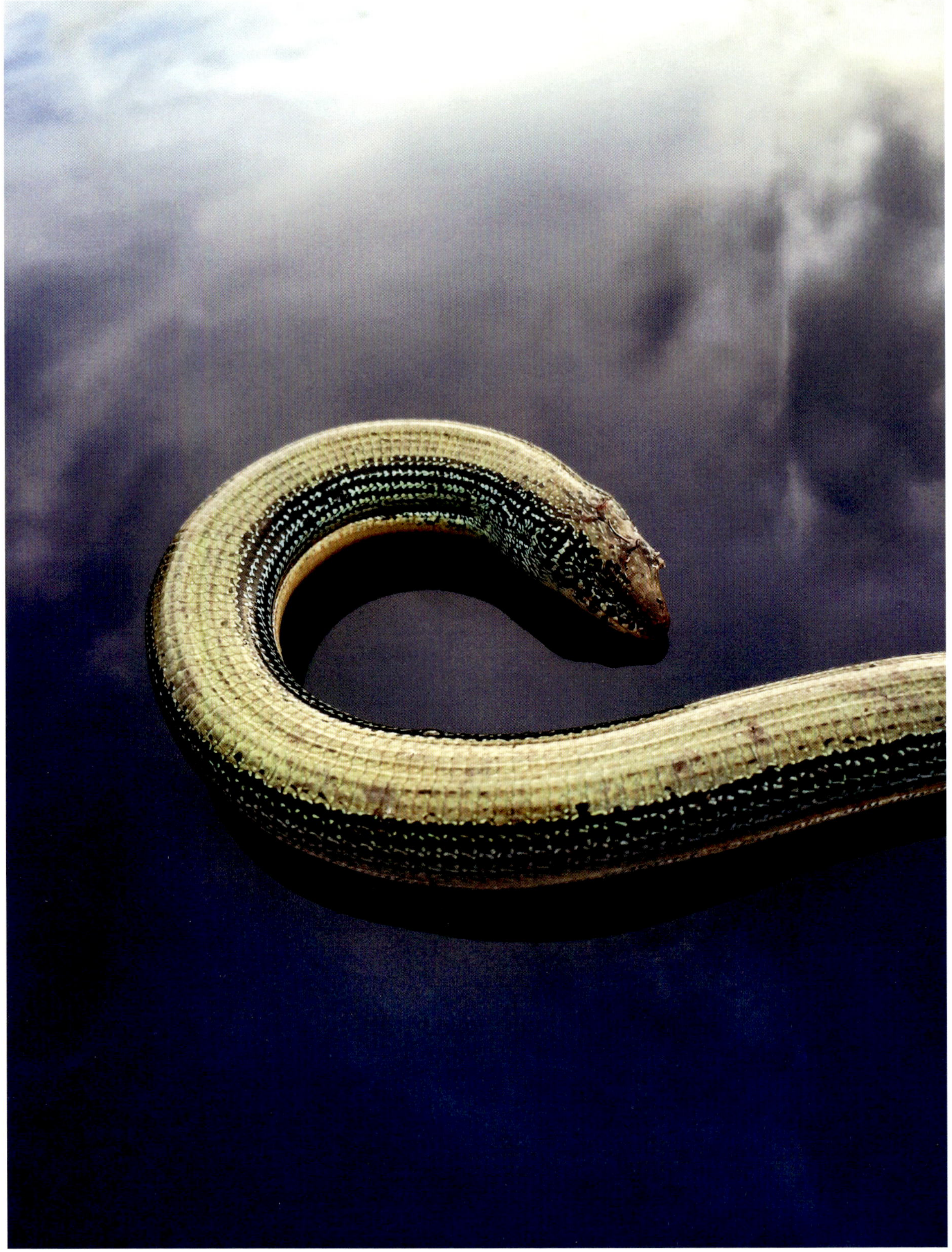

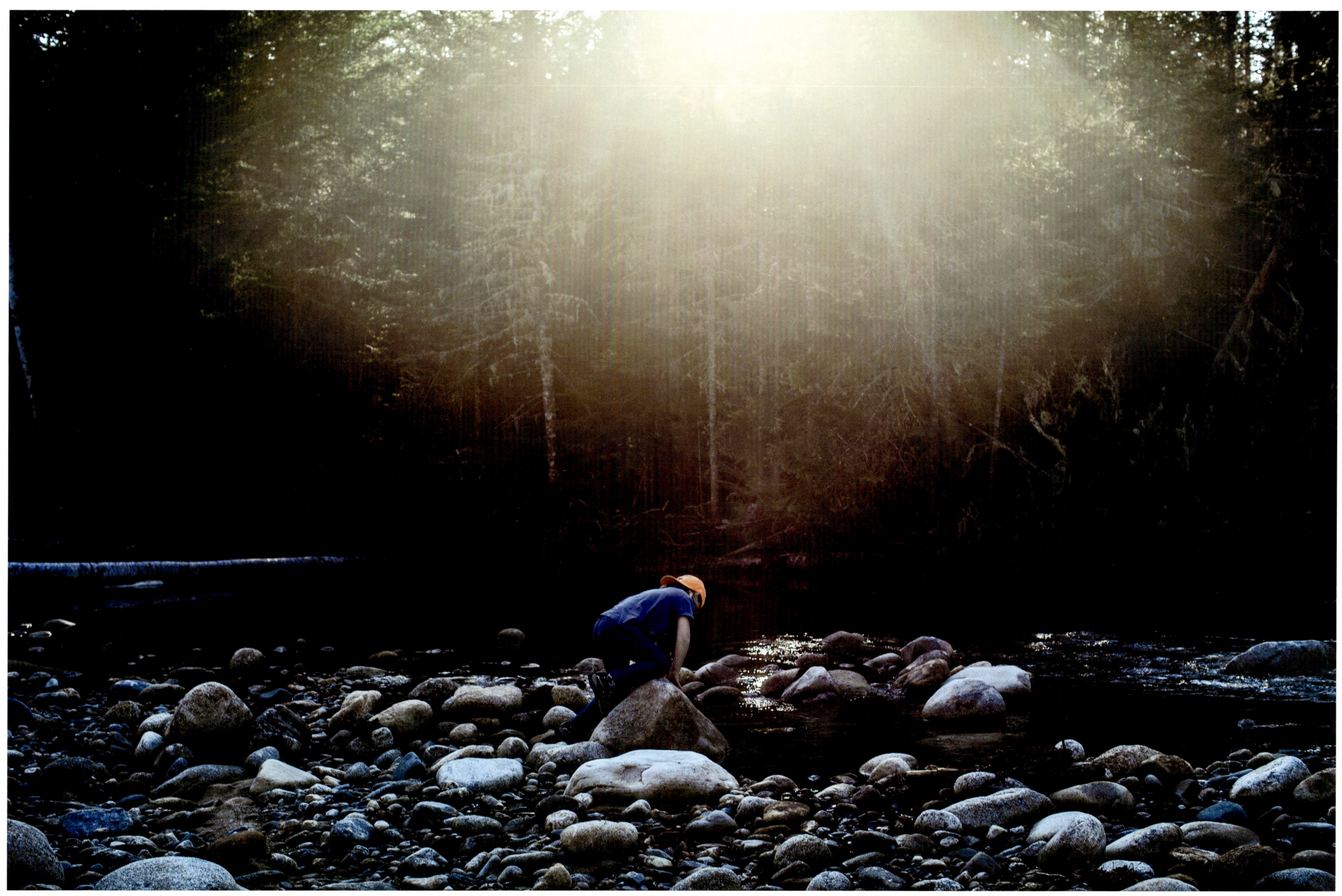

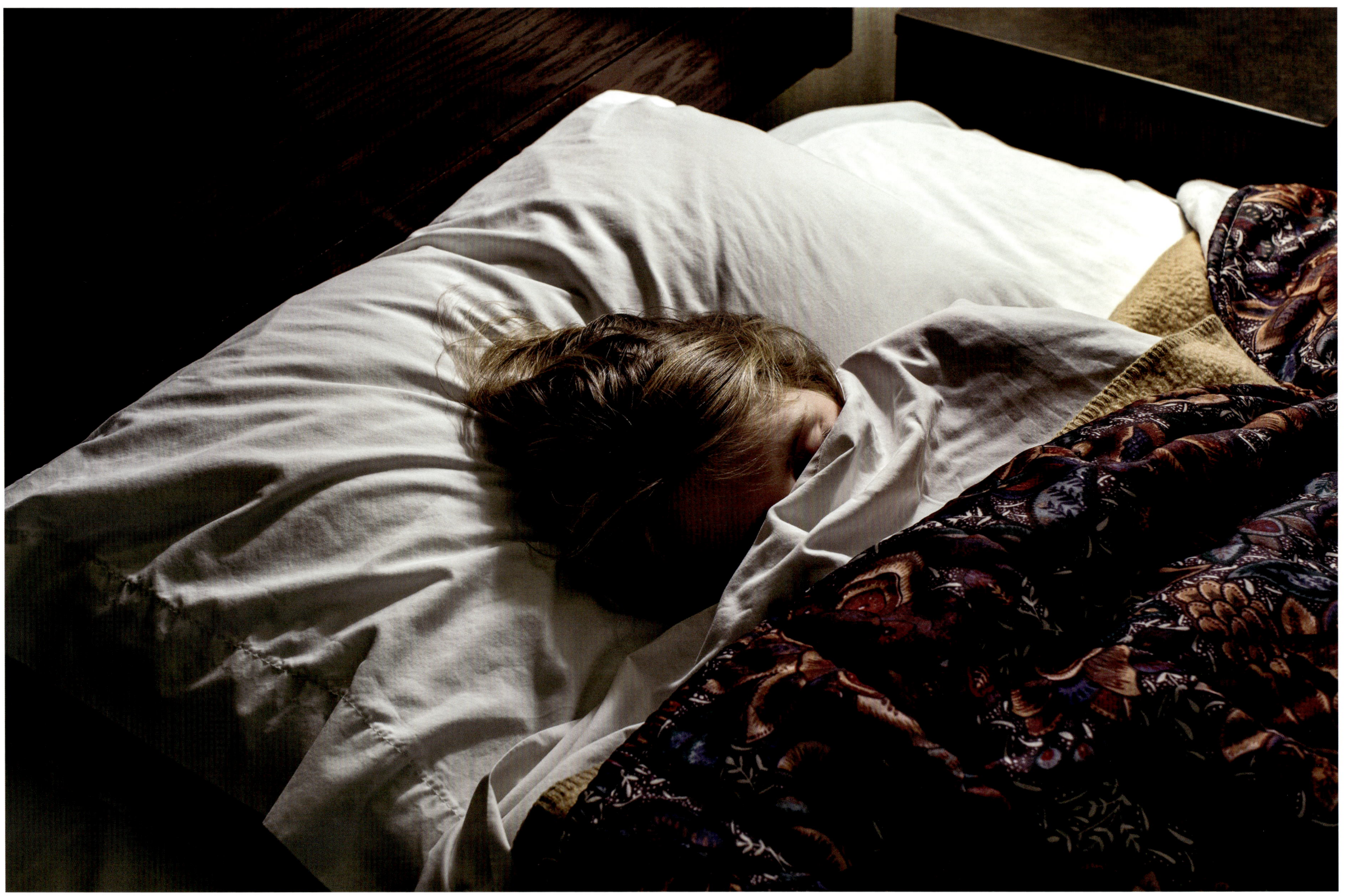

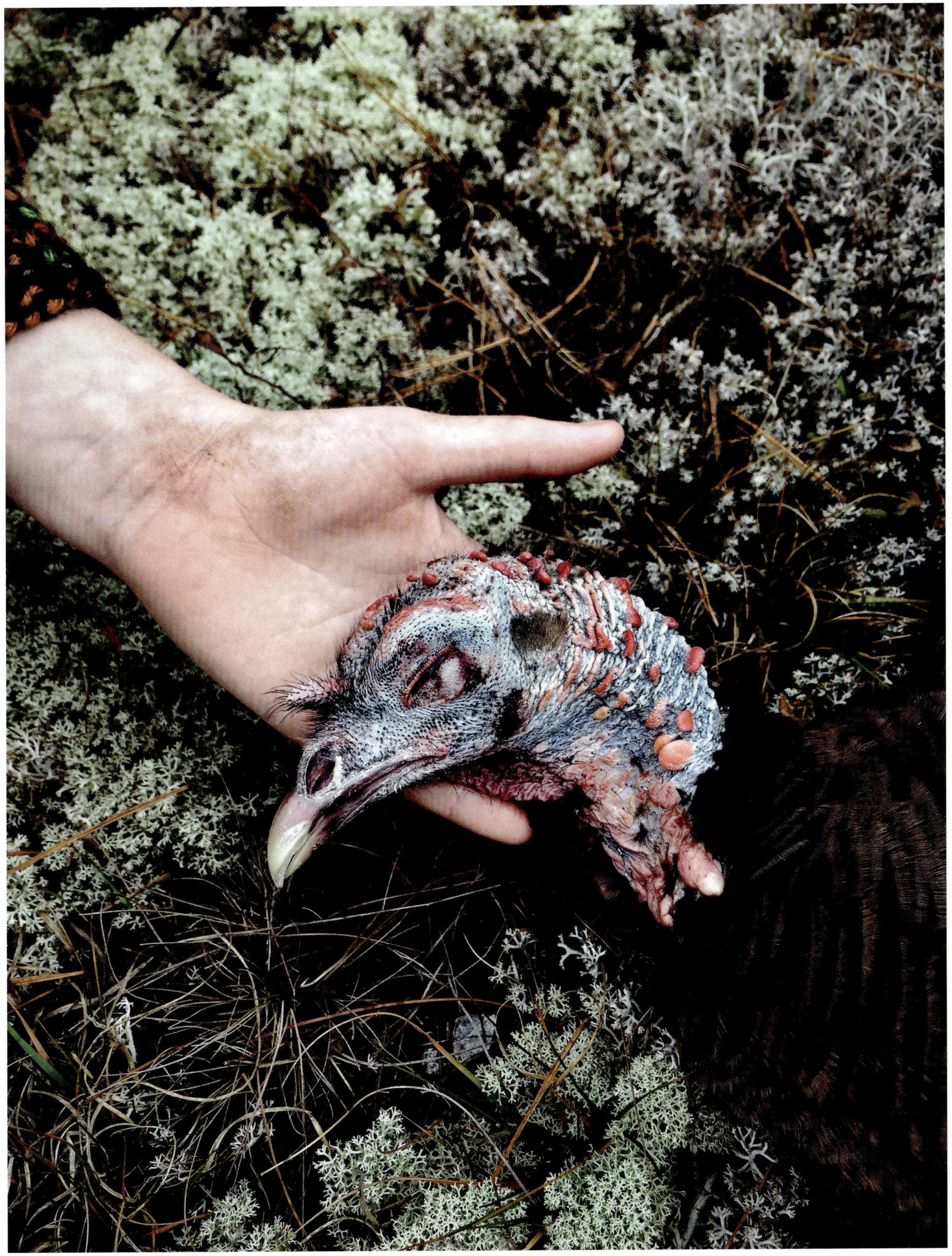

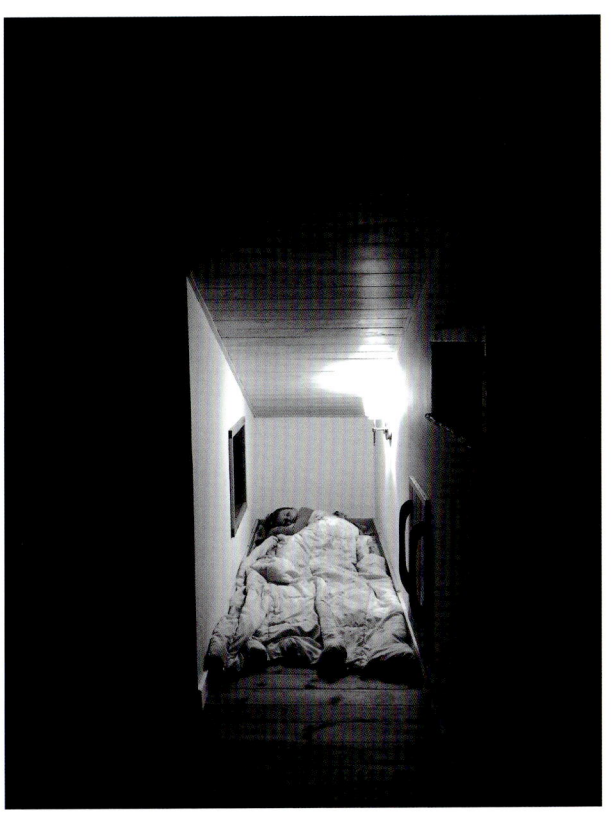

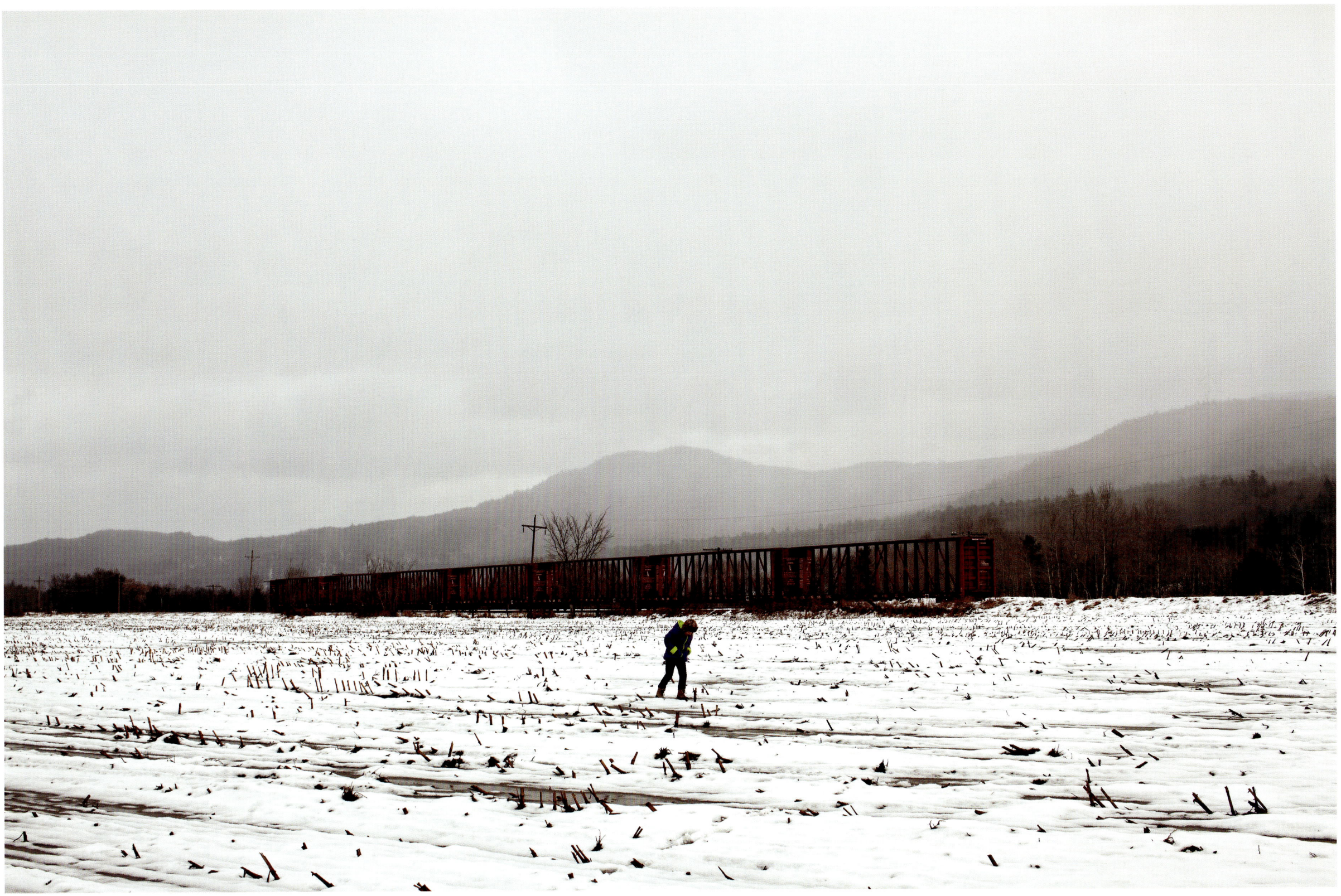

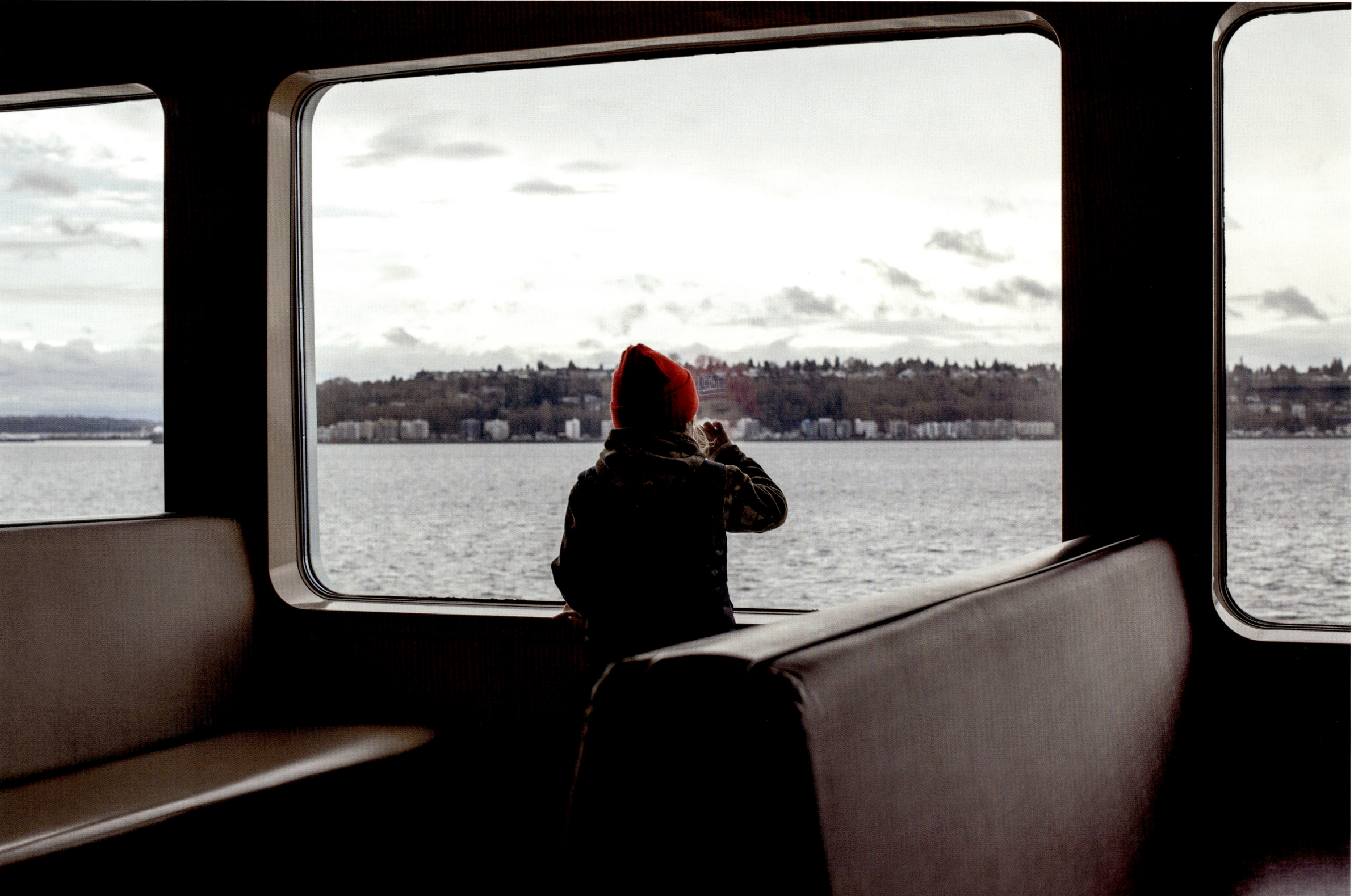

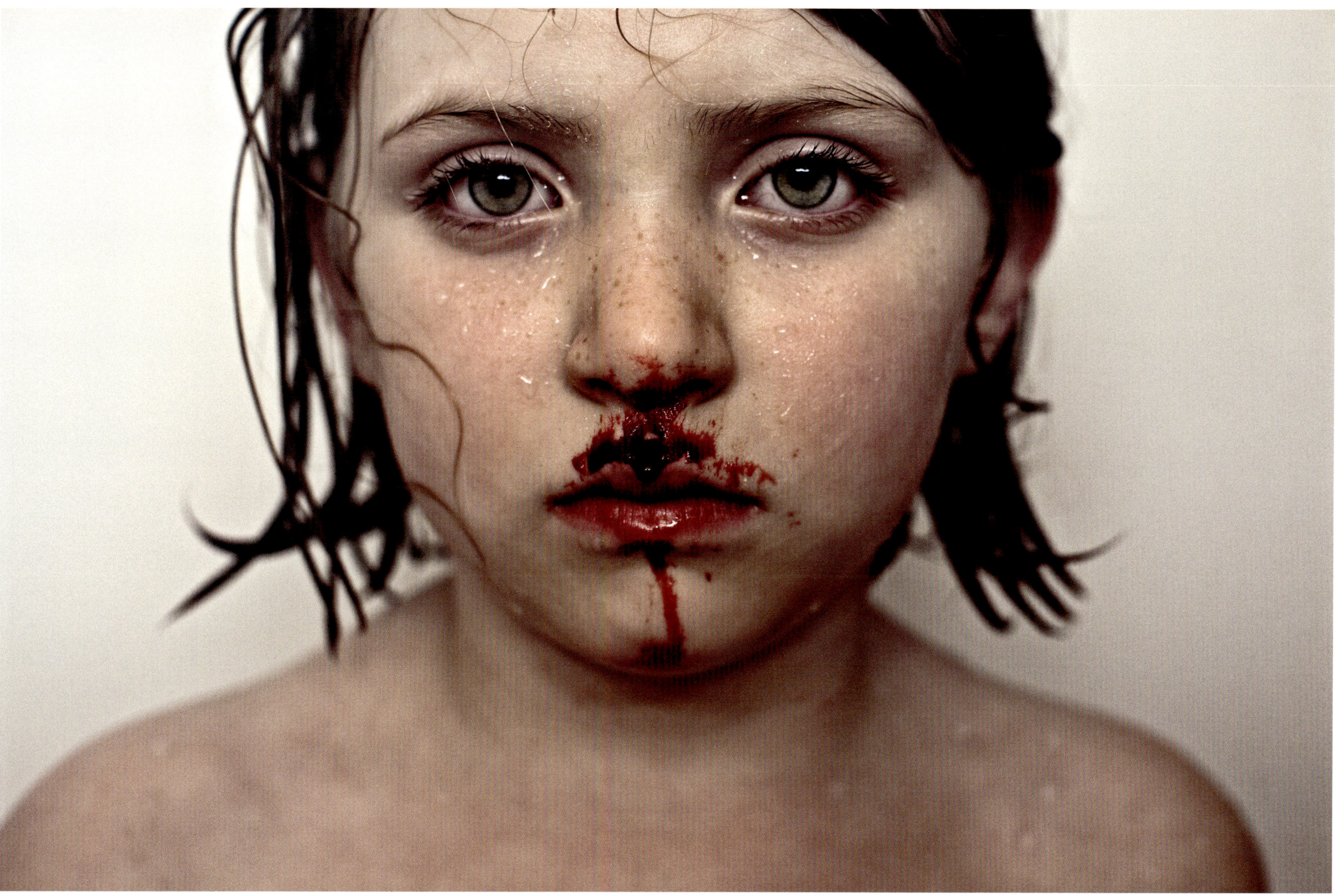

WALK IN THE
WOODS WHERE
IT'S WET.

STAND IN THE
SAND WHERE
IT'S DRY.

WADE IN THE RIVER
THAT TWISTS
AND TURNS
AND REACH FOR
THE BLUE
OF THE SKY.

DALLAS
CLAYTON

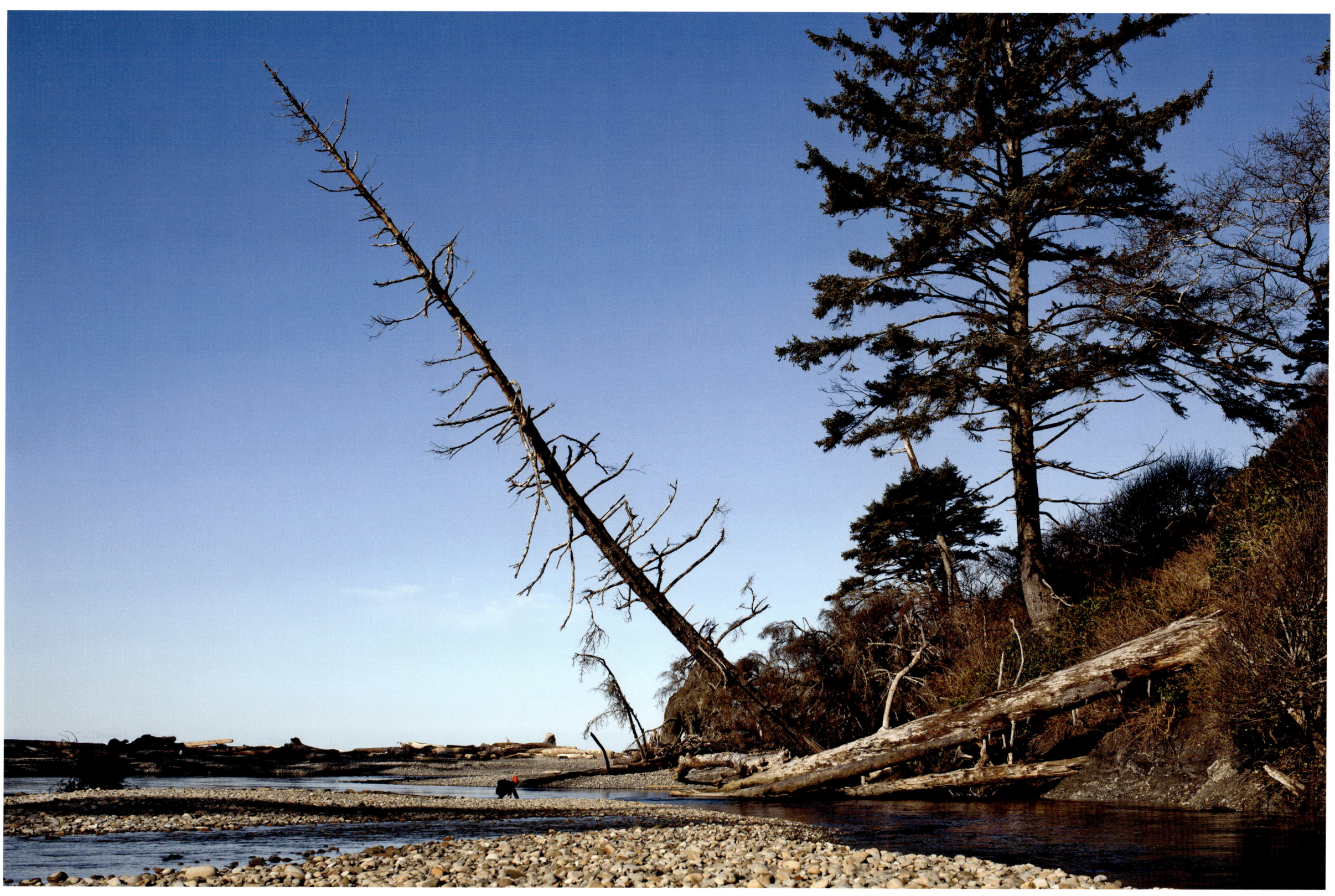

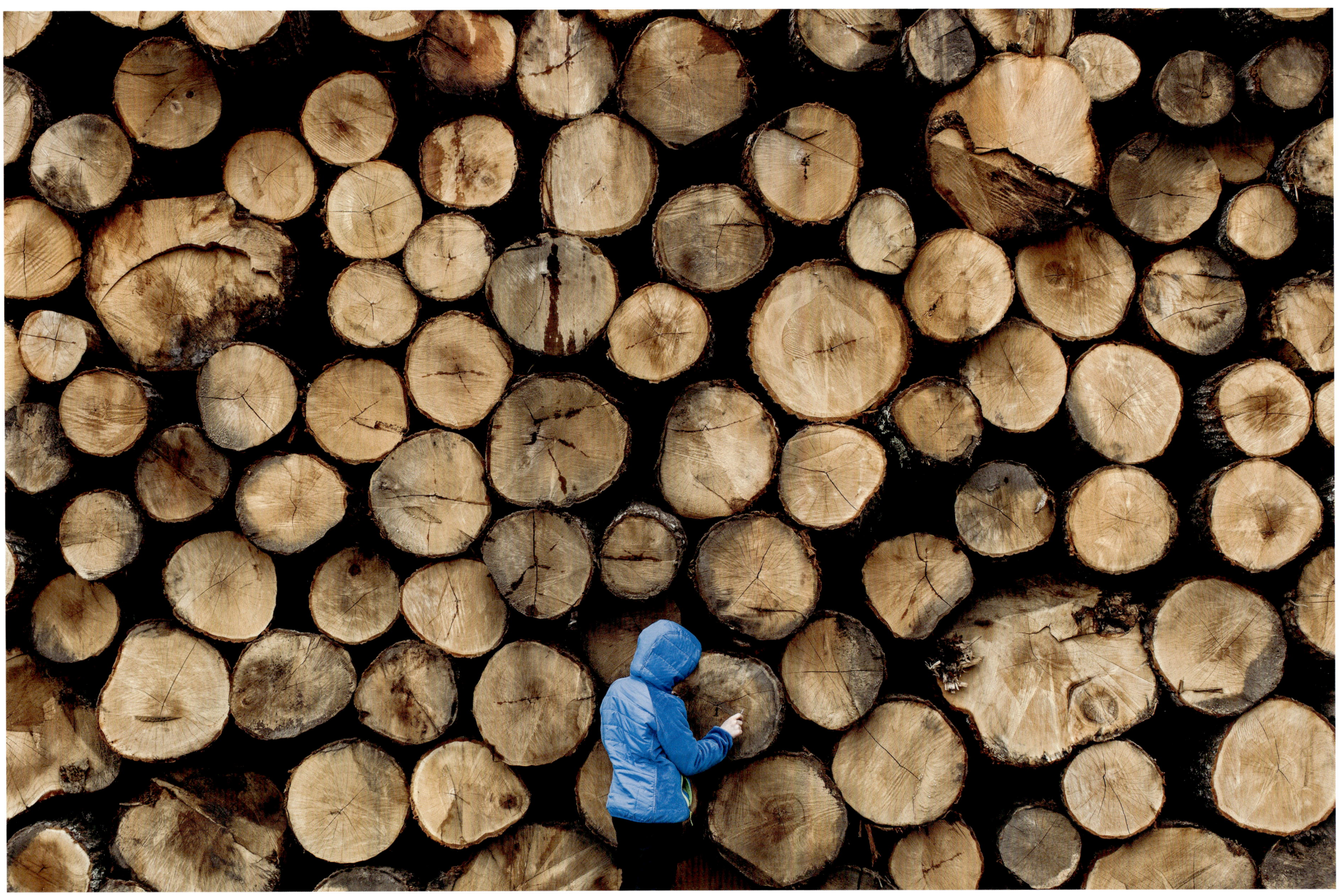

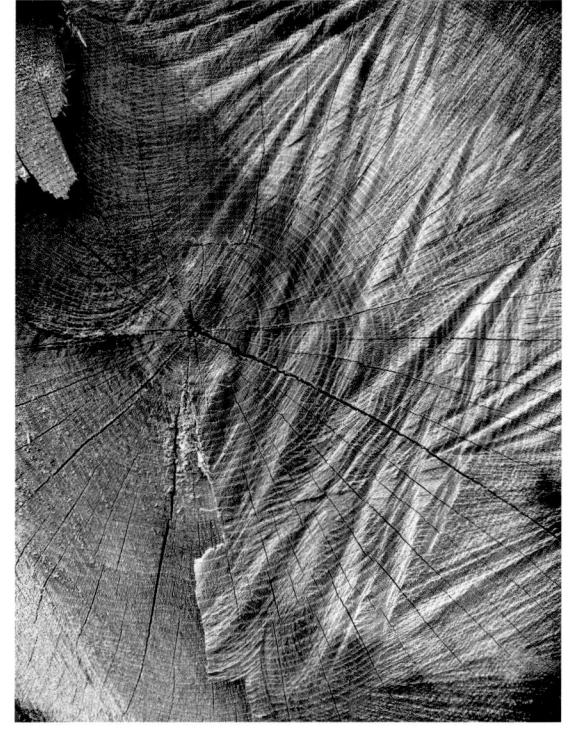
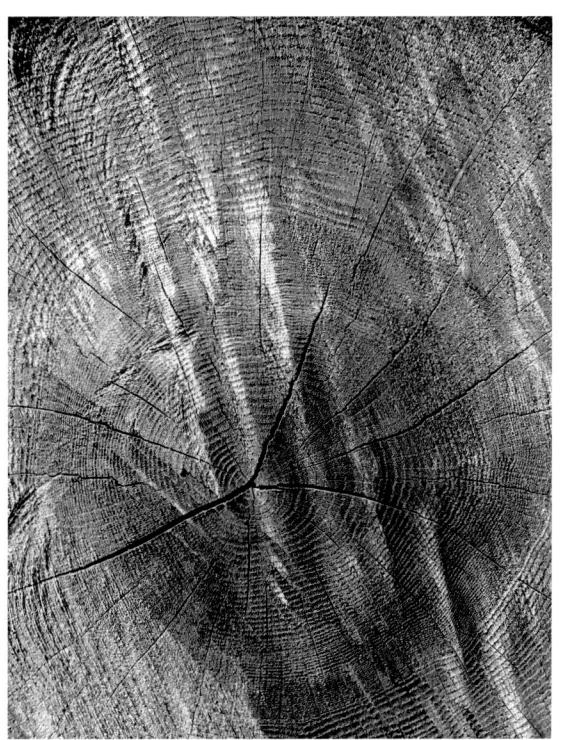
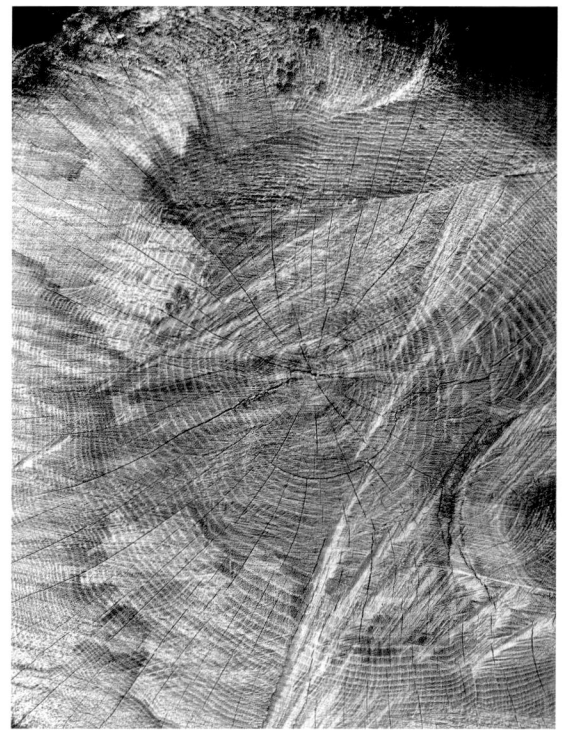
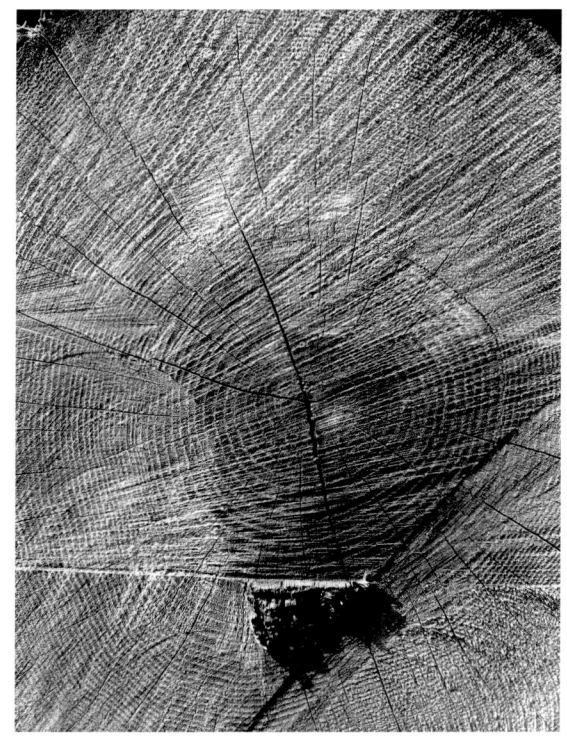
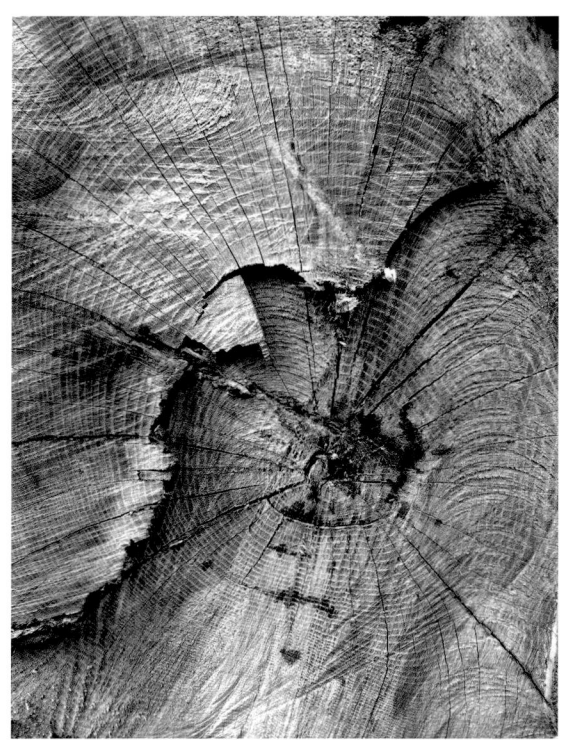
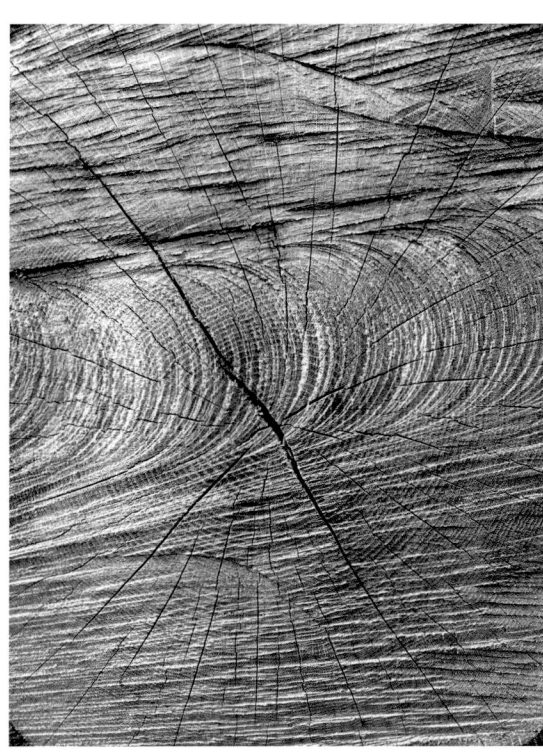
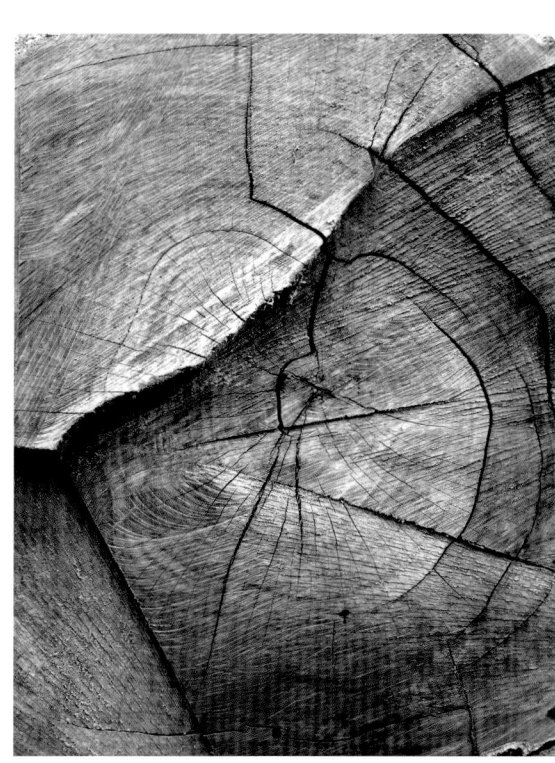
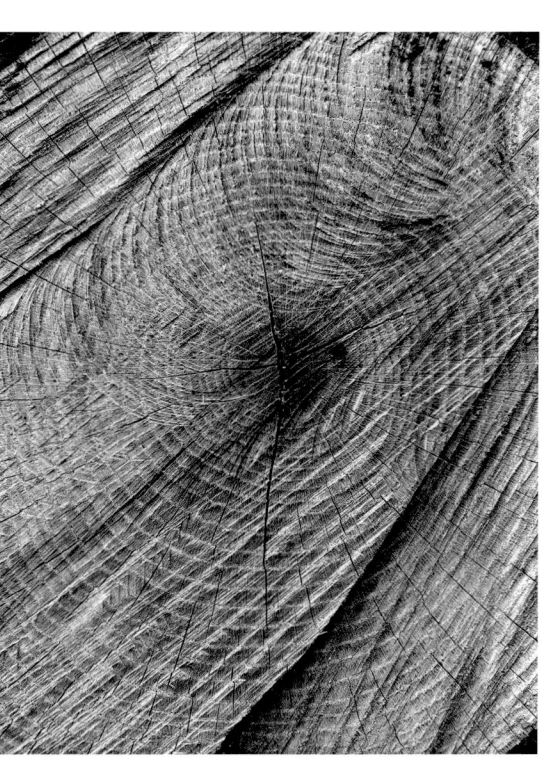

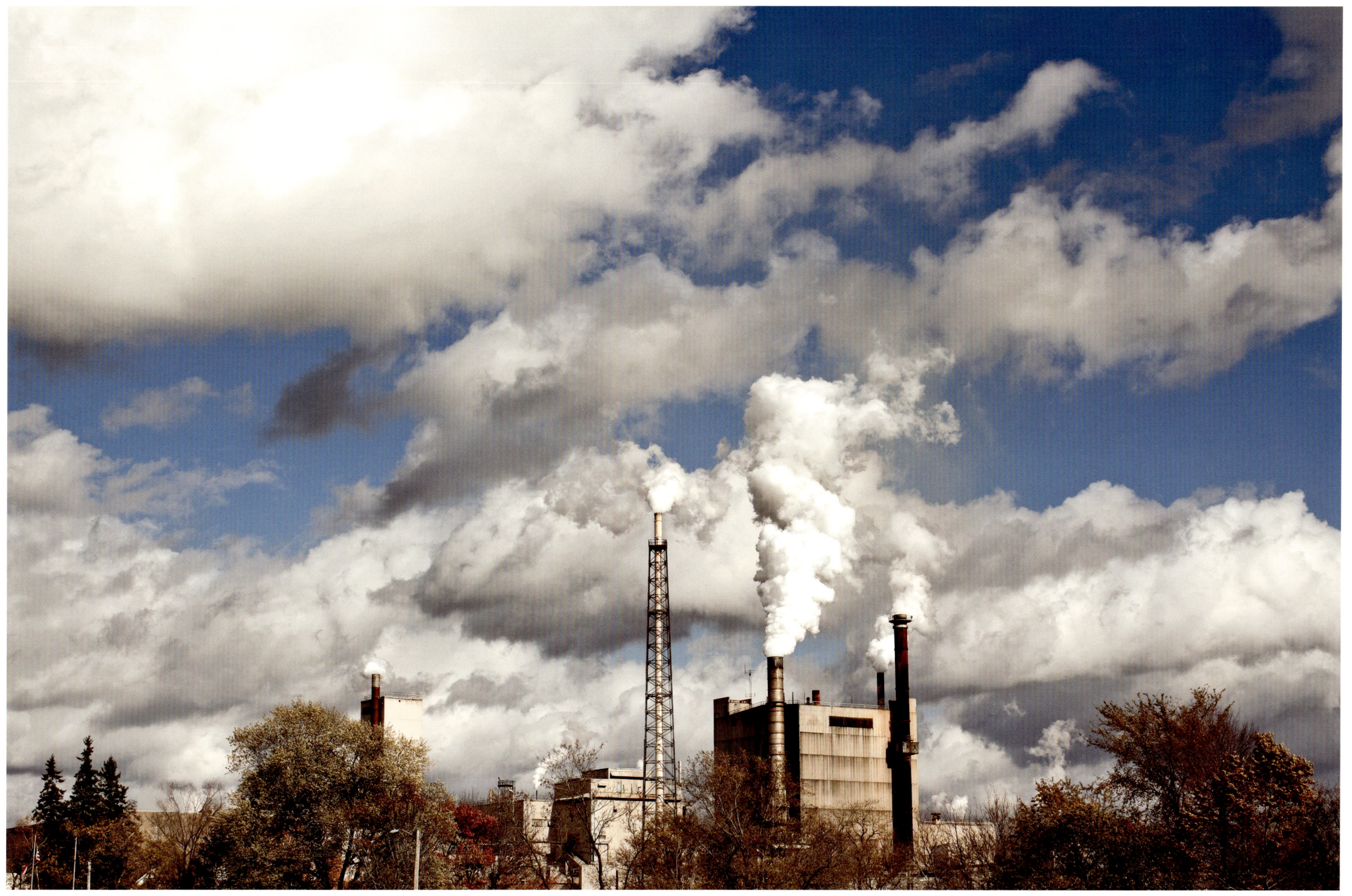

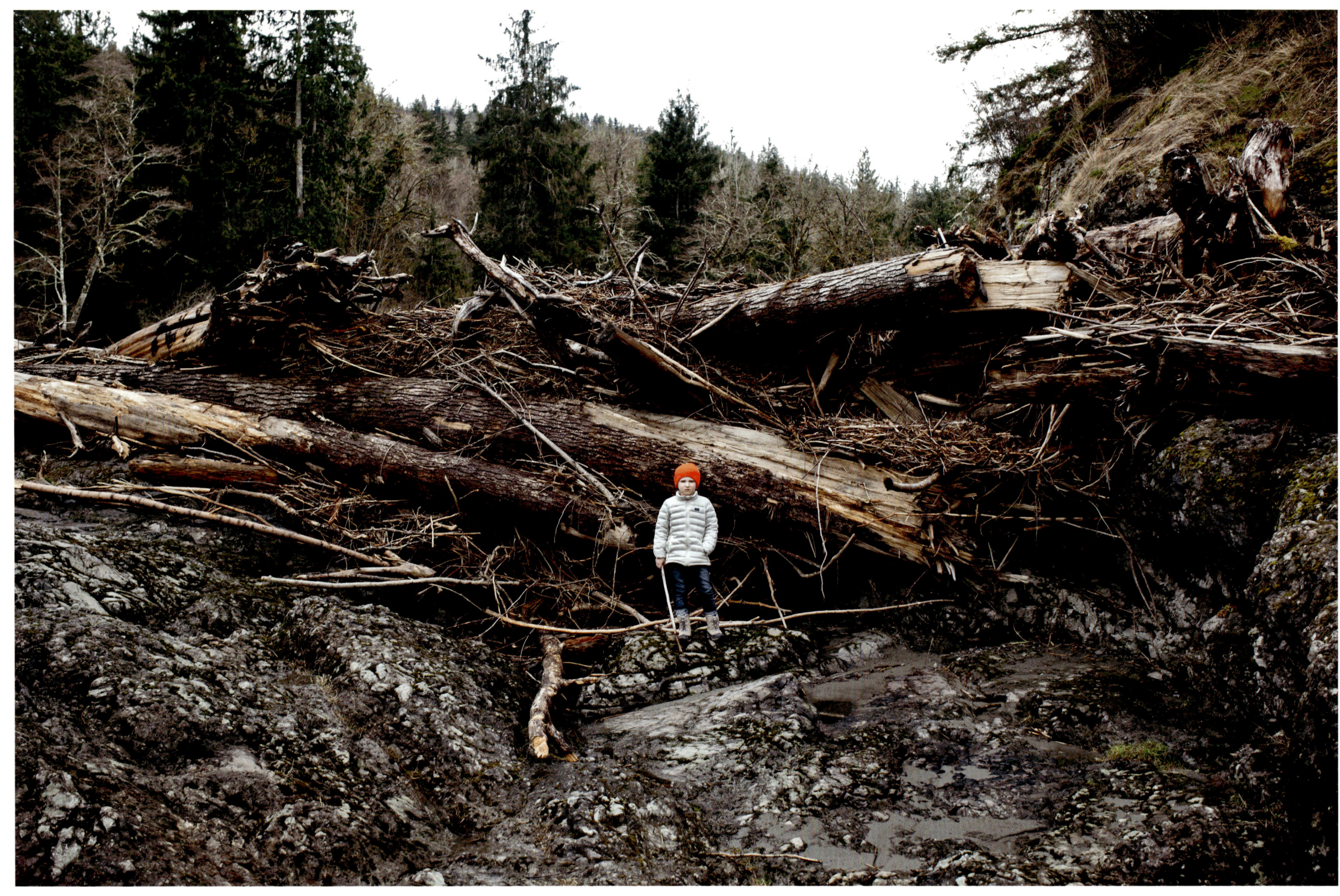

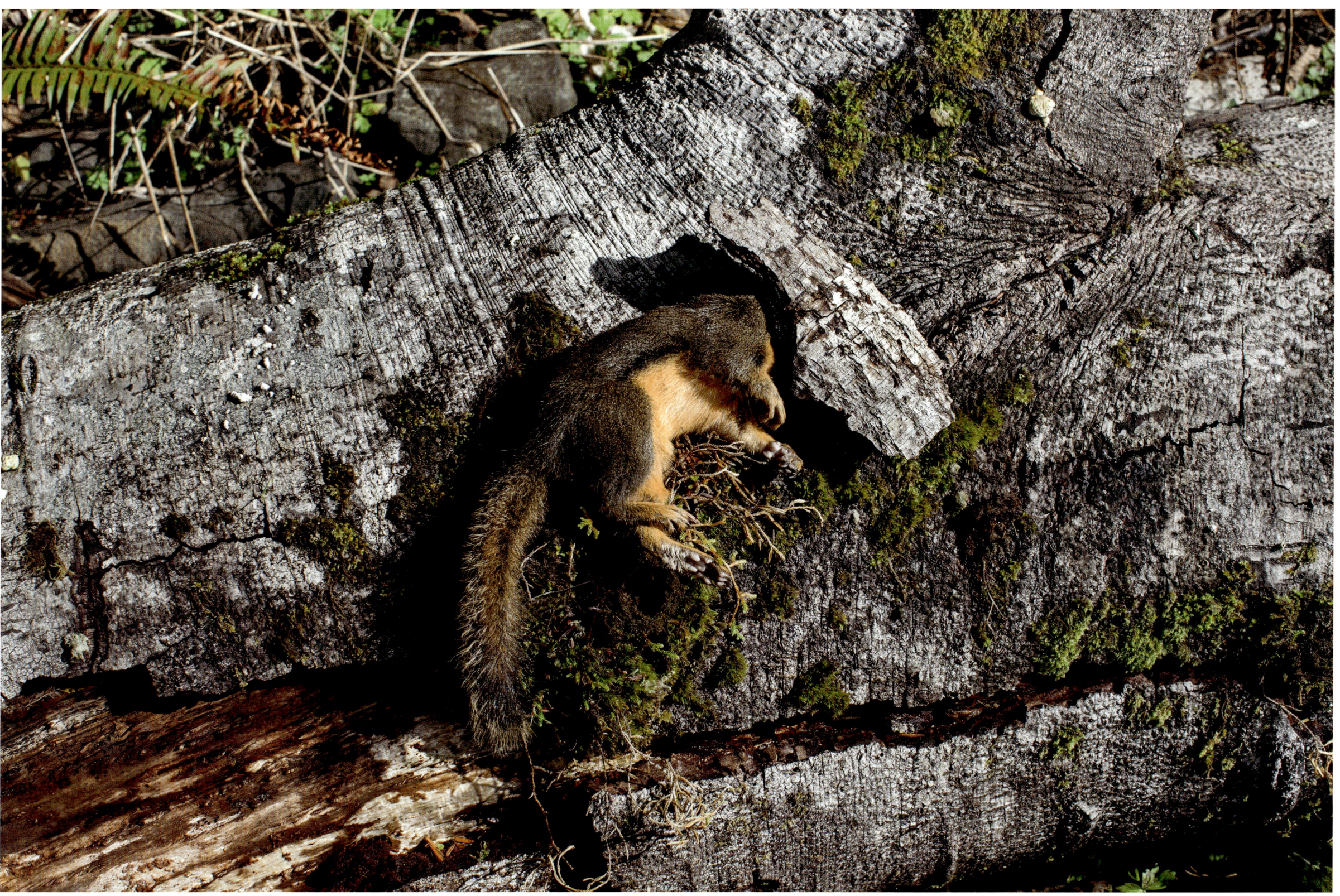

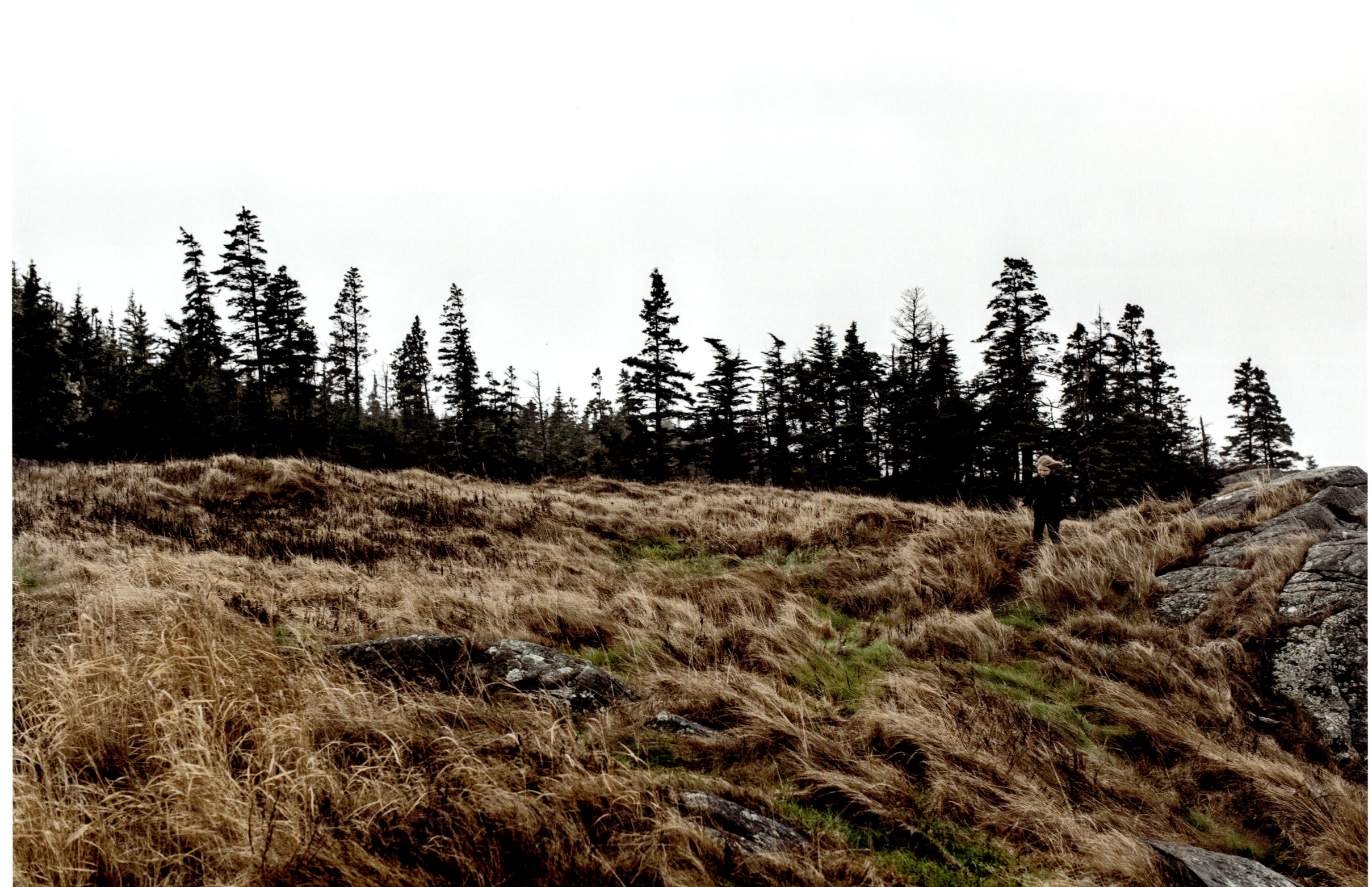

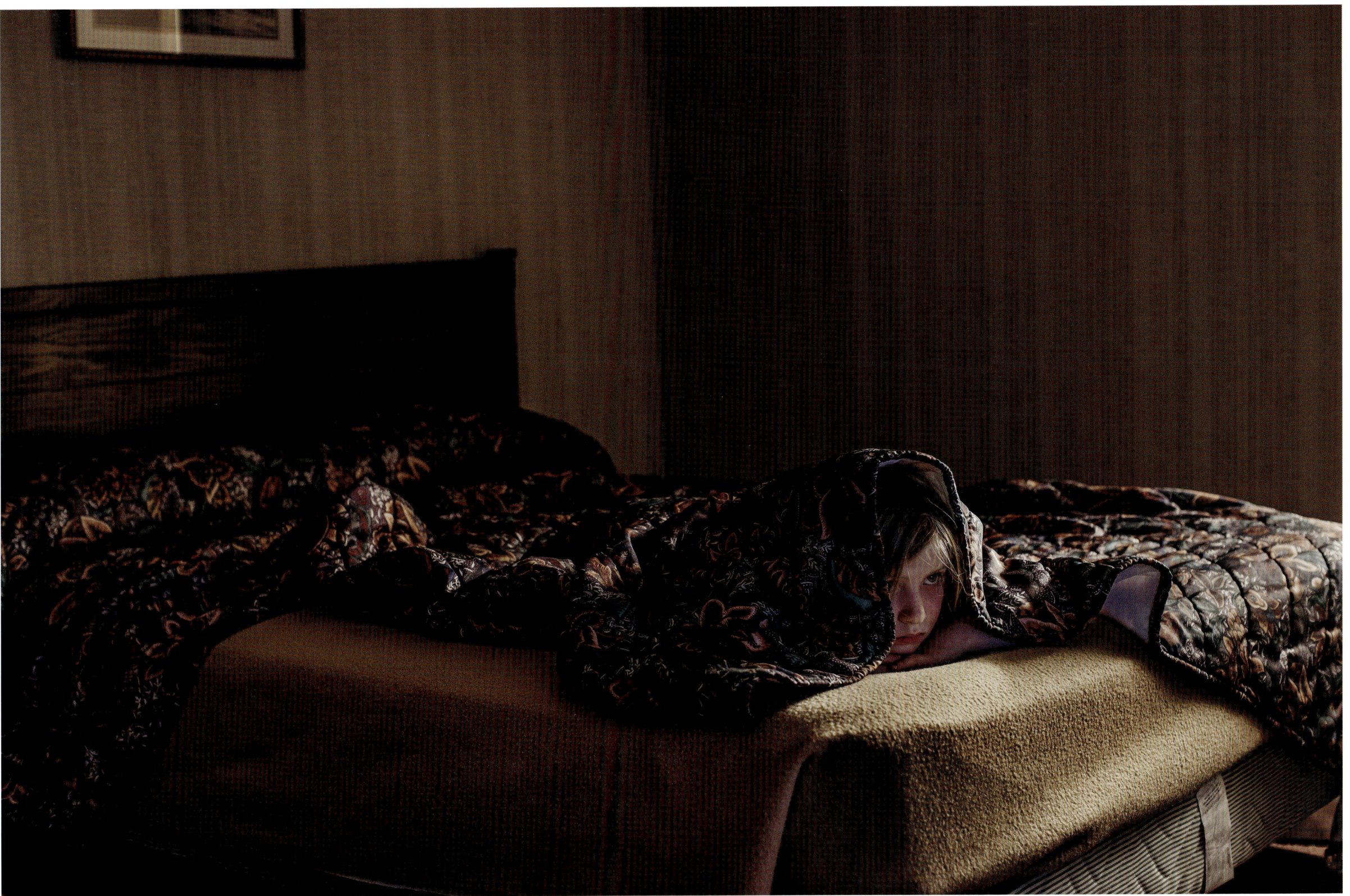

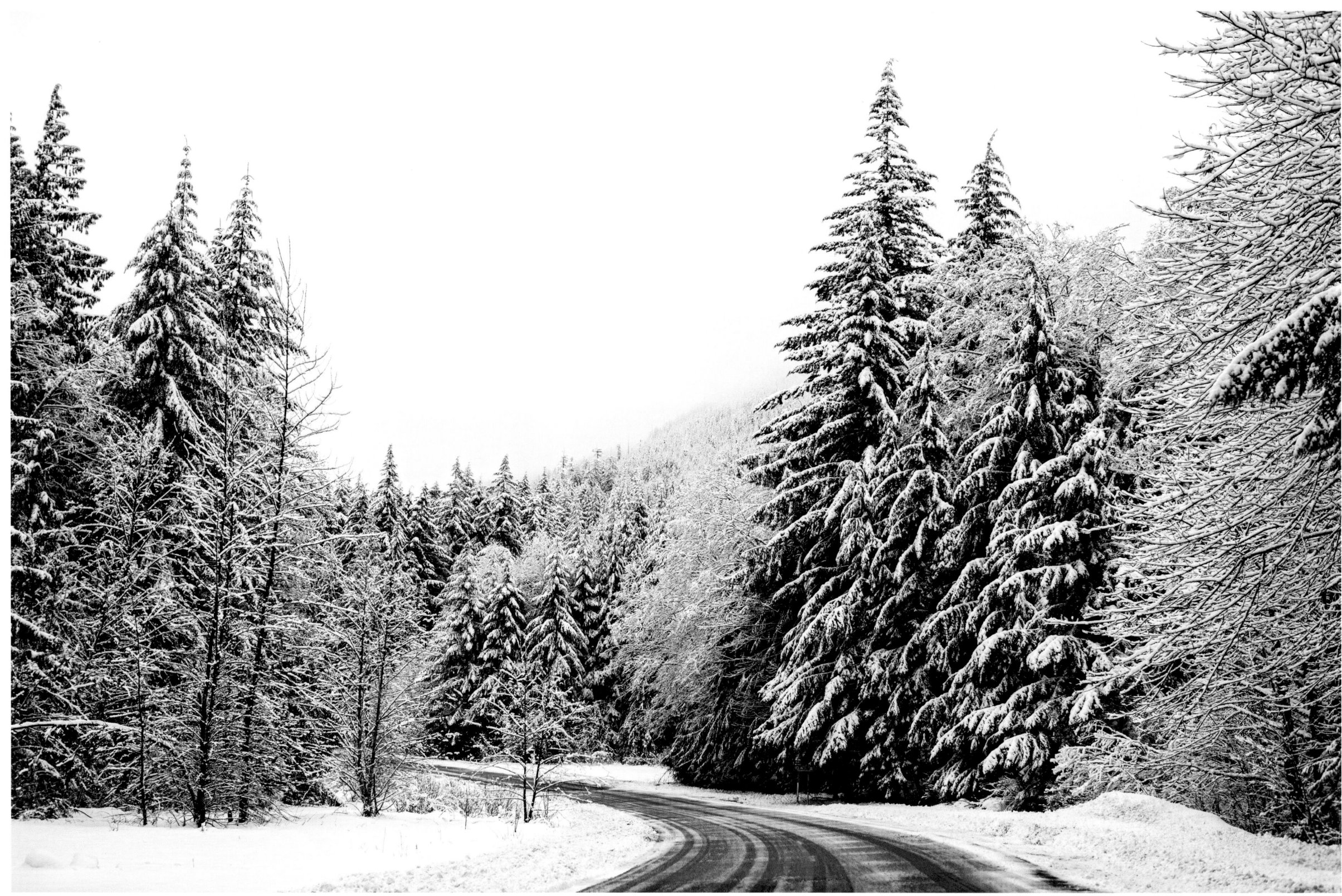

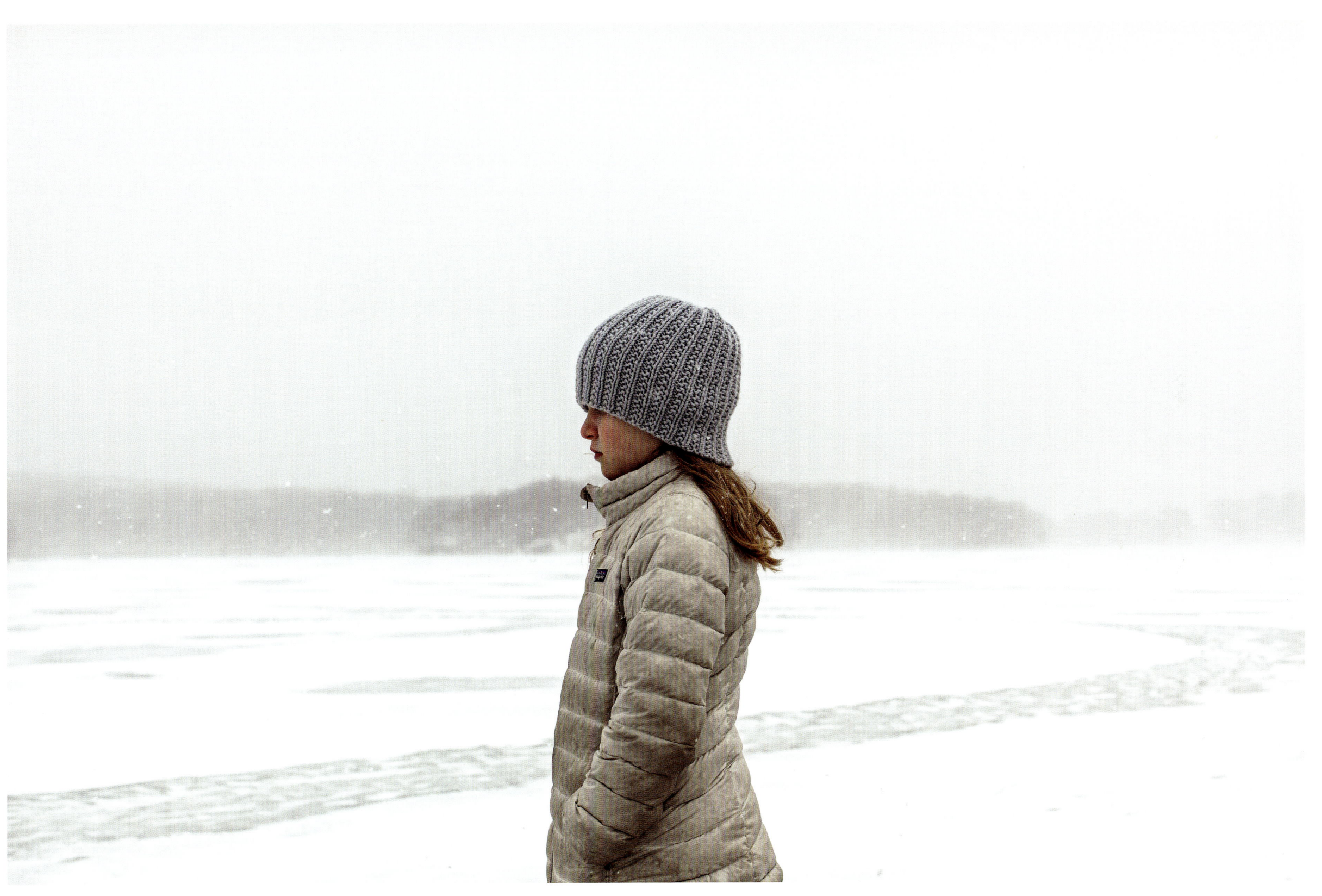

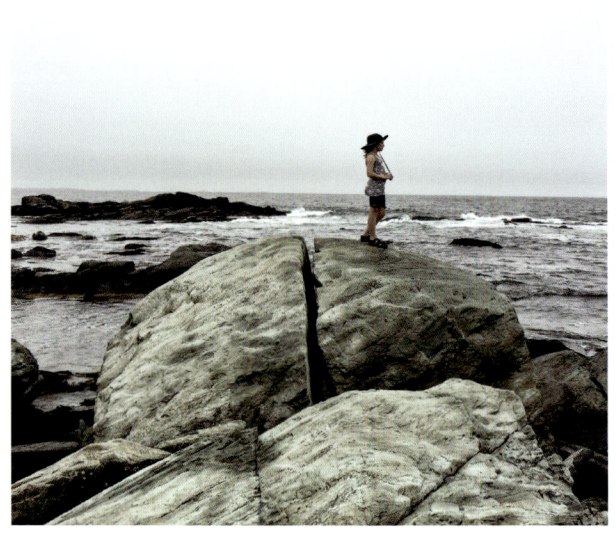

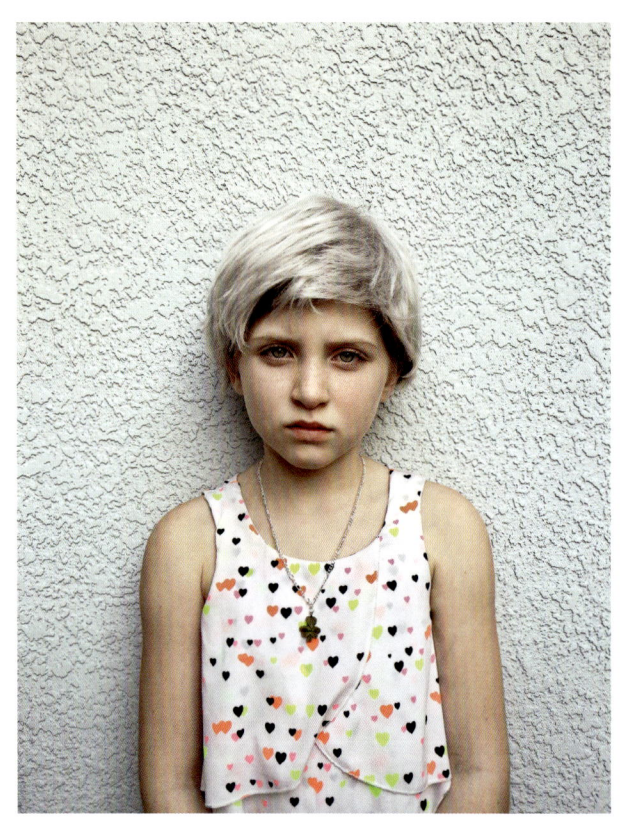

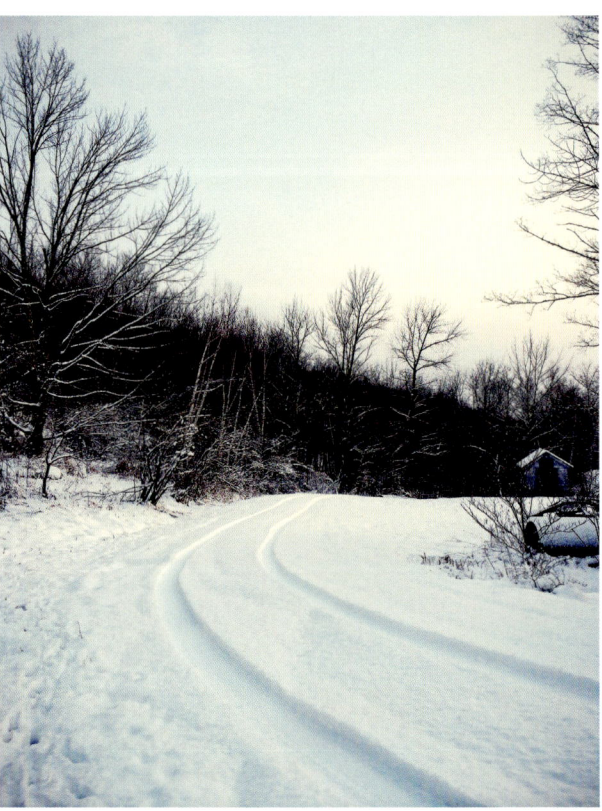

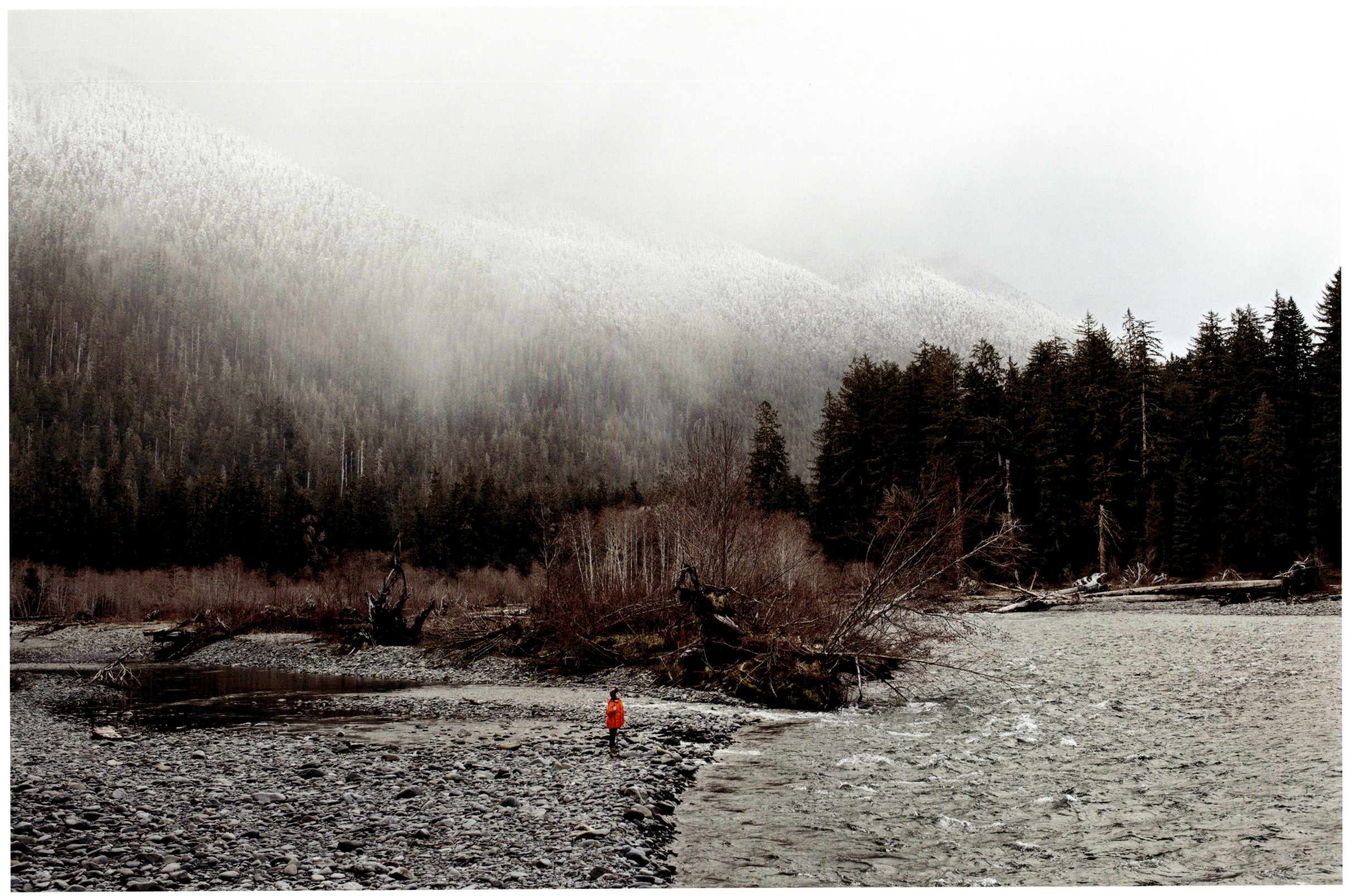

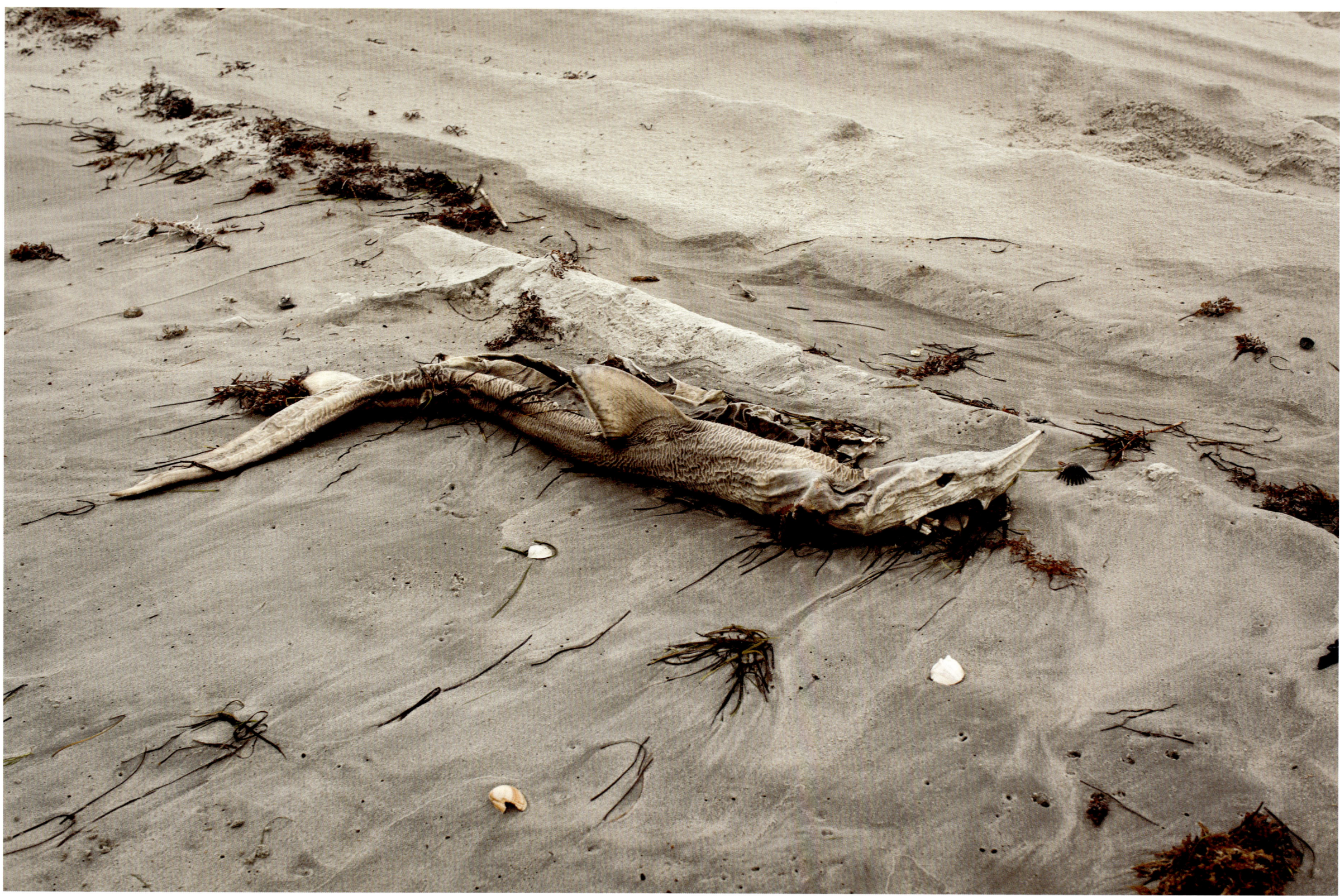

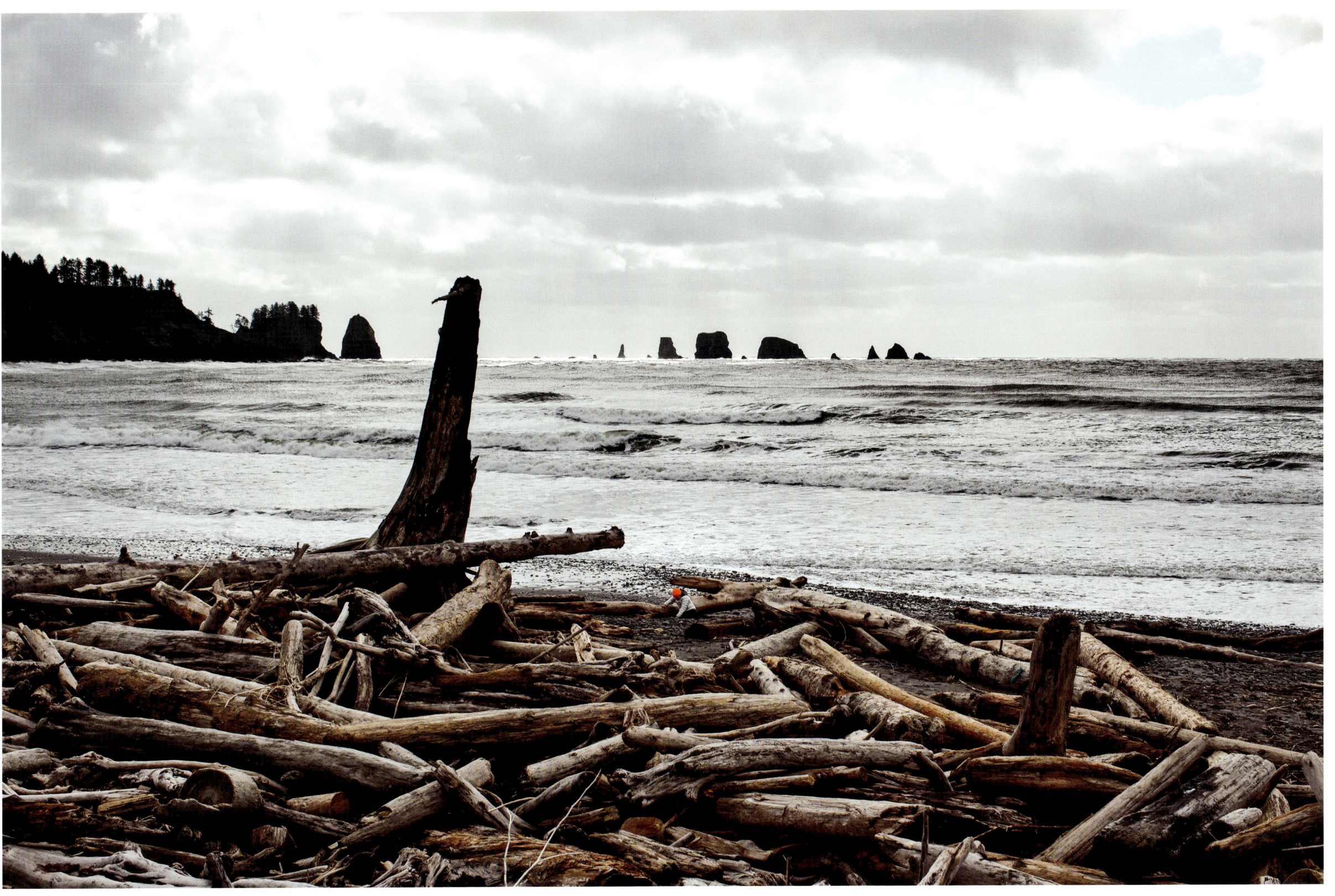

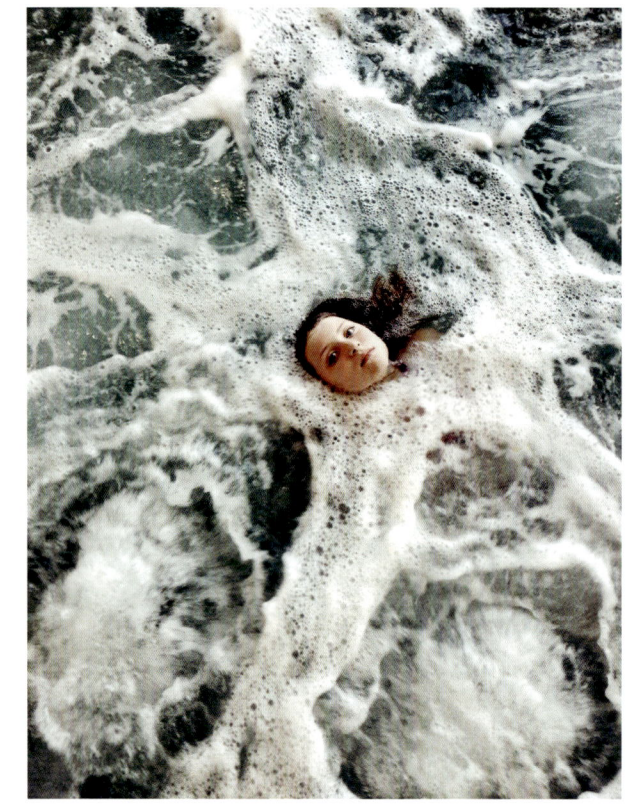
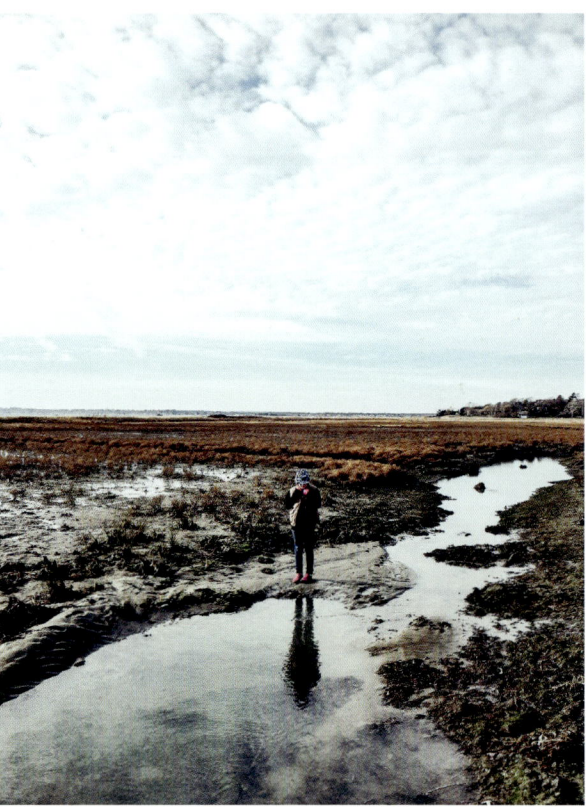

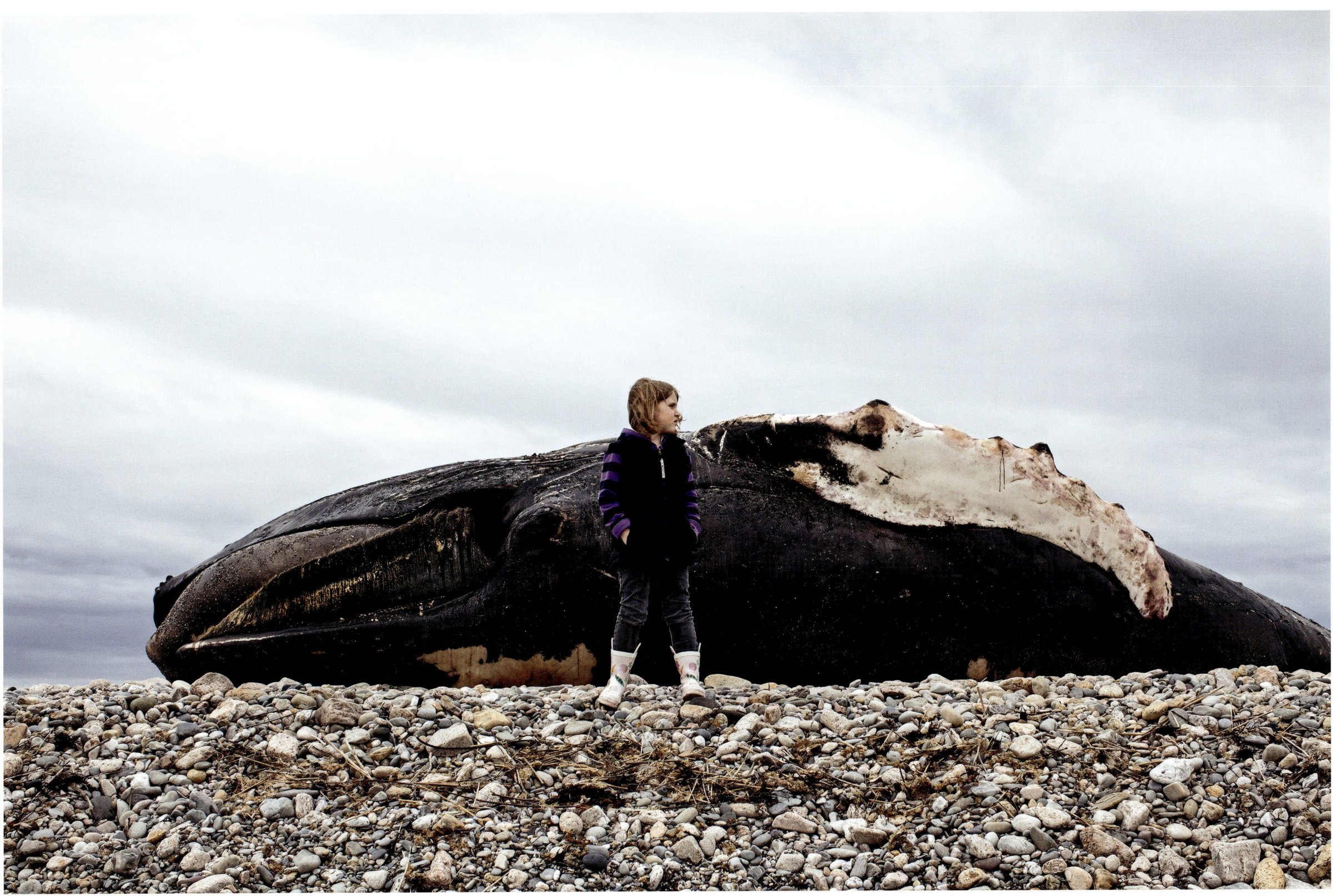

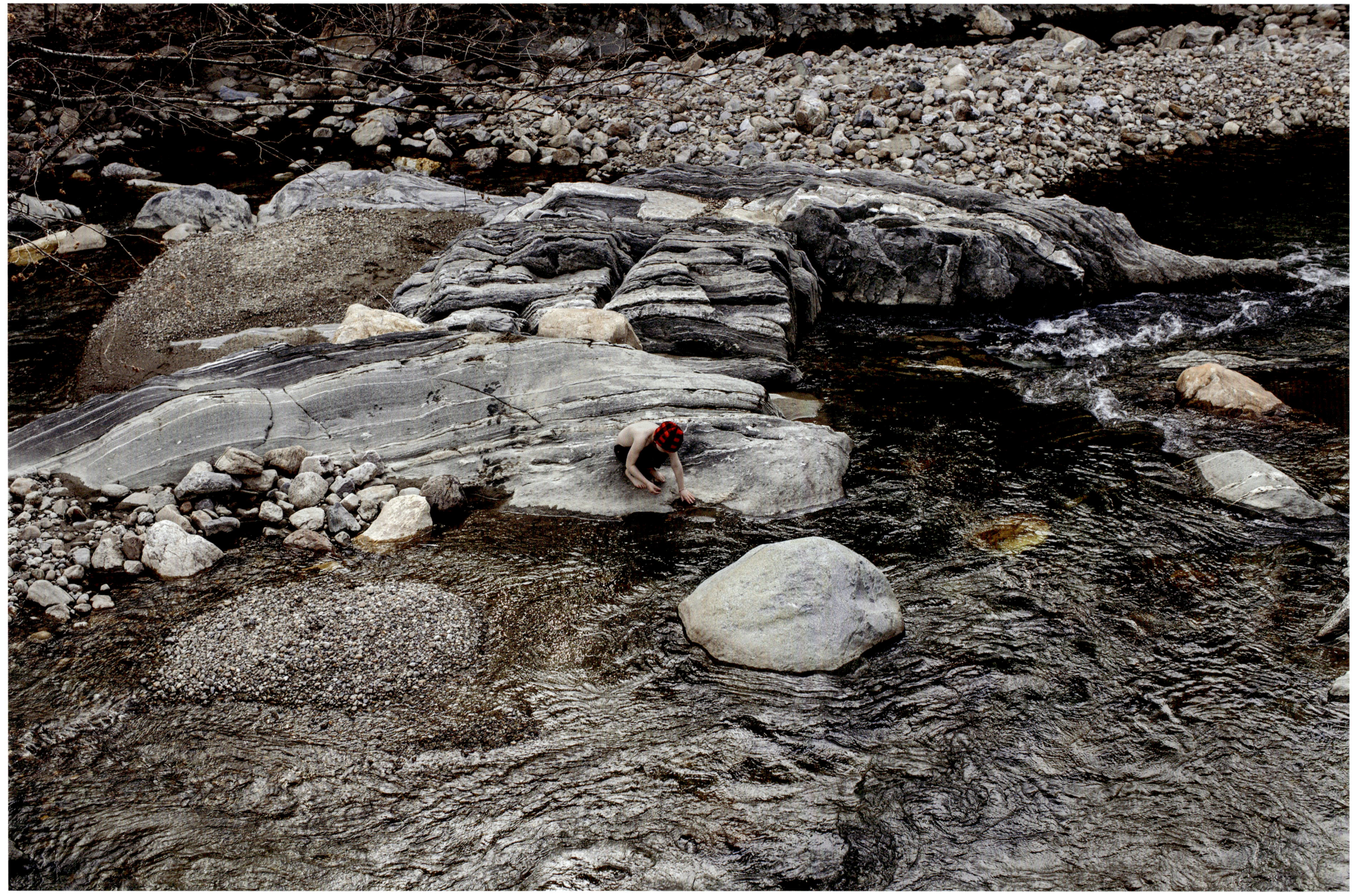

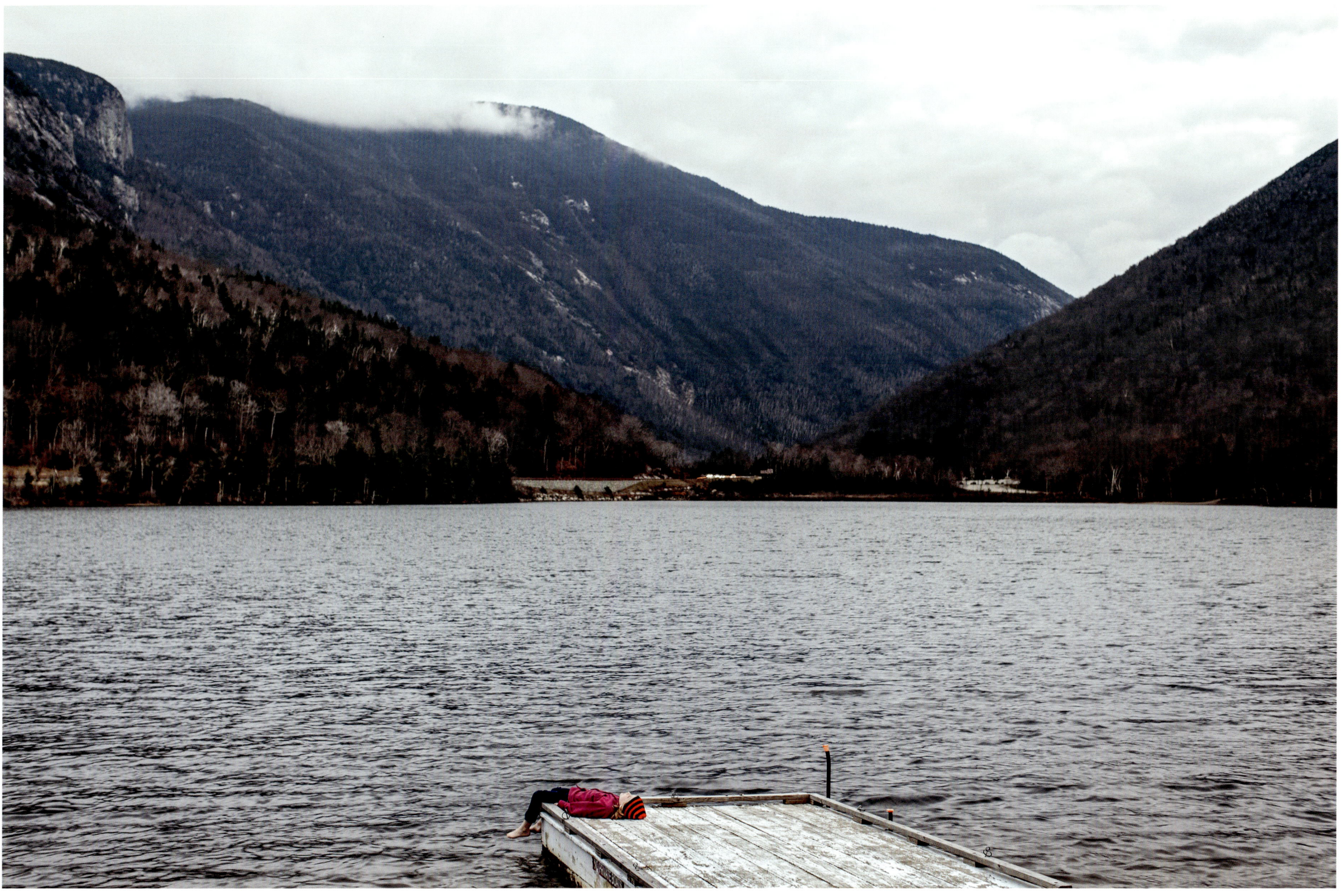

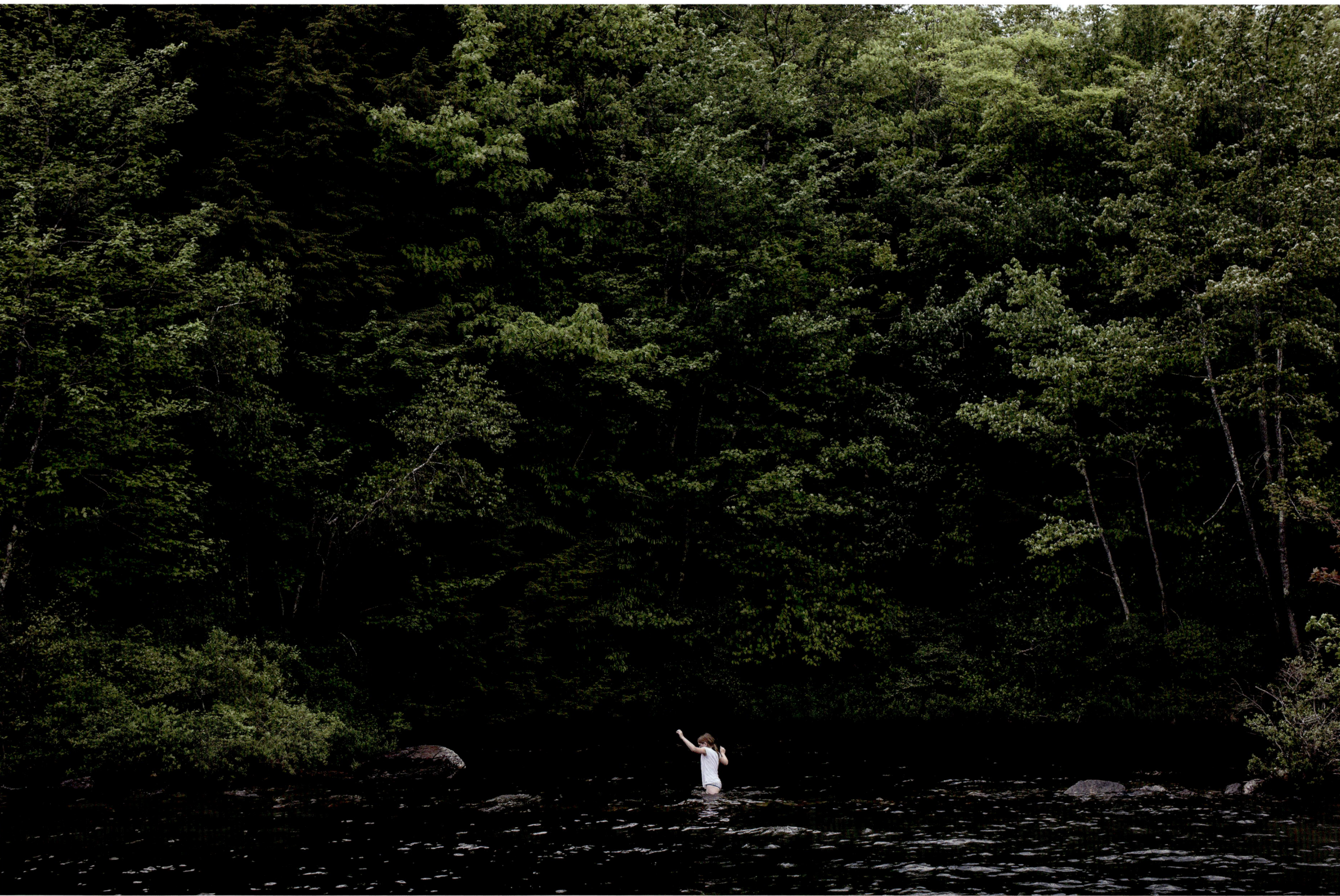

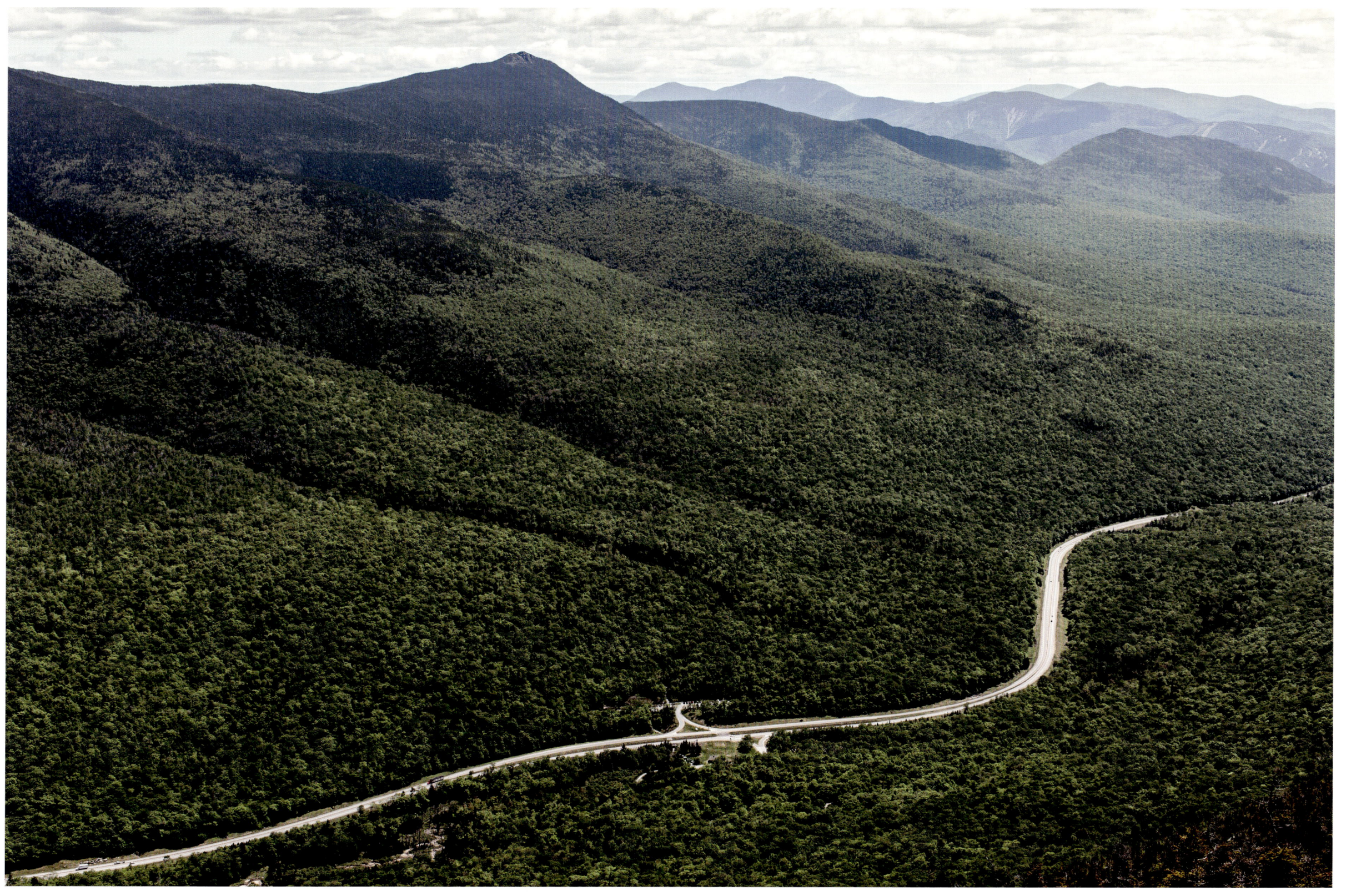

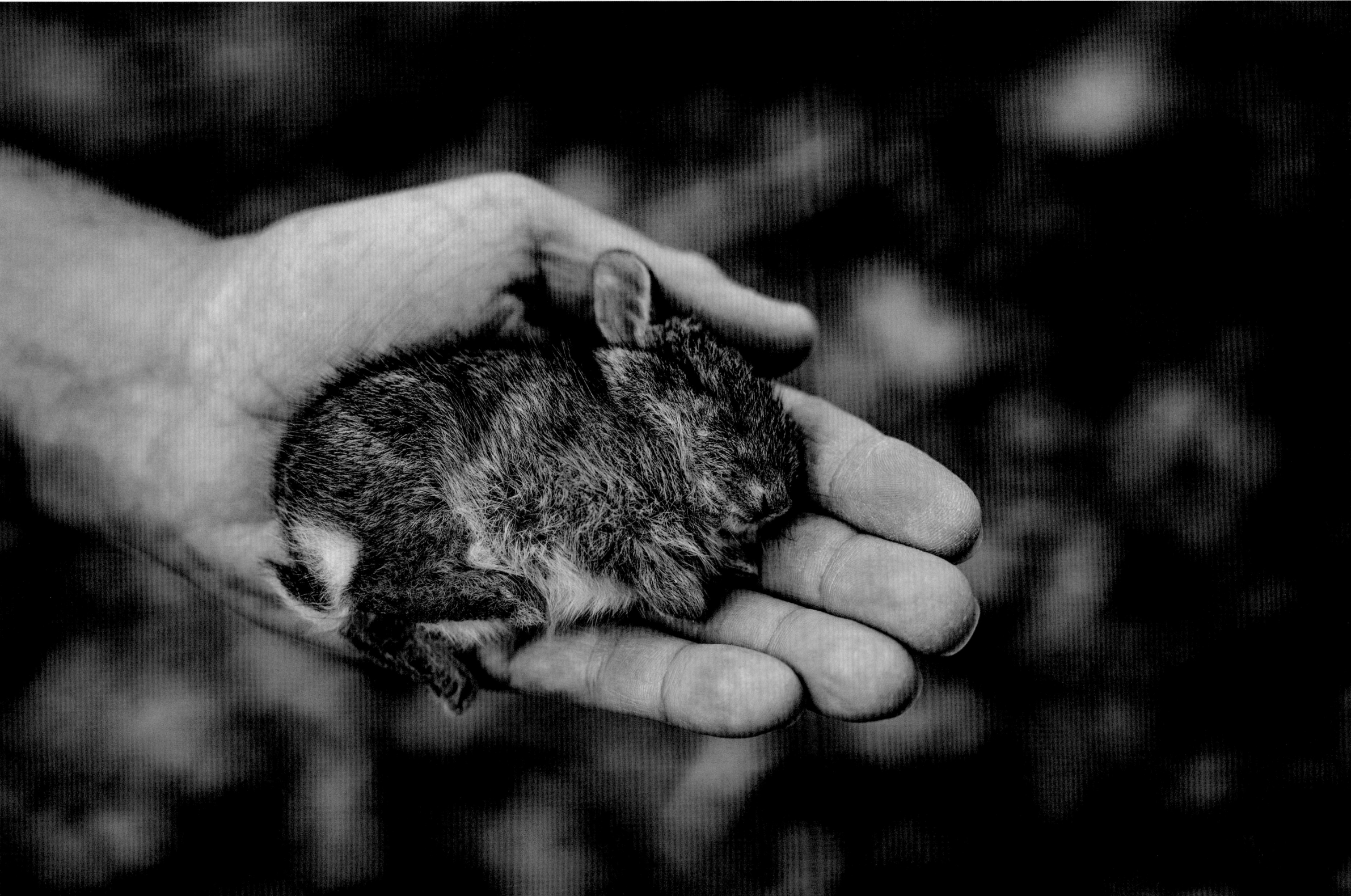

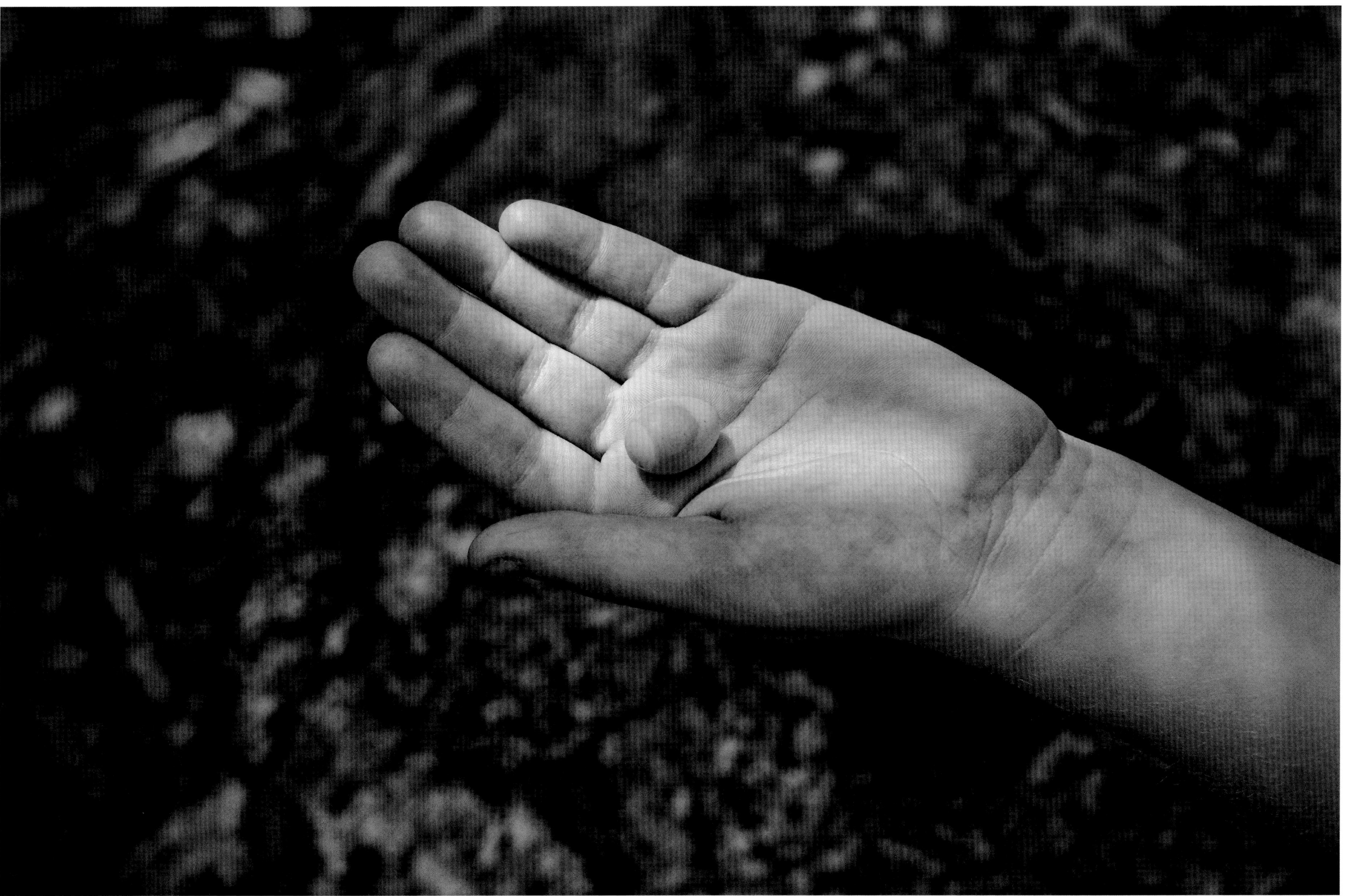

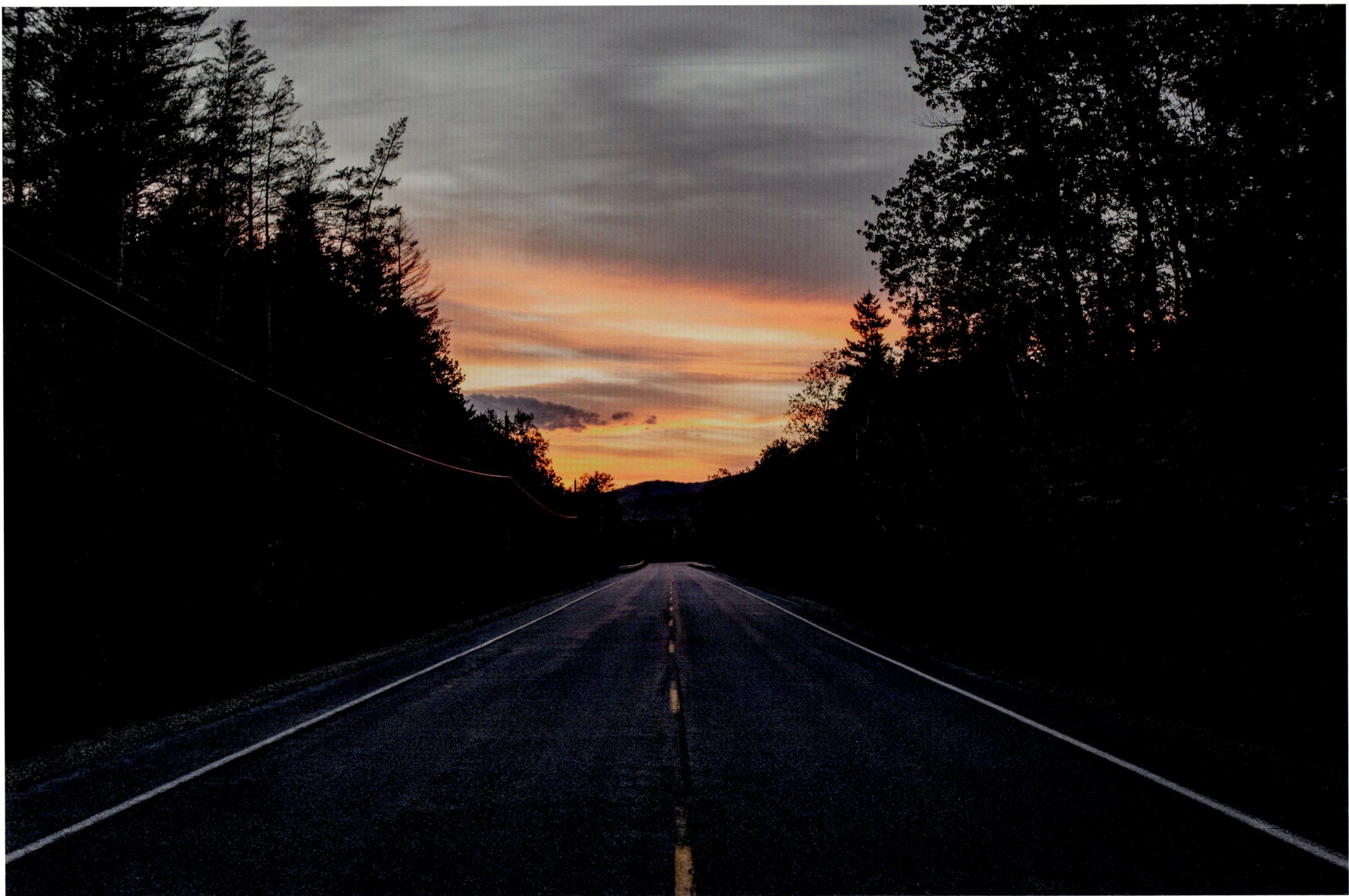

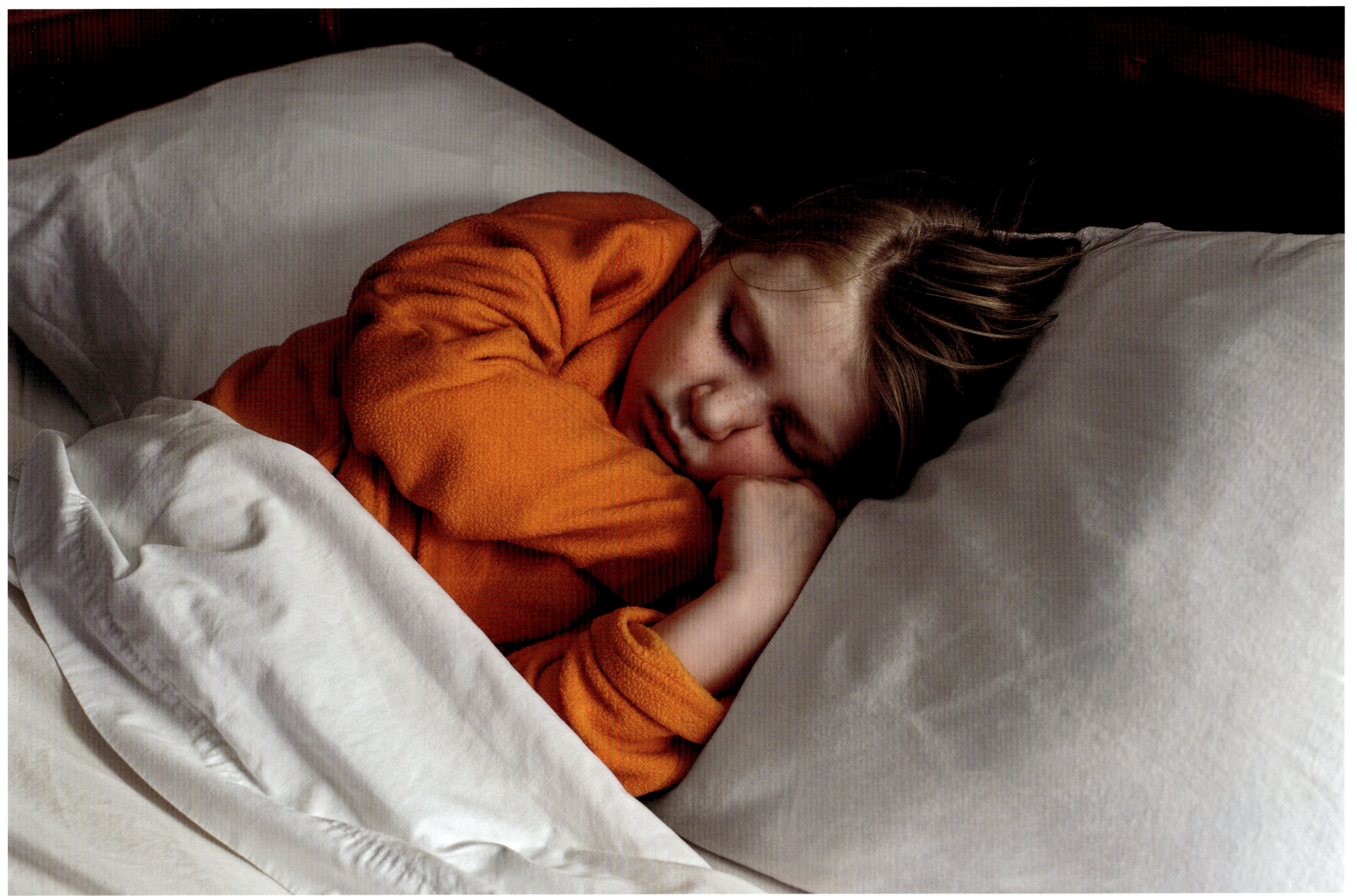

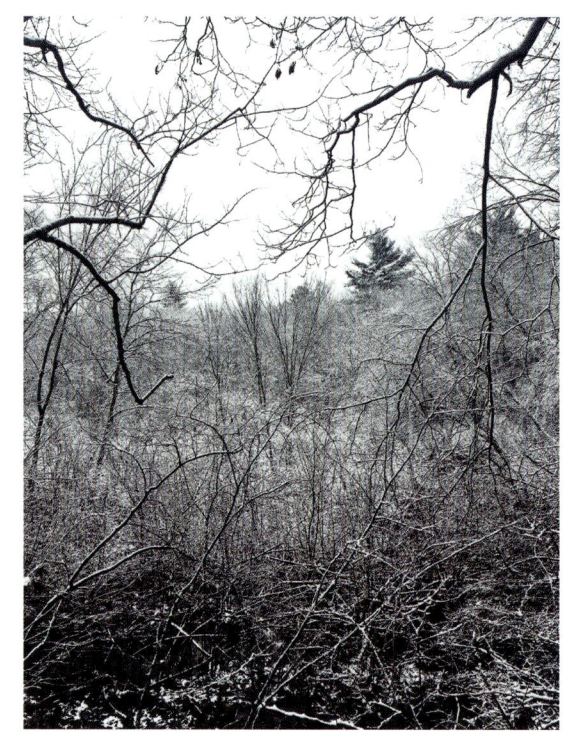

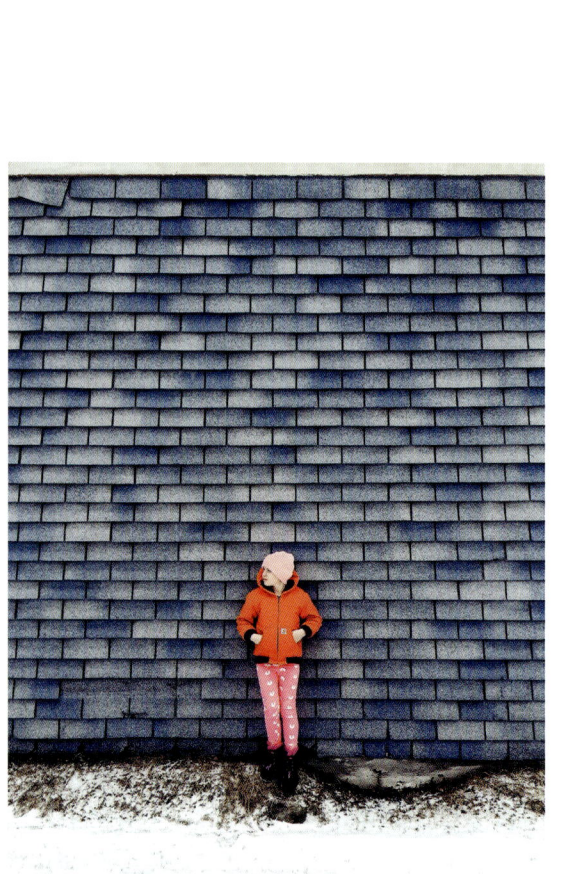

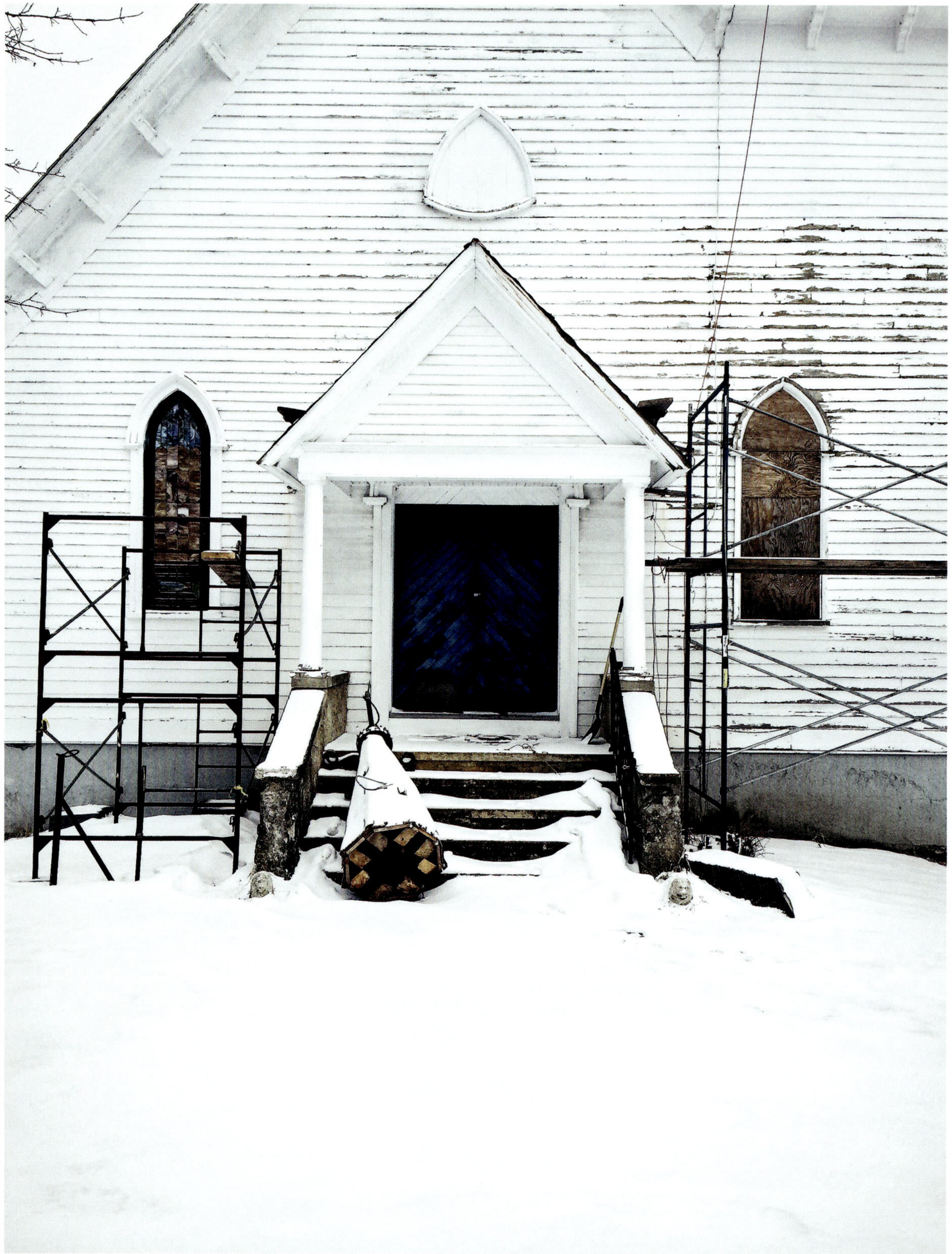

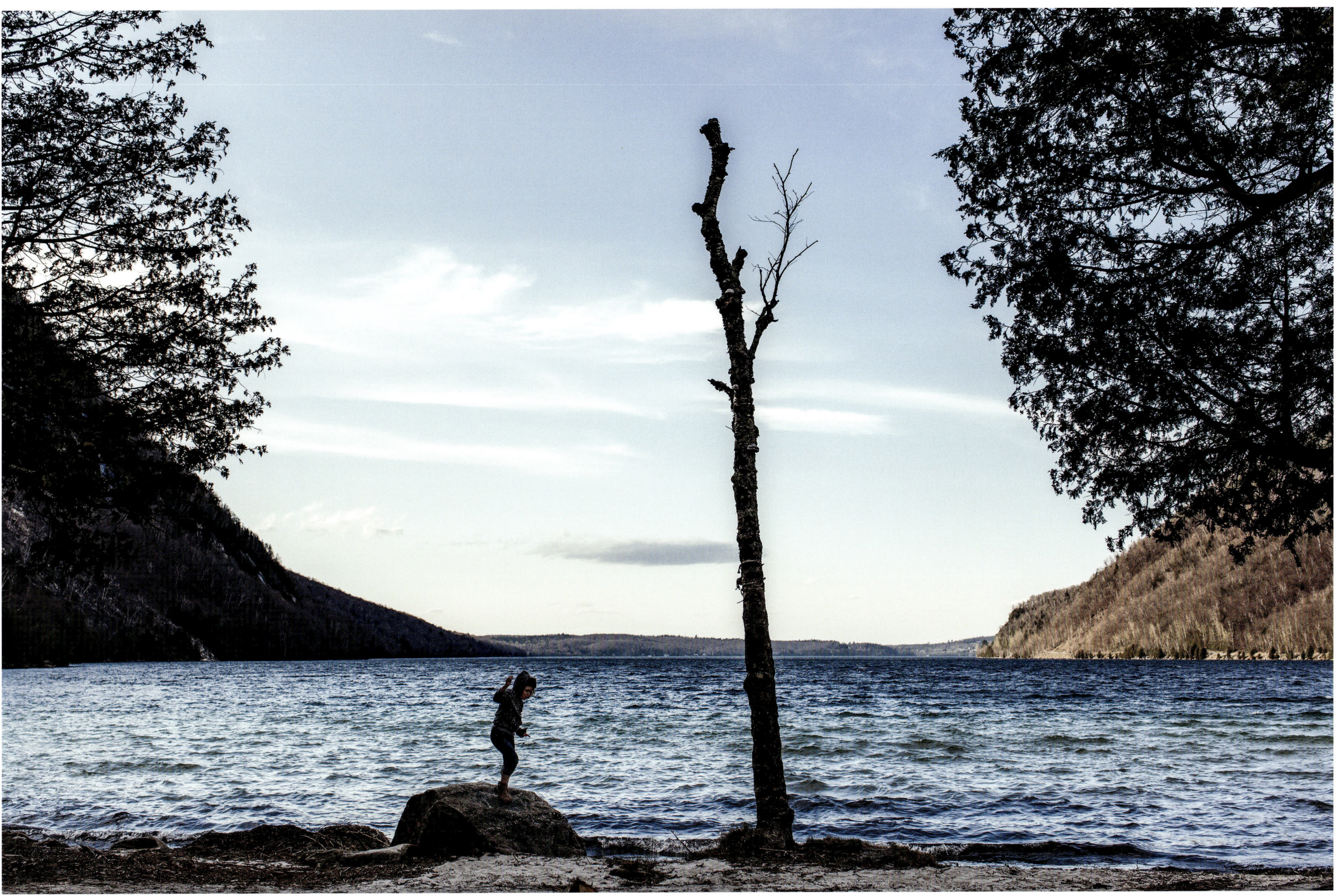

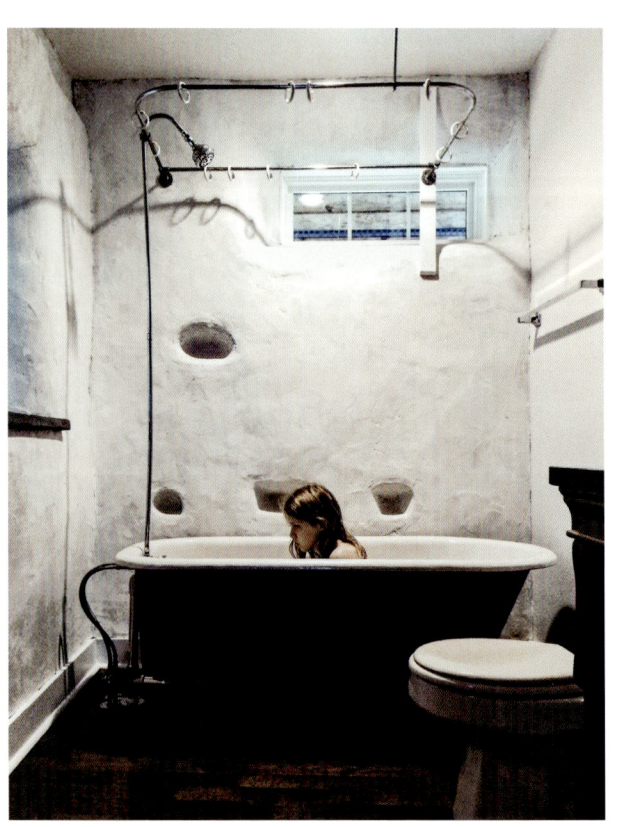

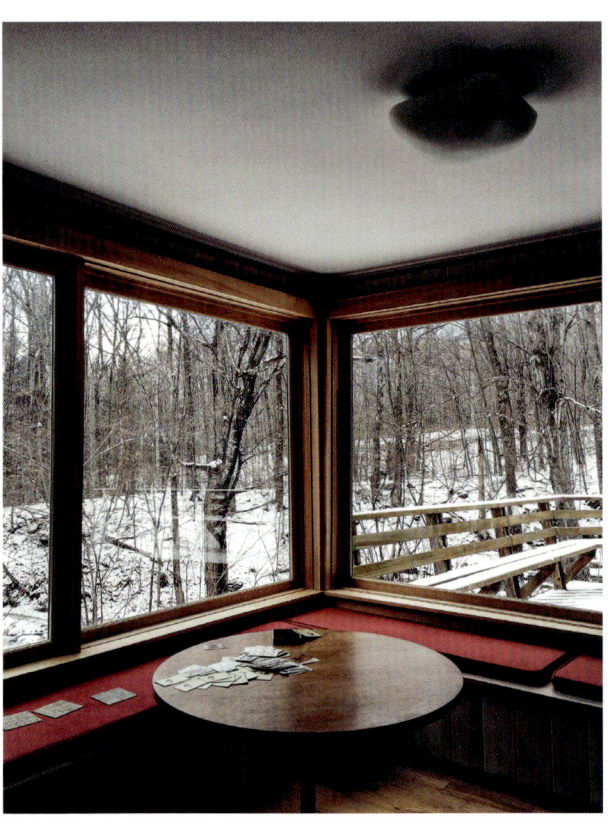

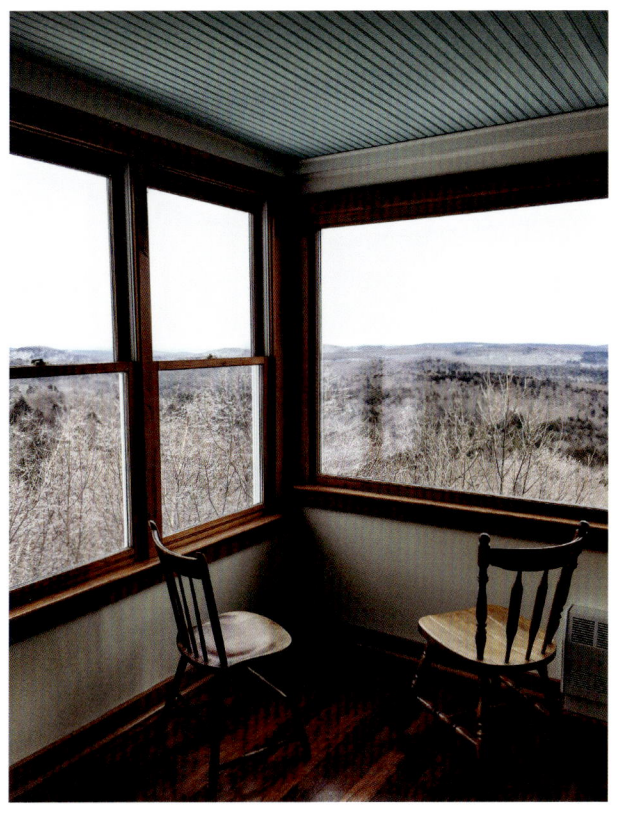

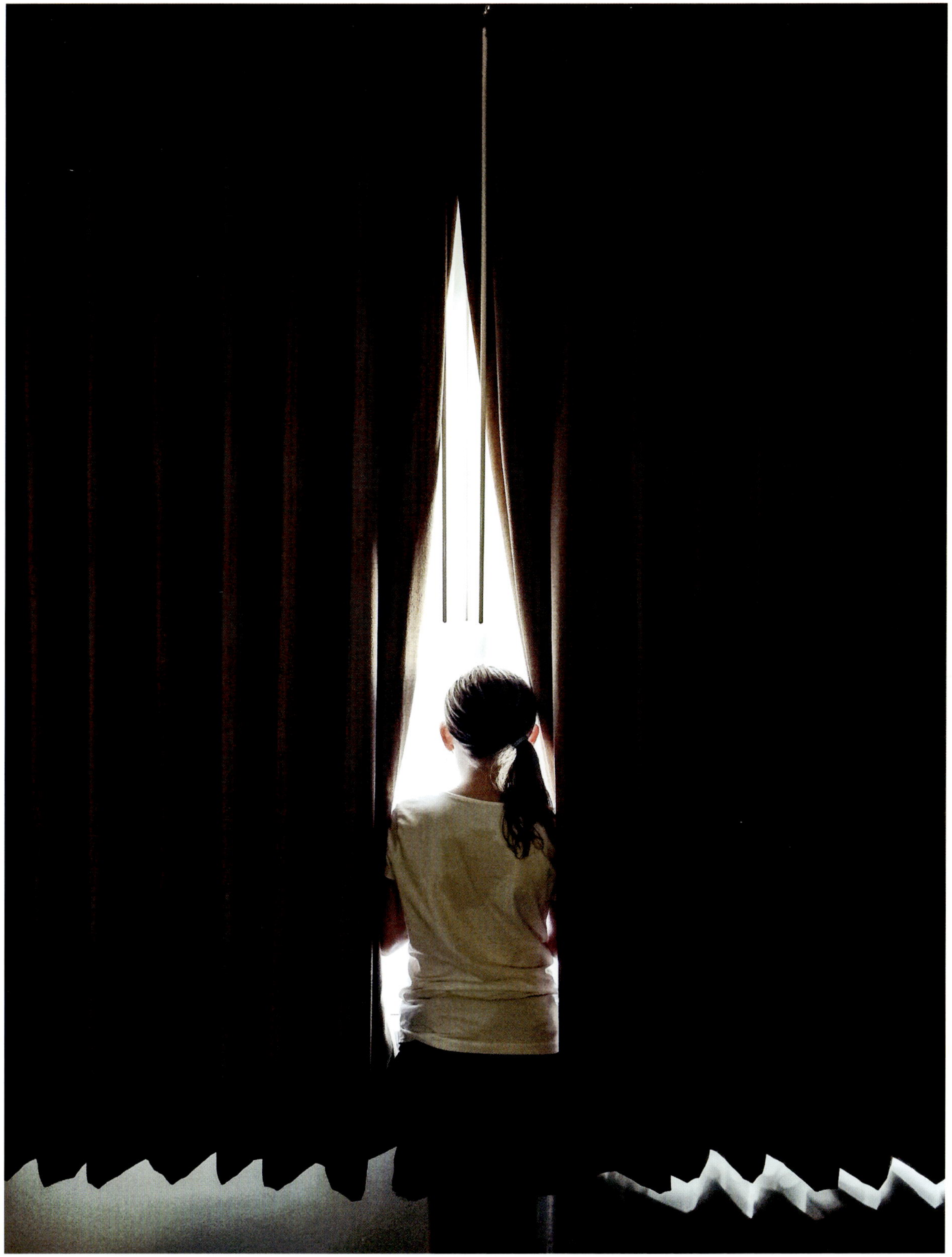

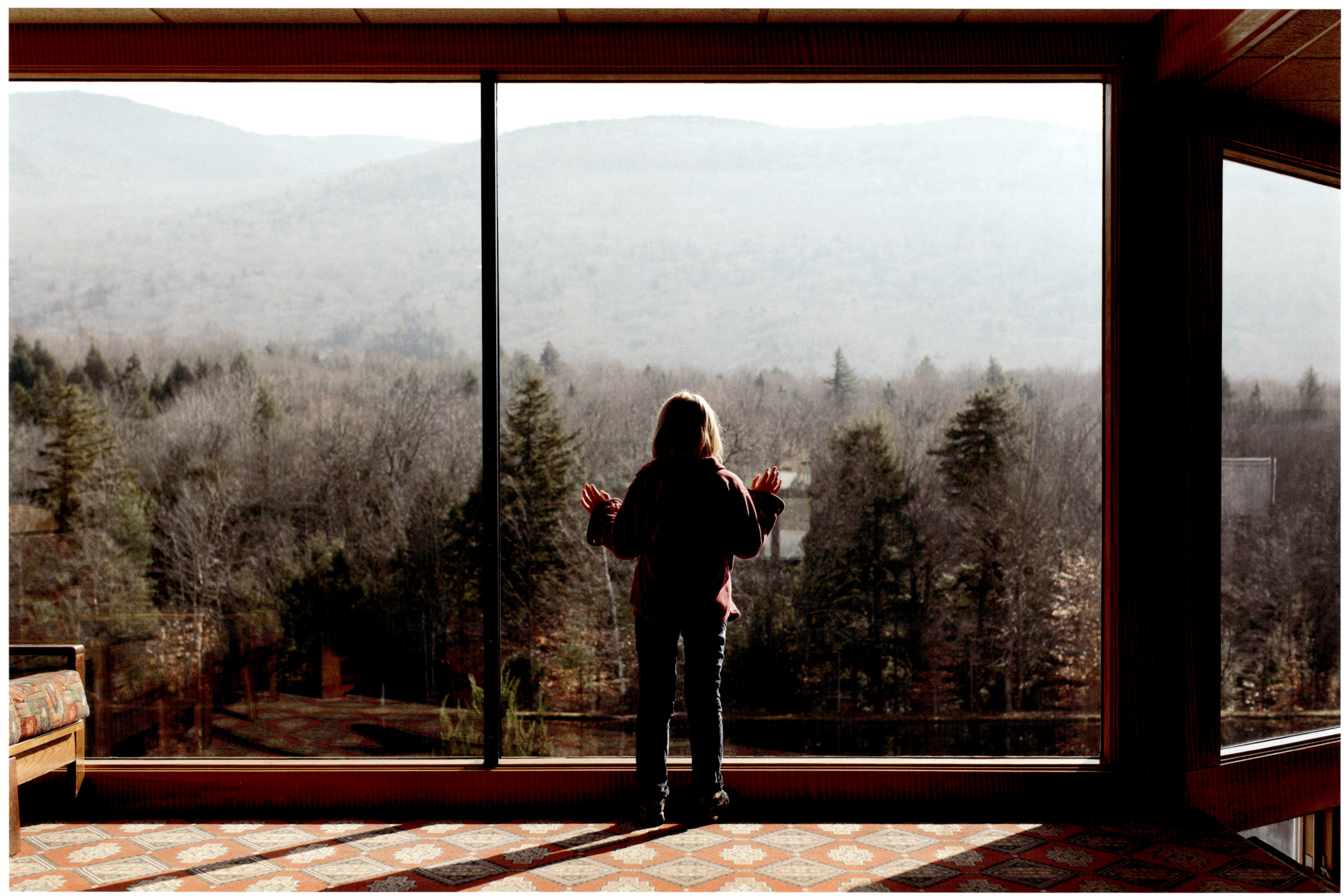

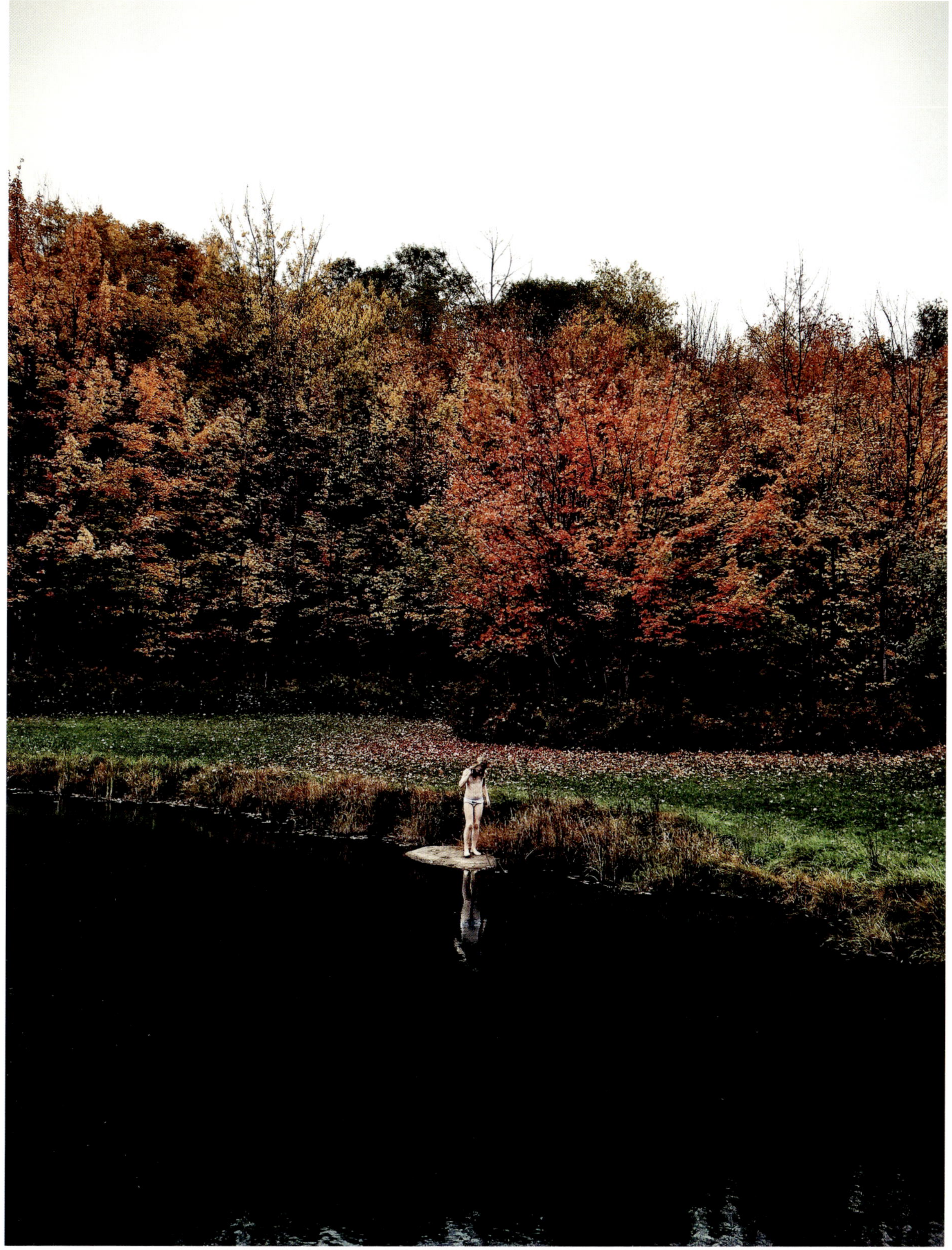

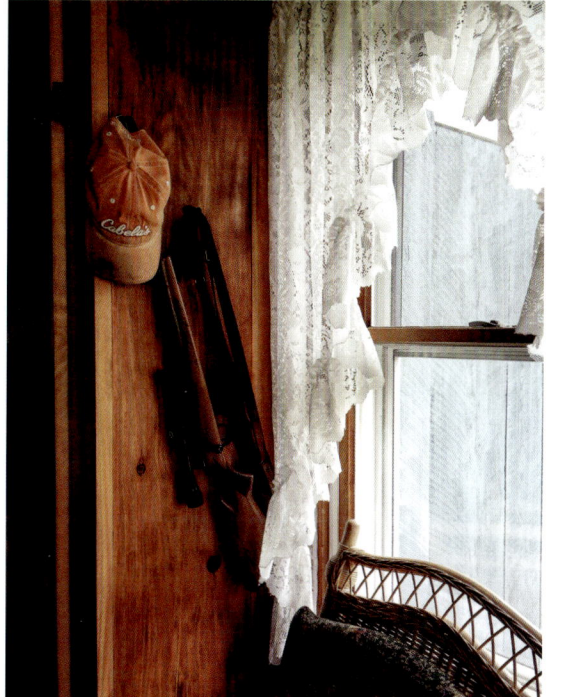
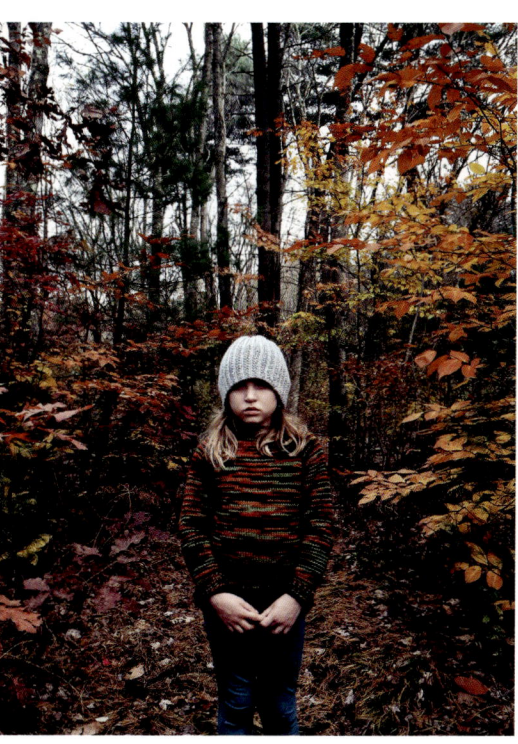

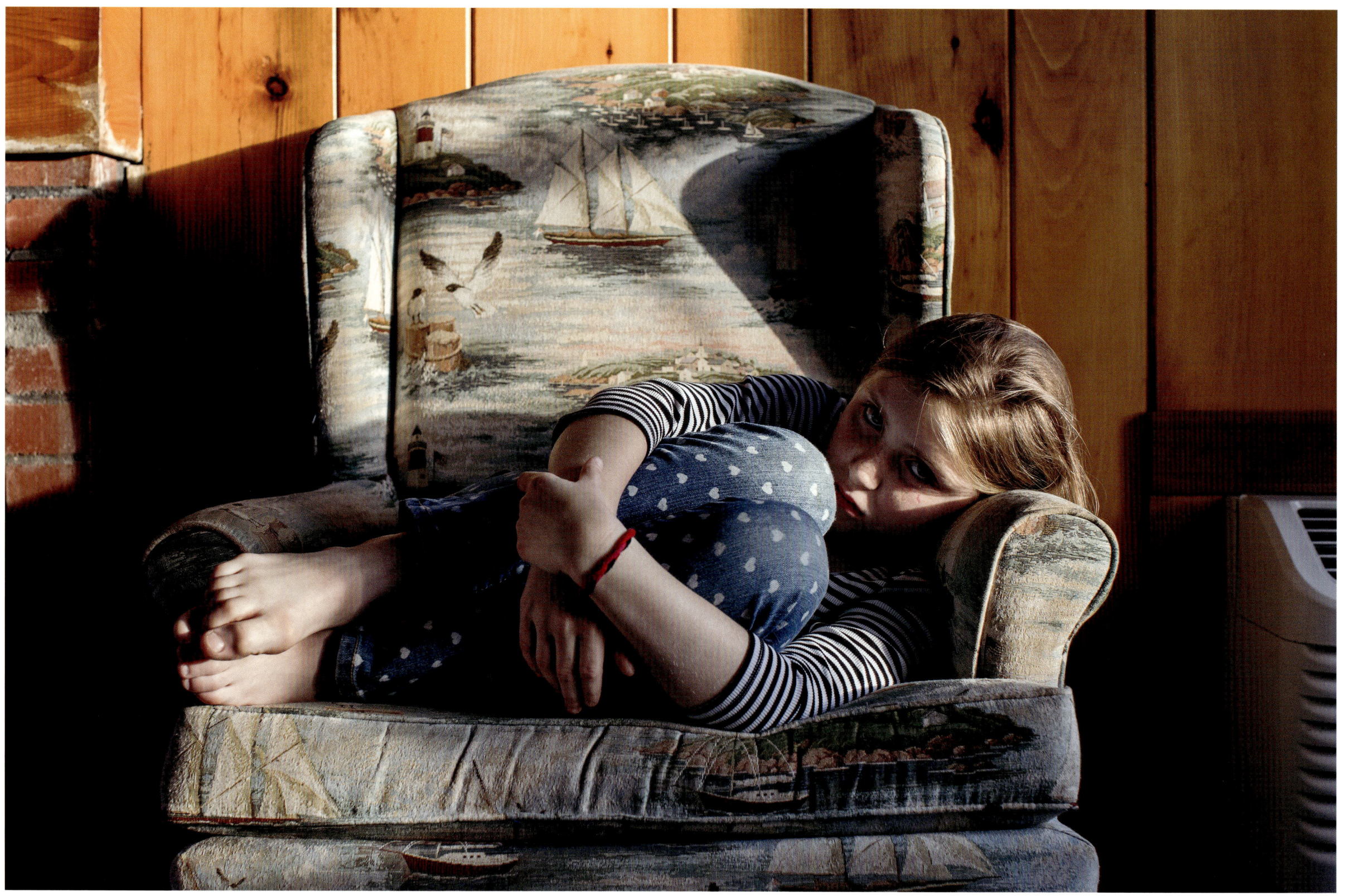

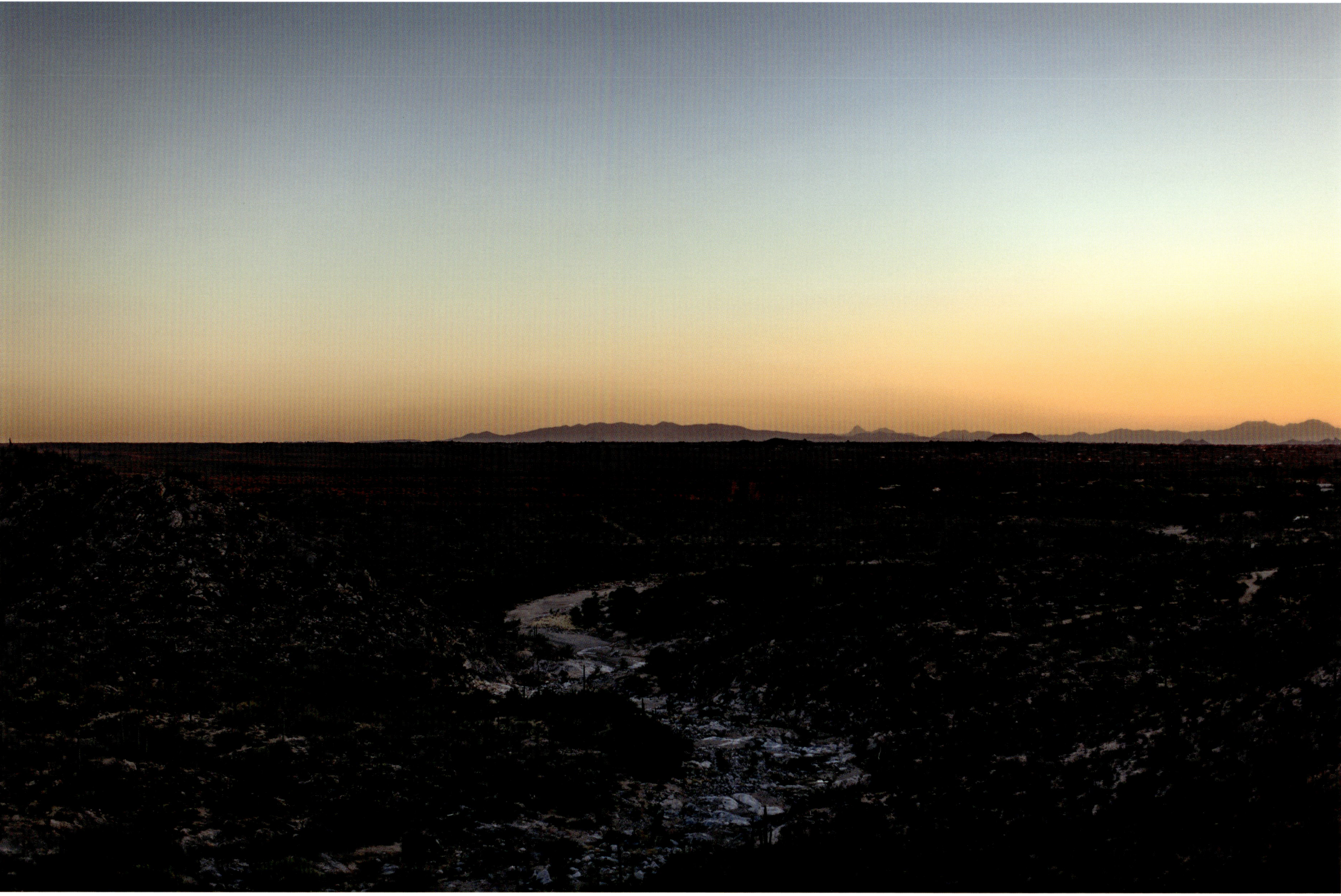

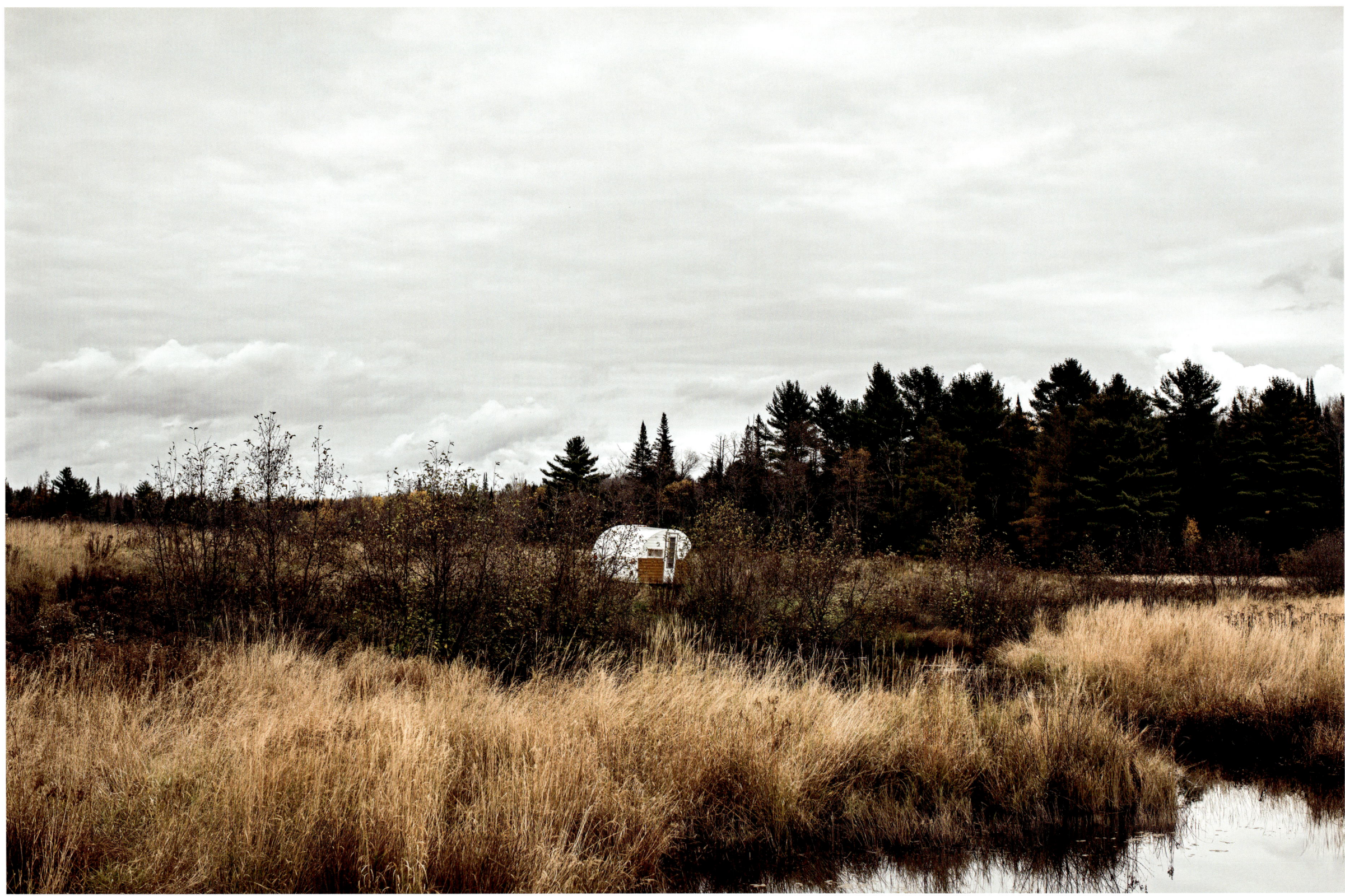

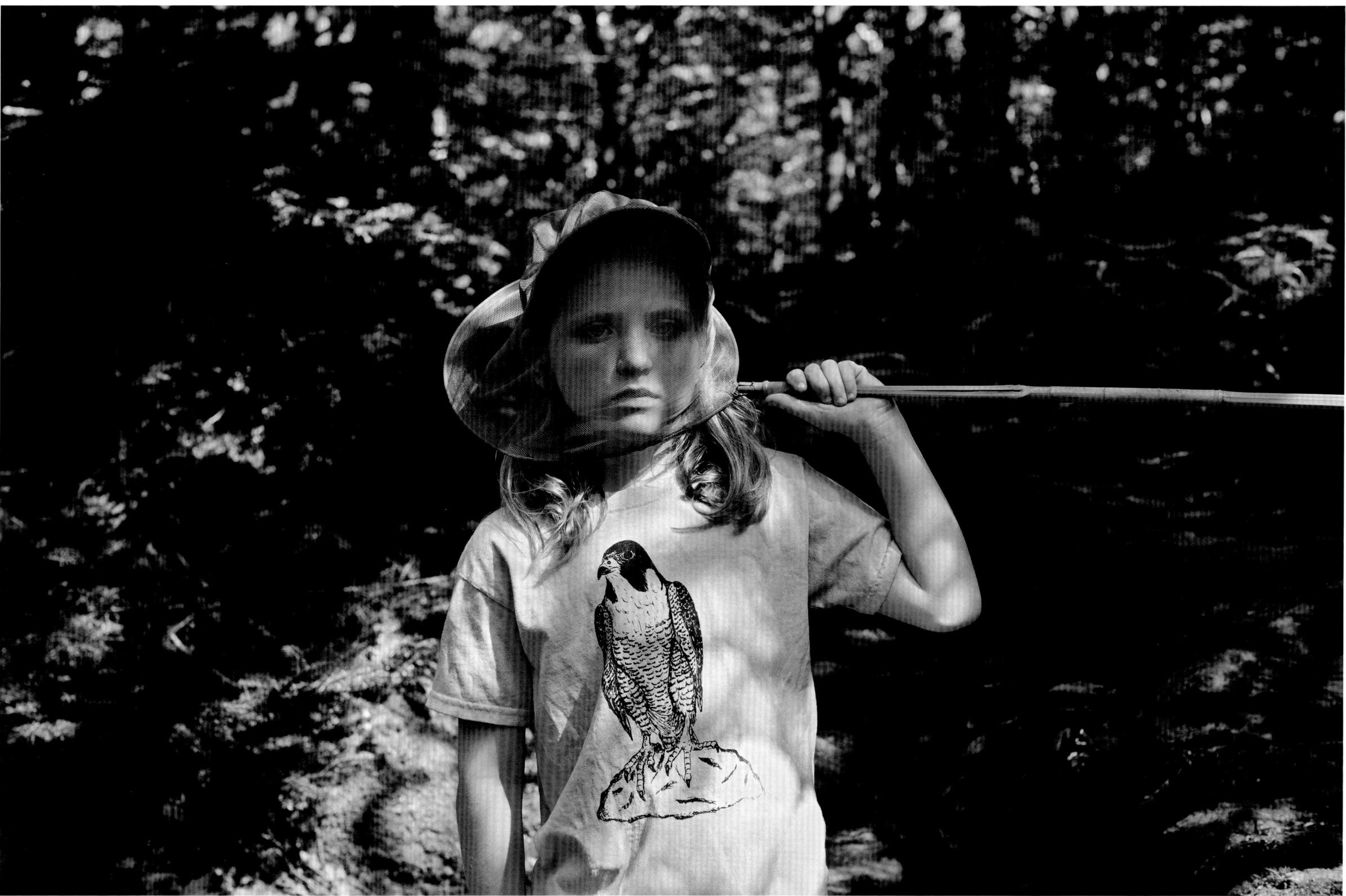

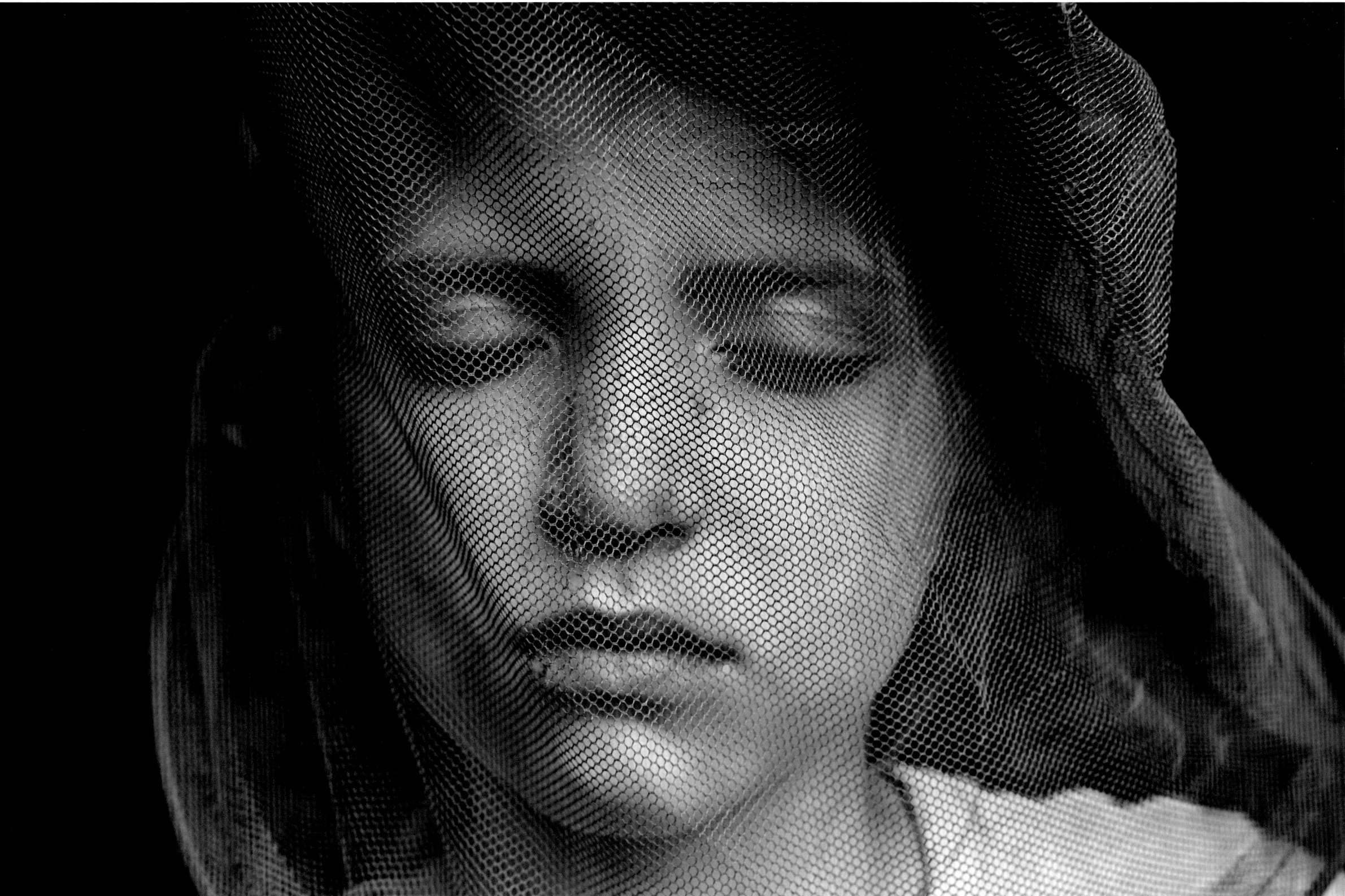

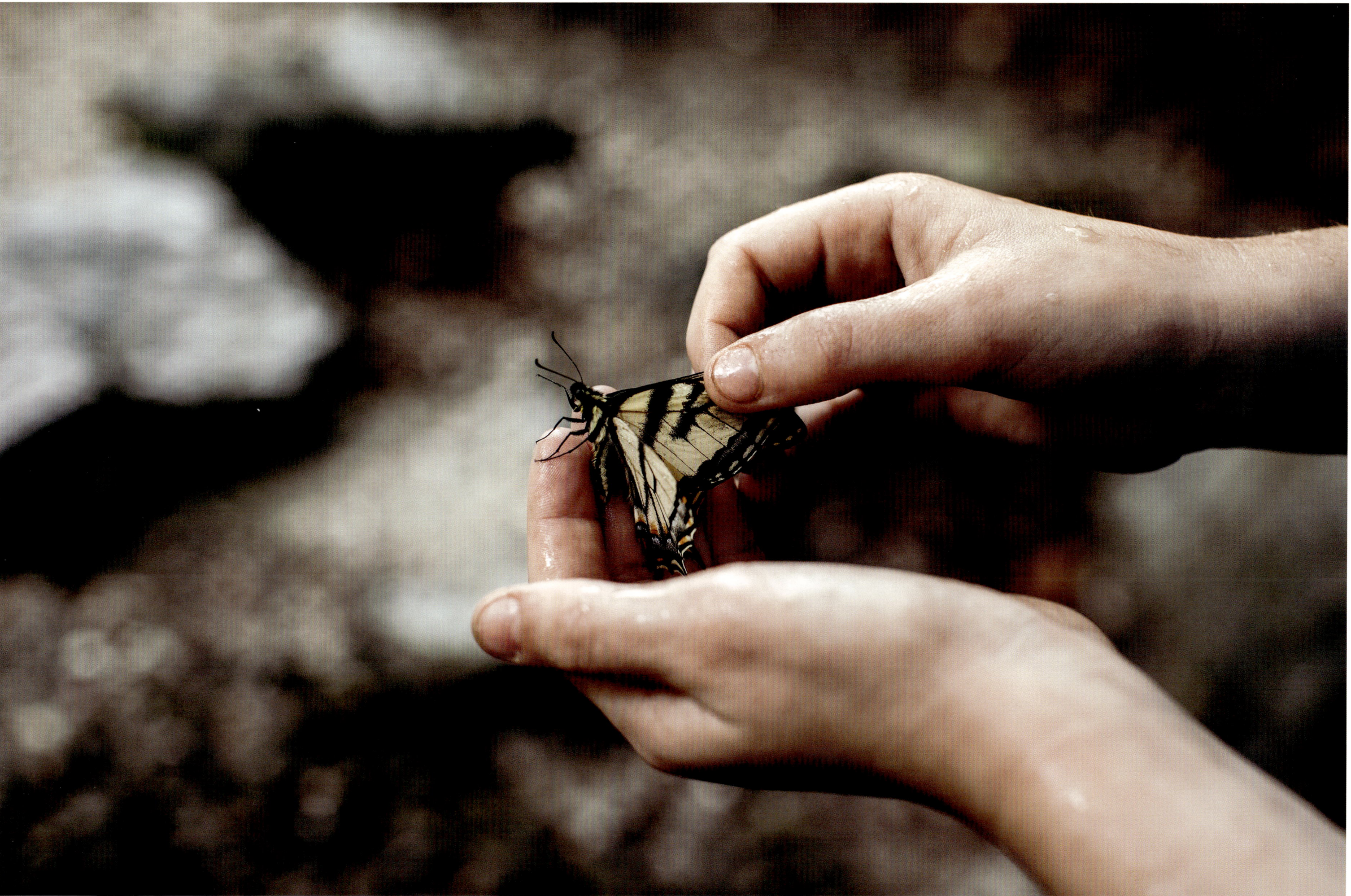

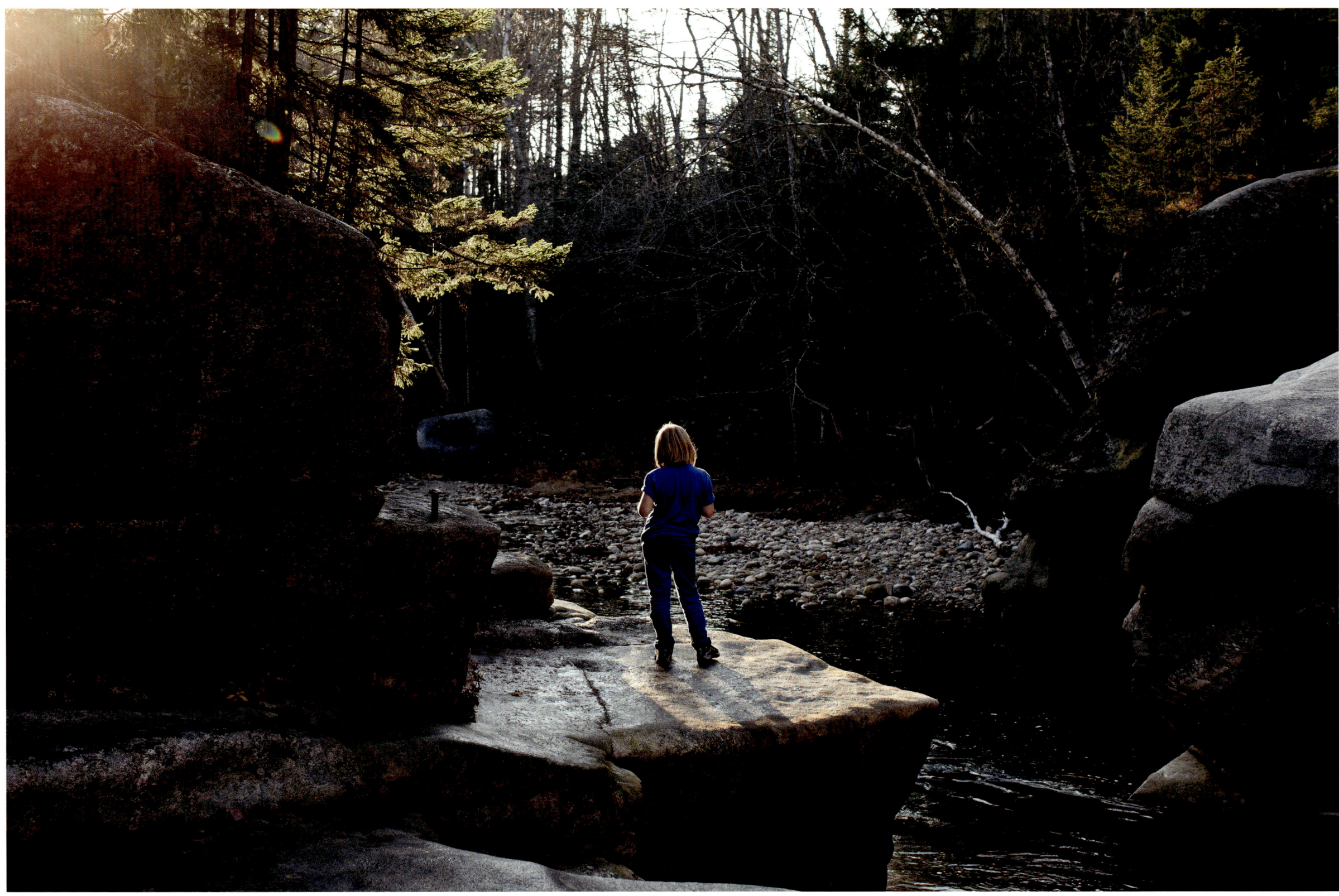

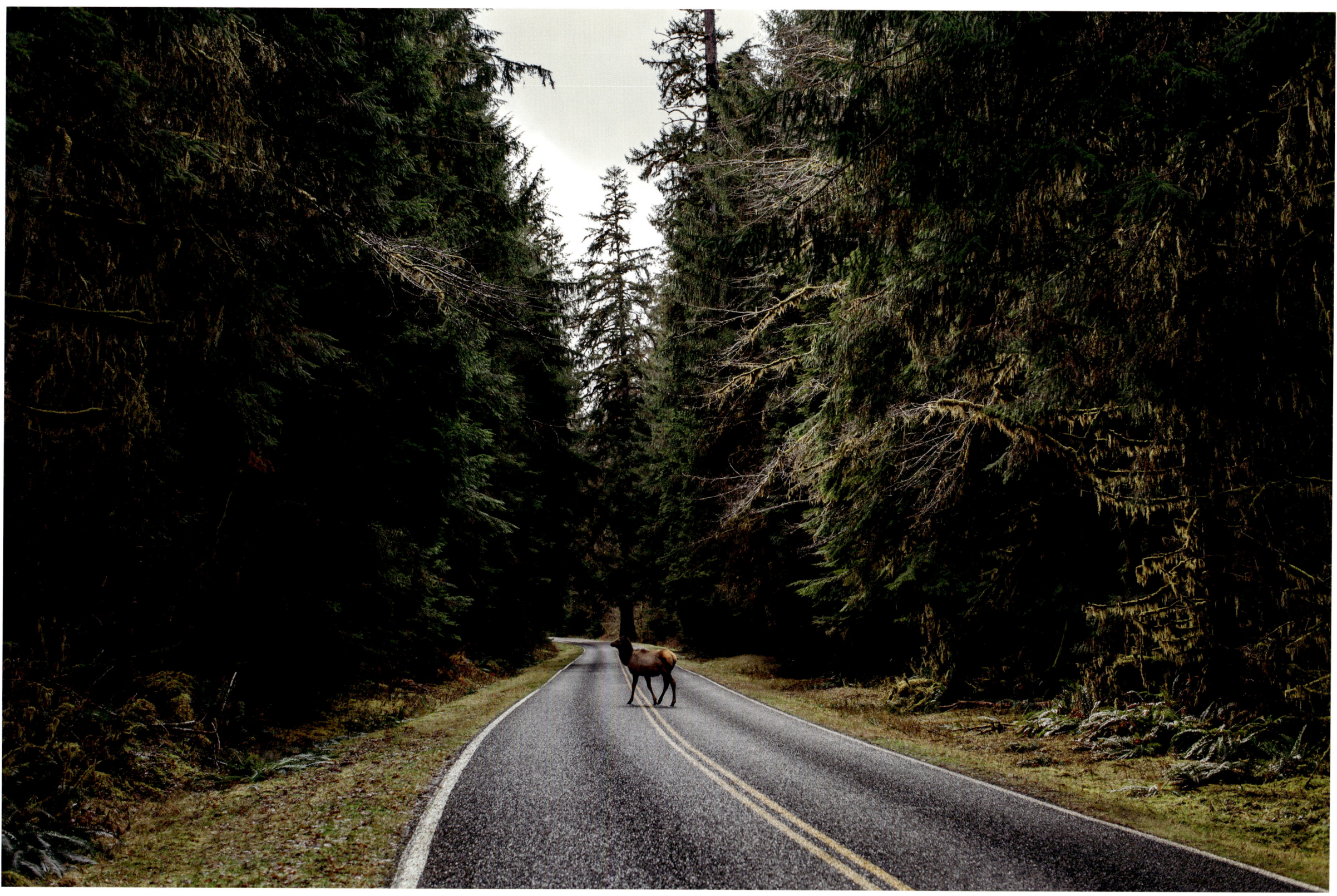

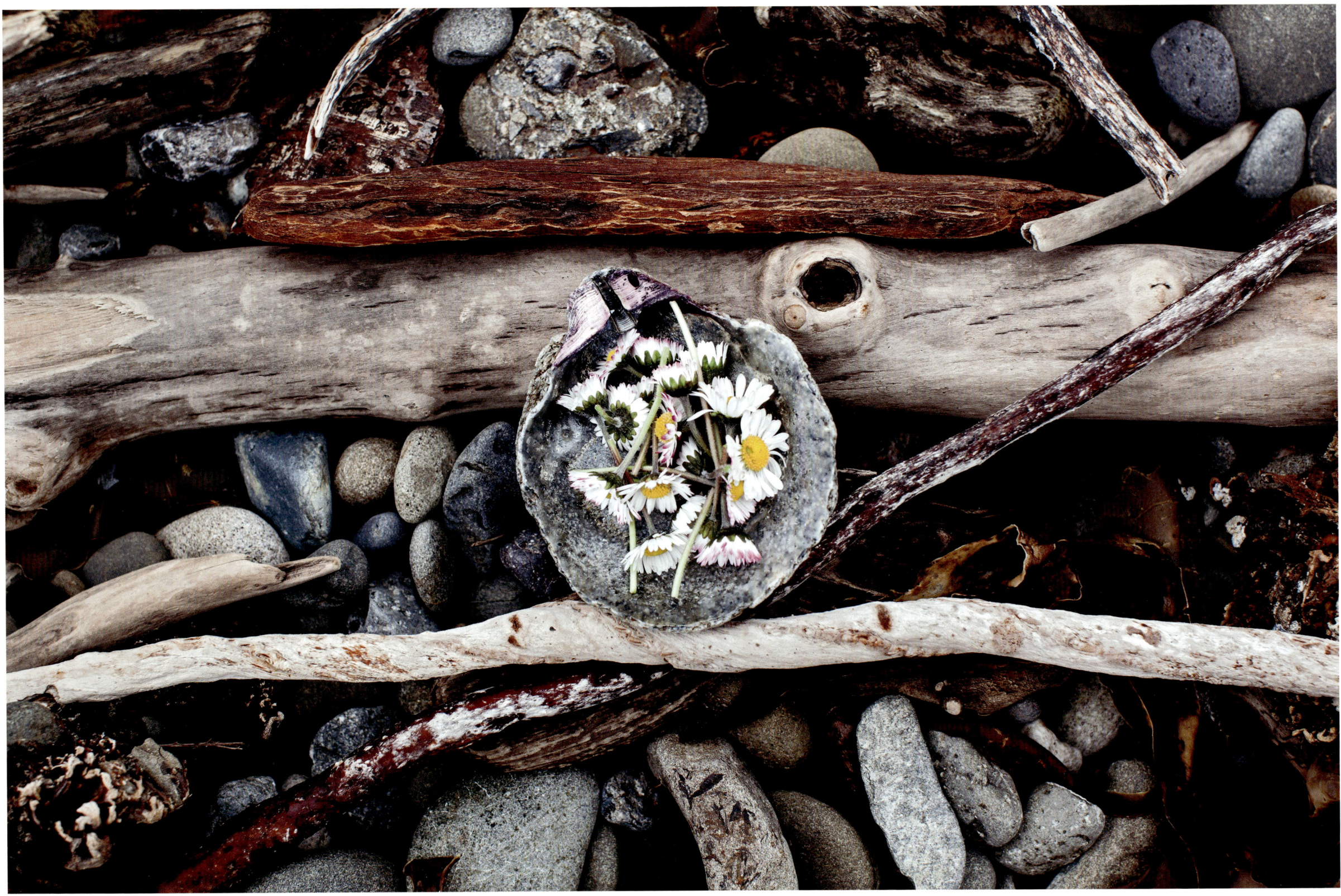

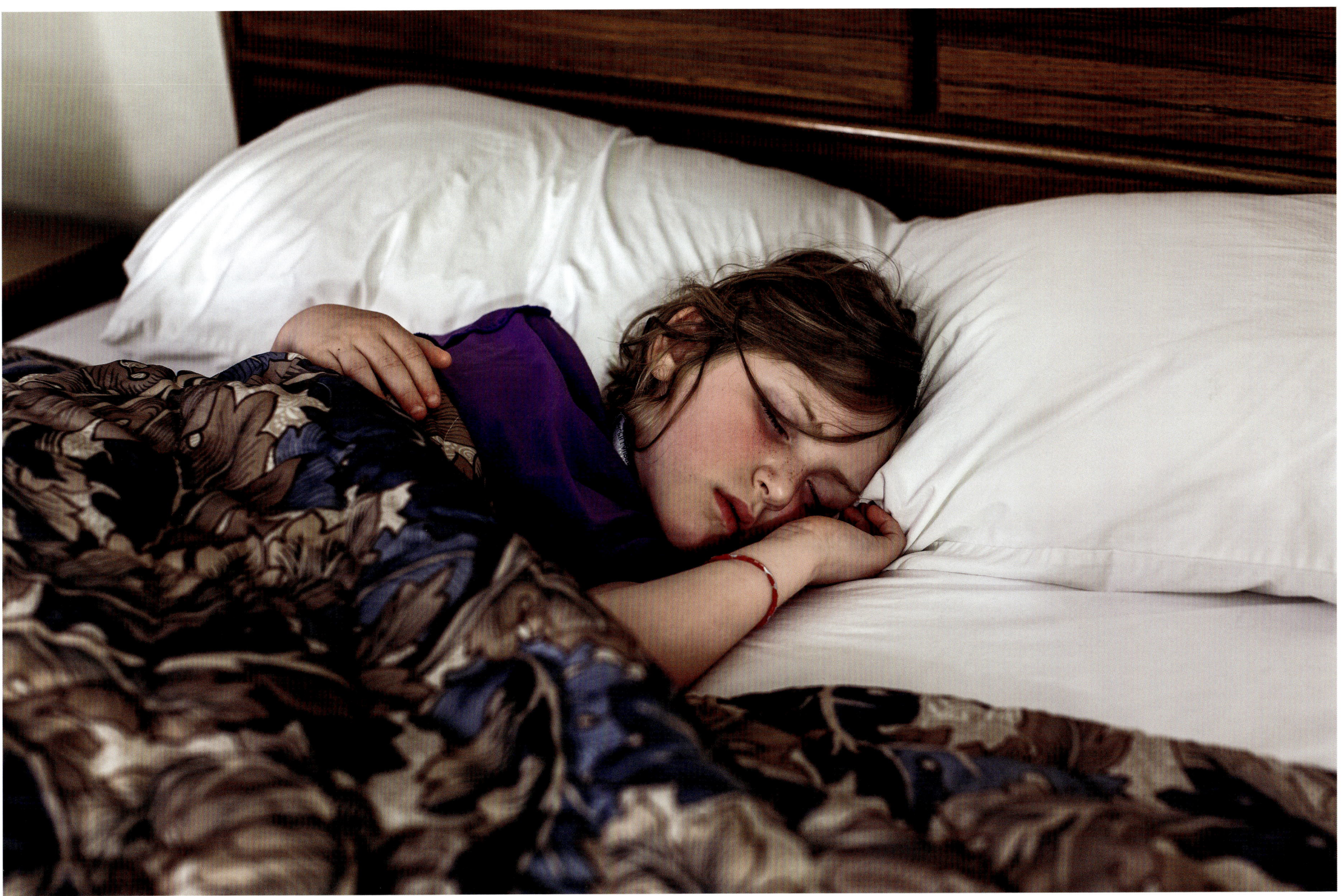

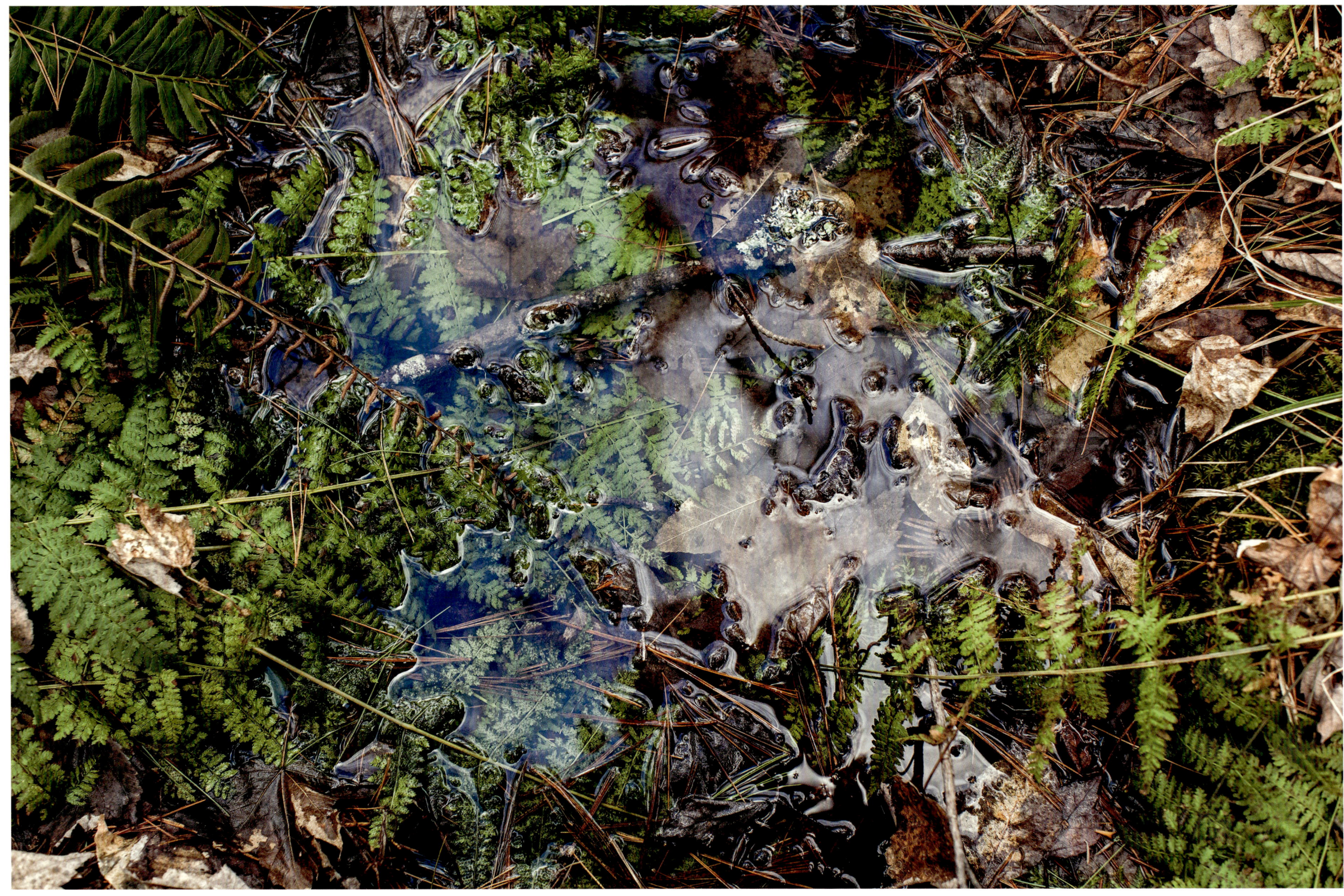

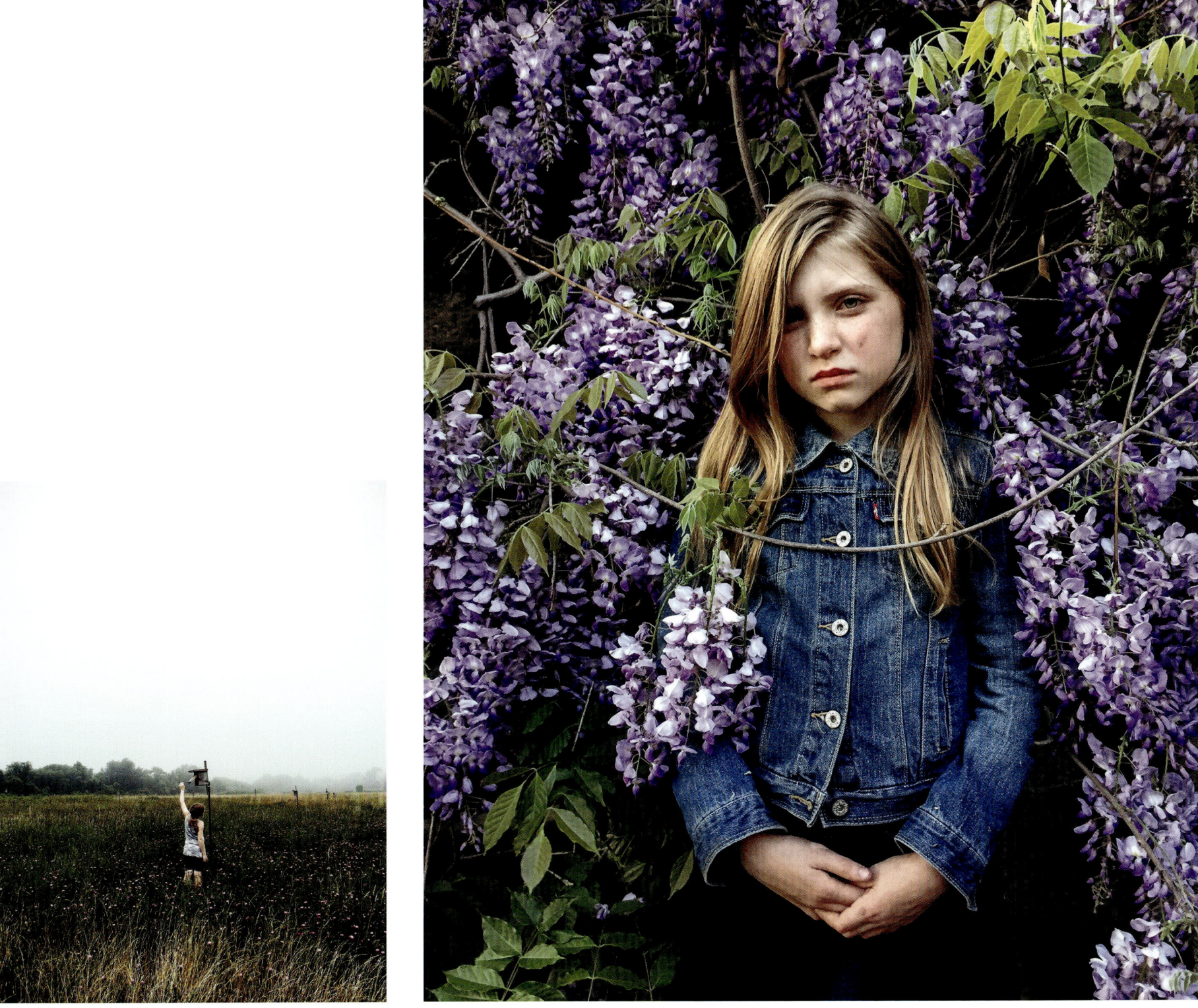

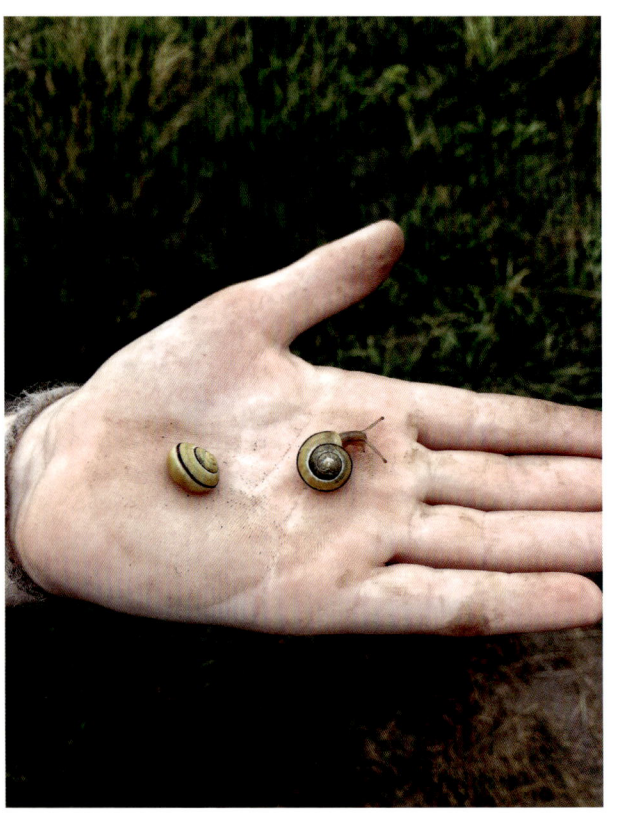

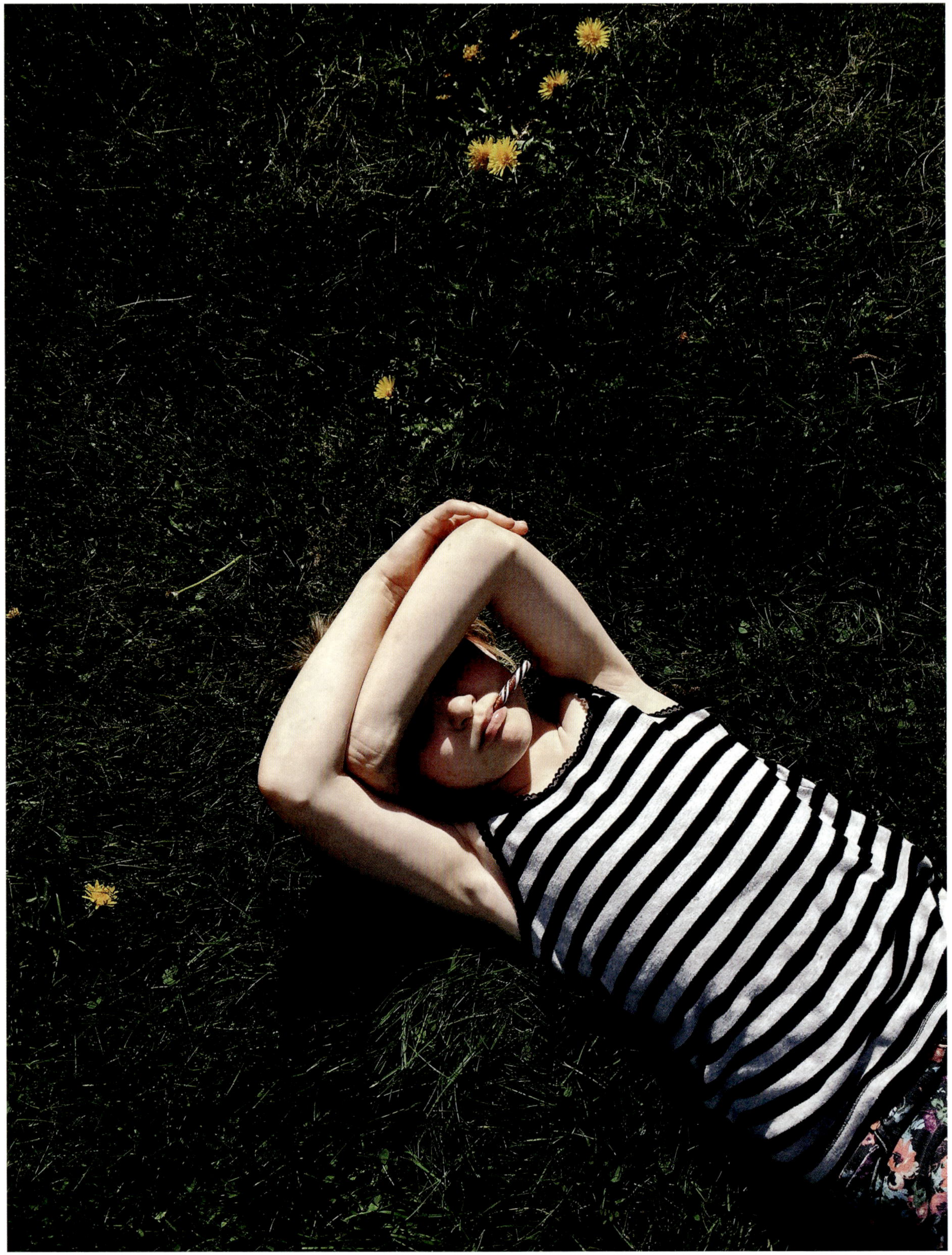

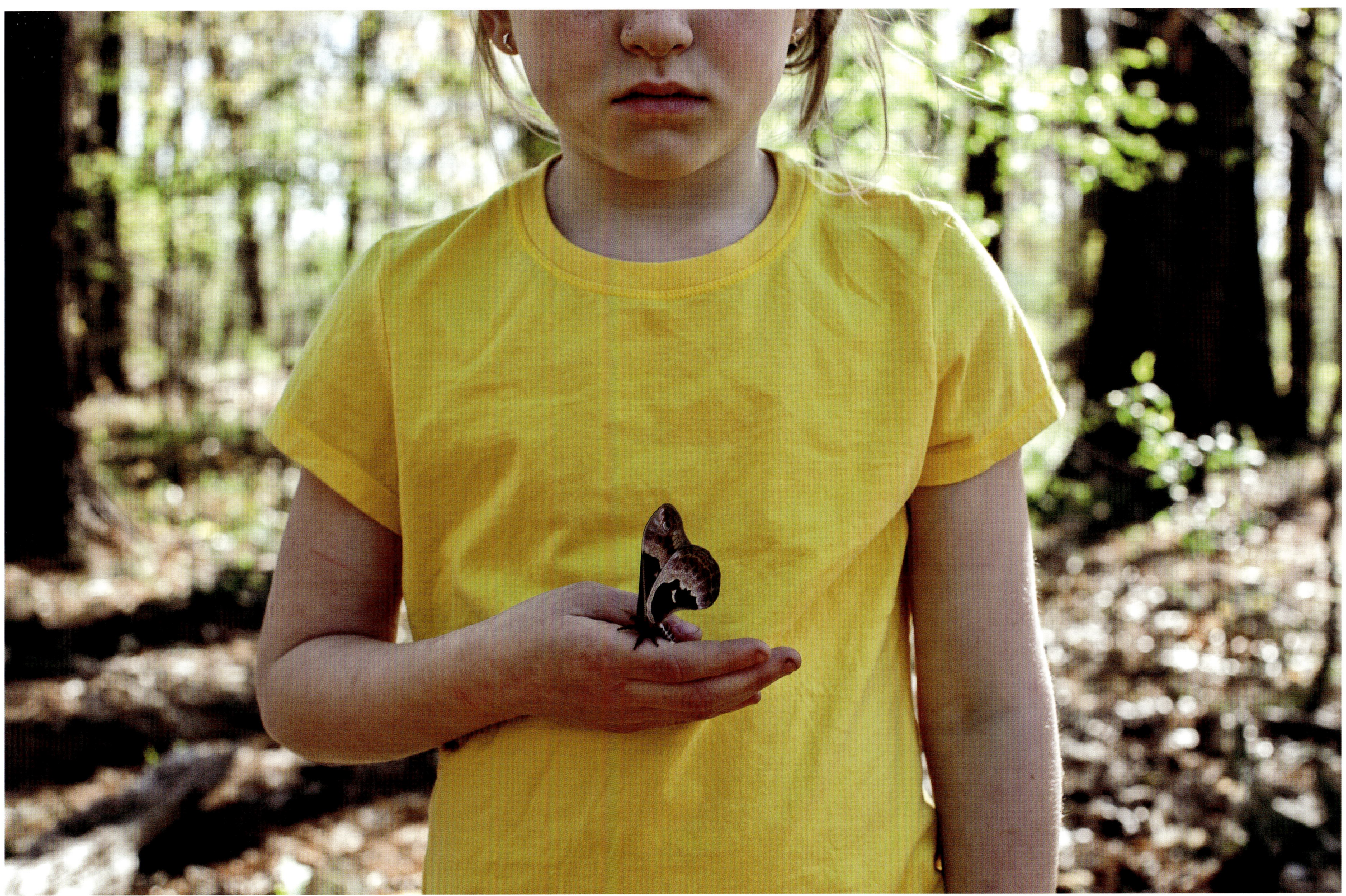

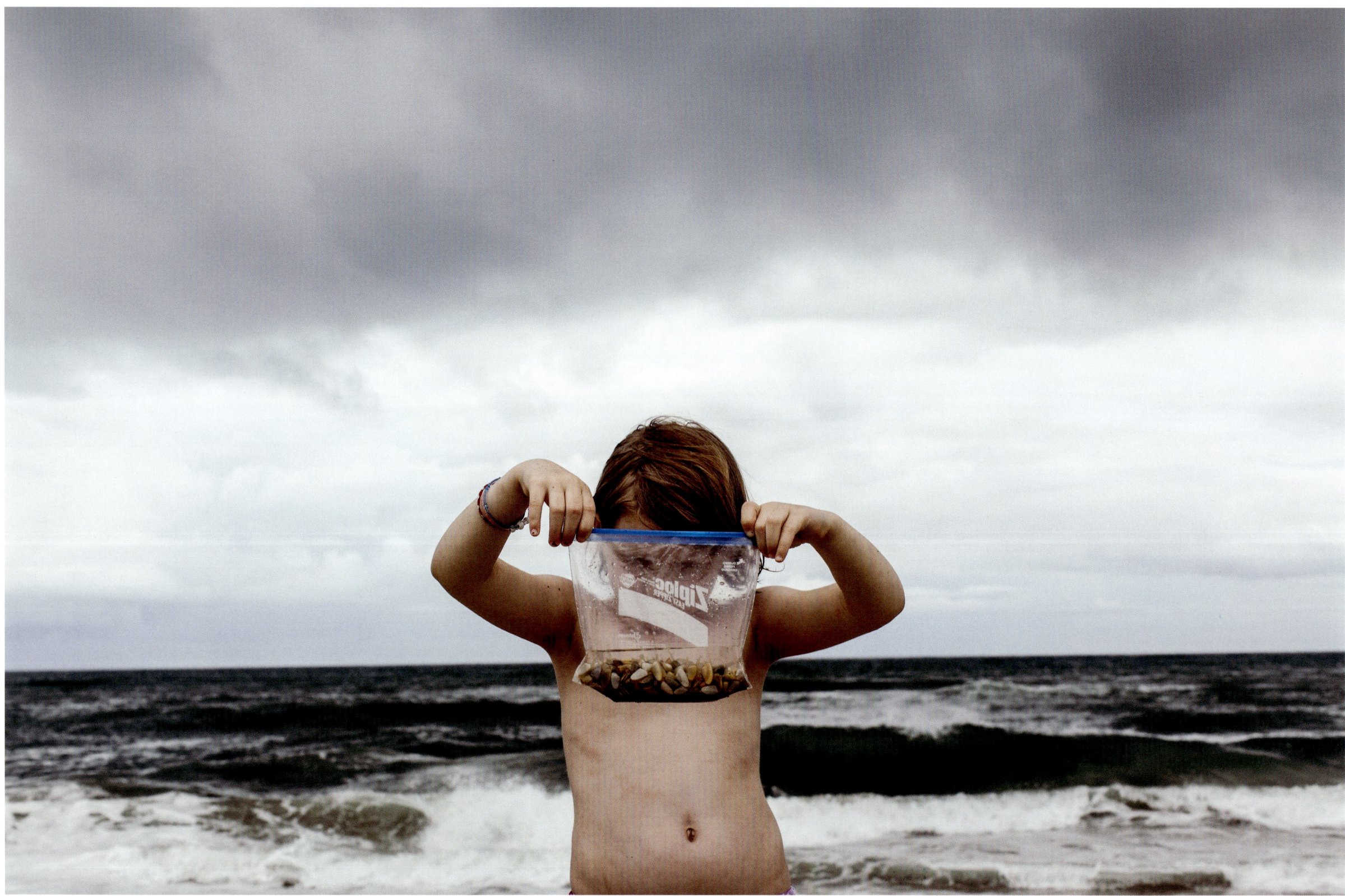

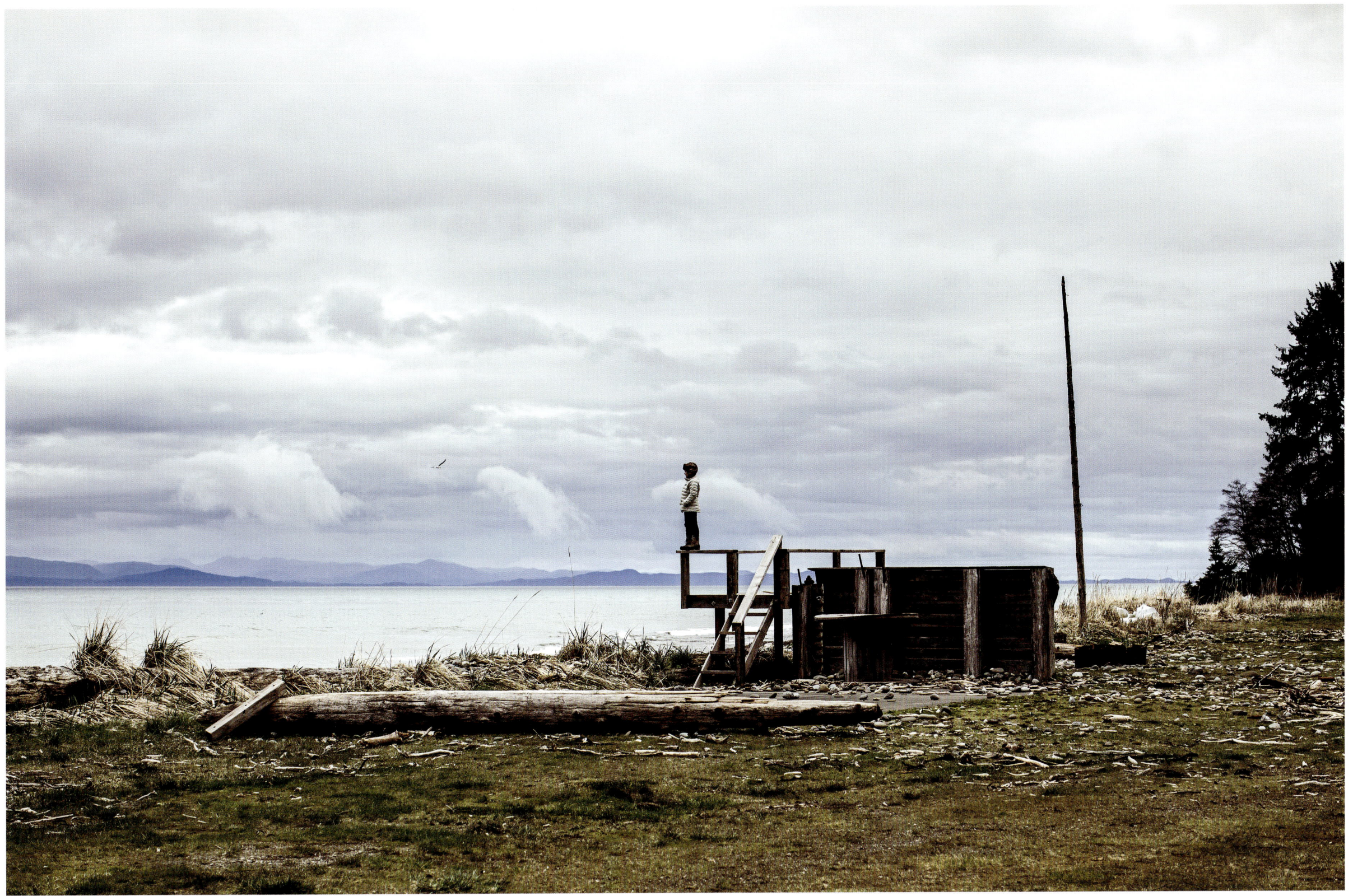

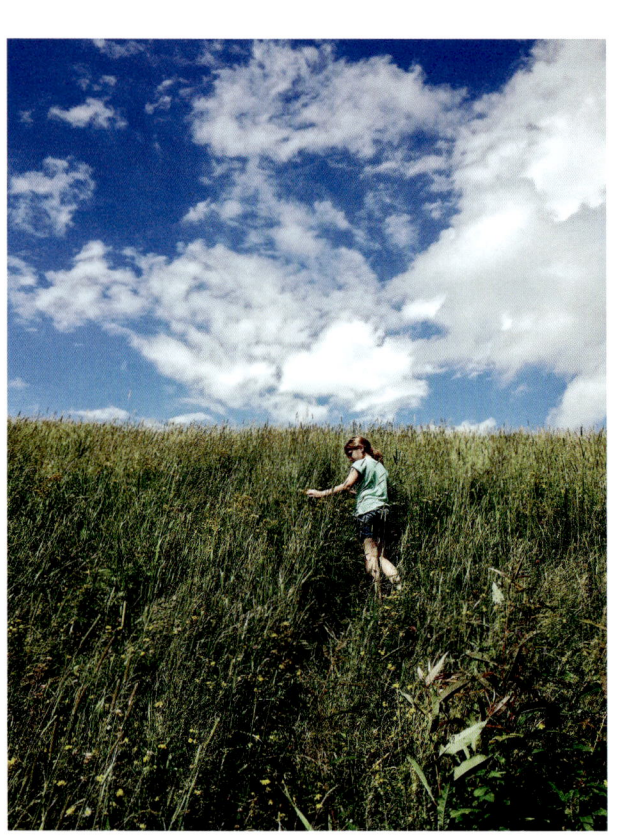

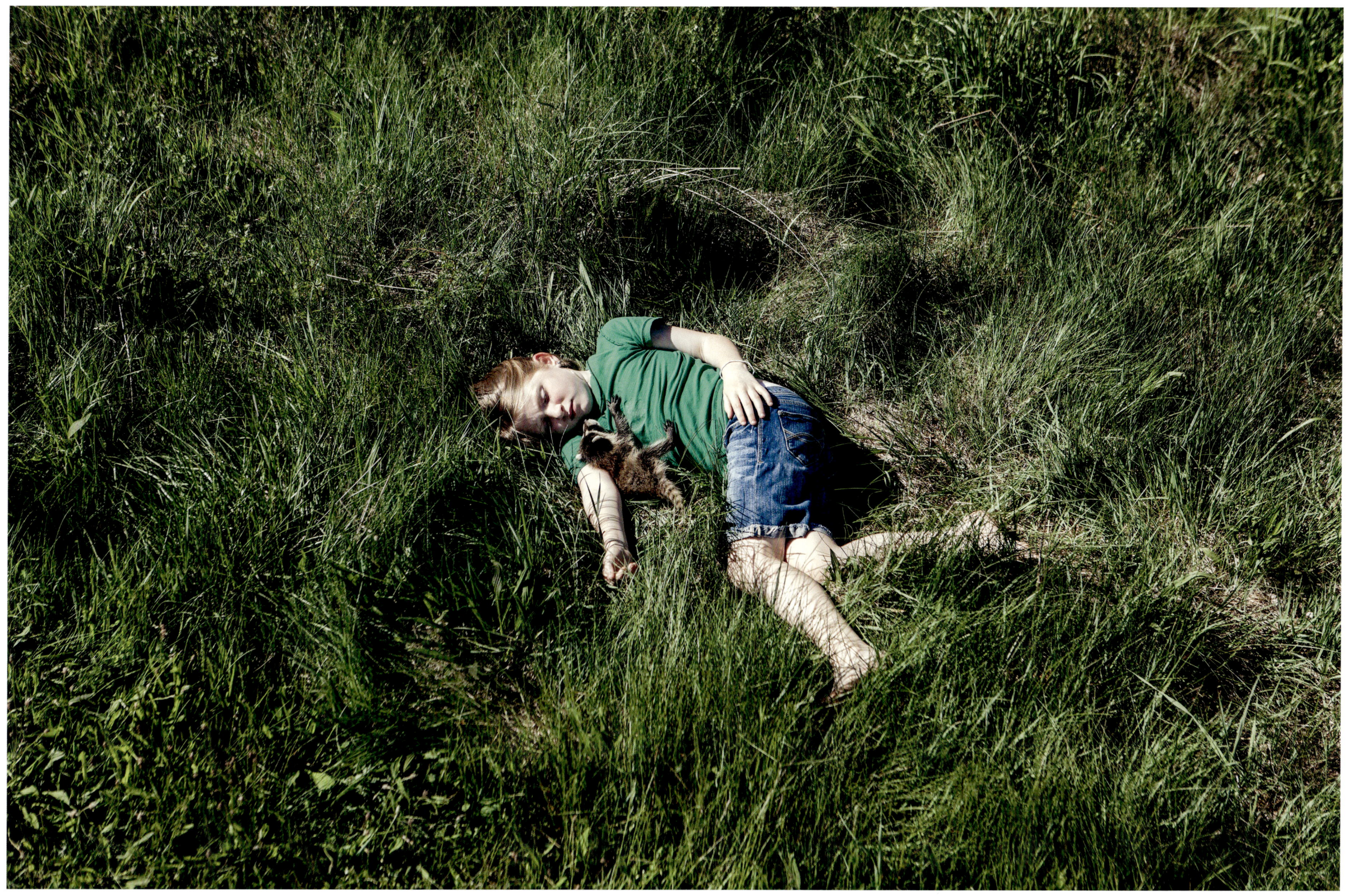

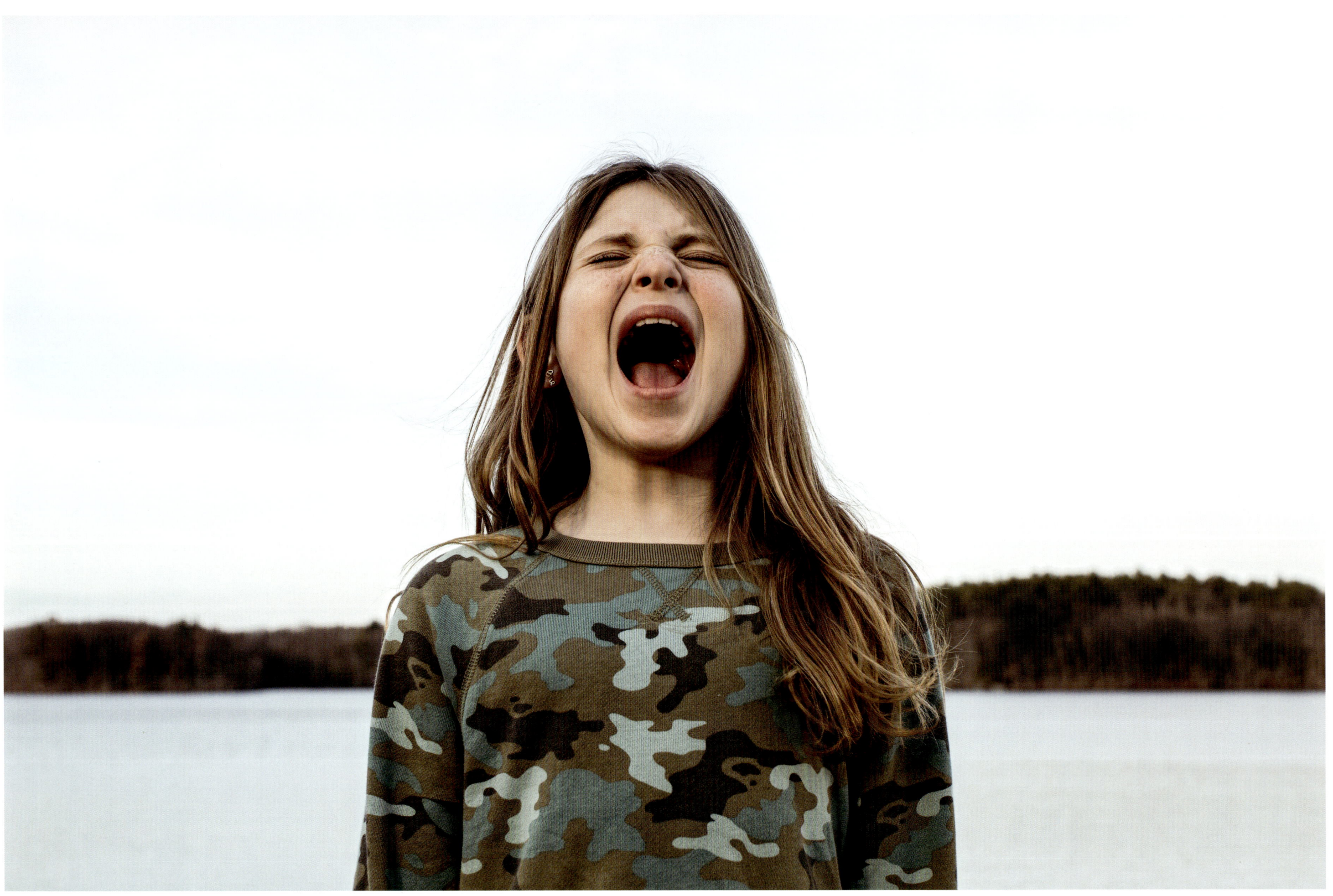

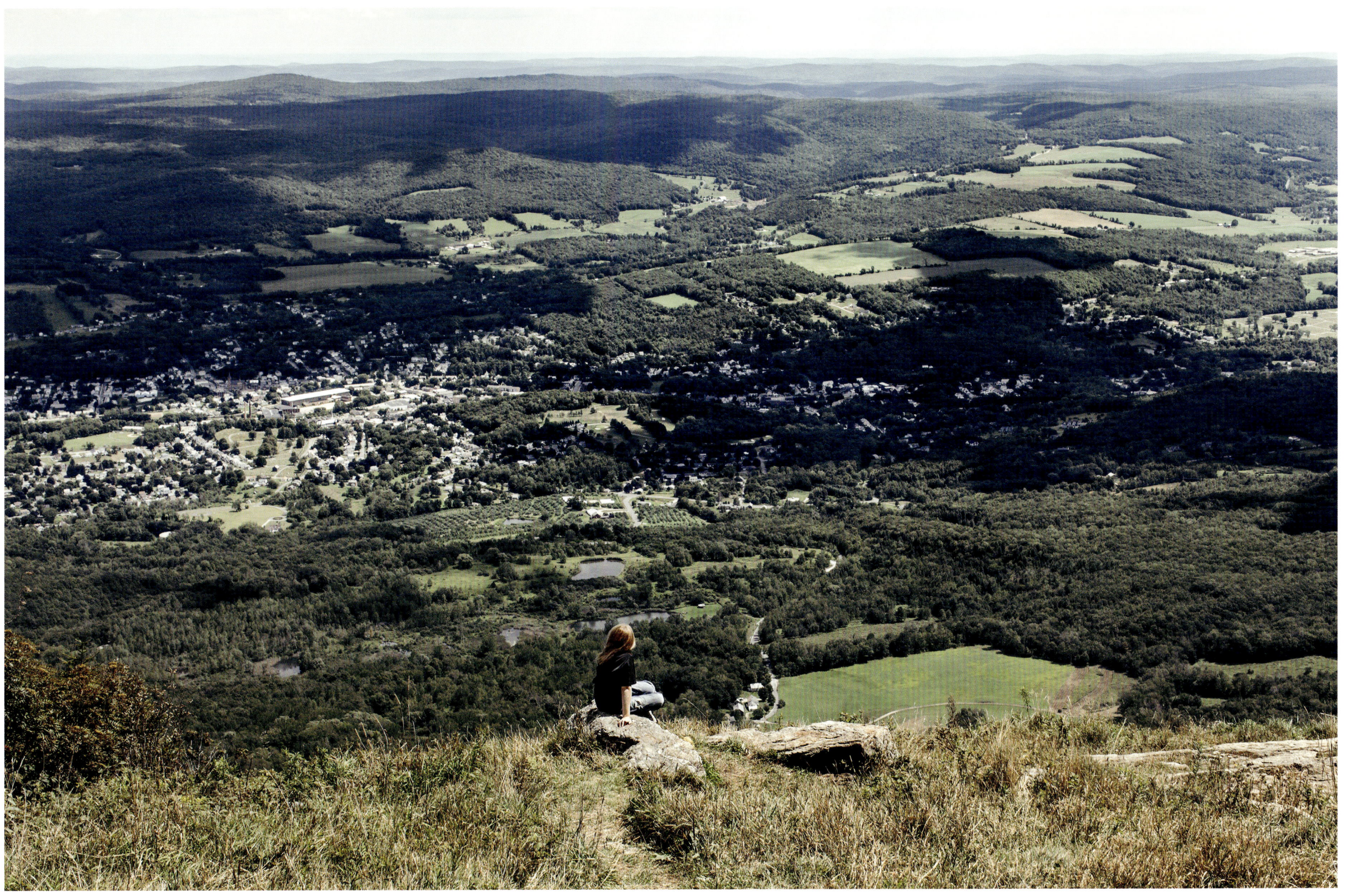

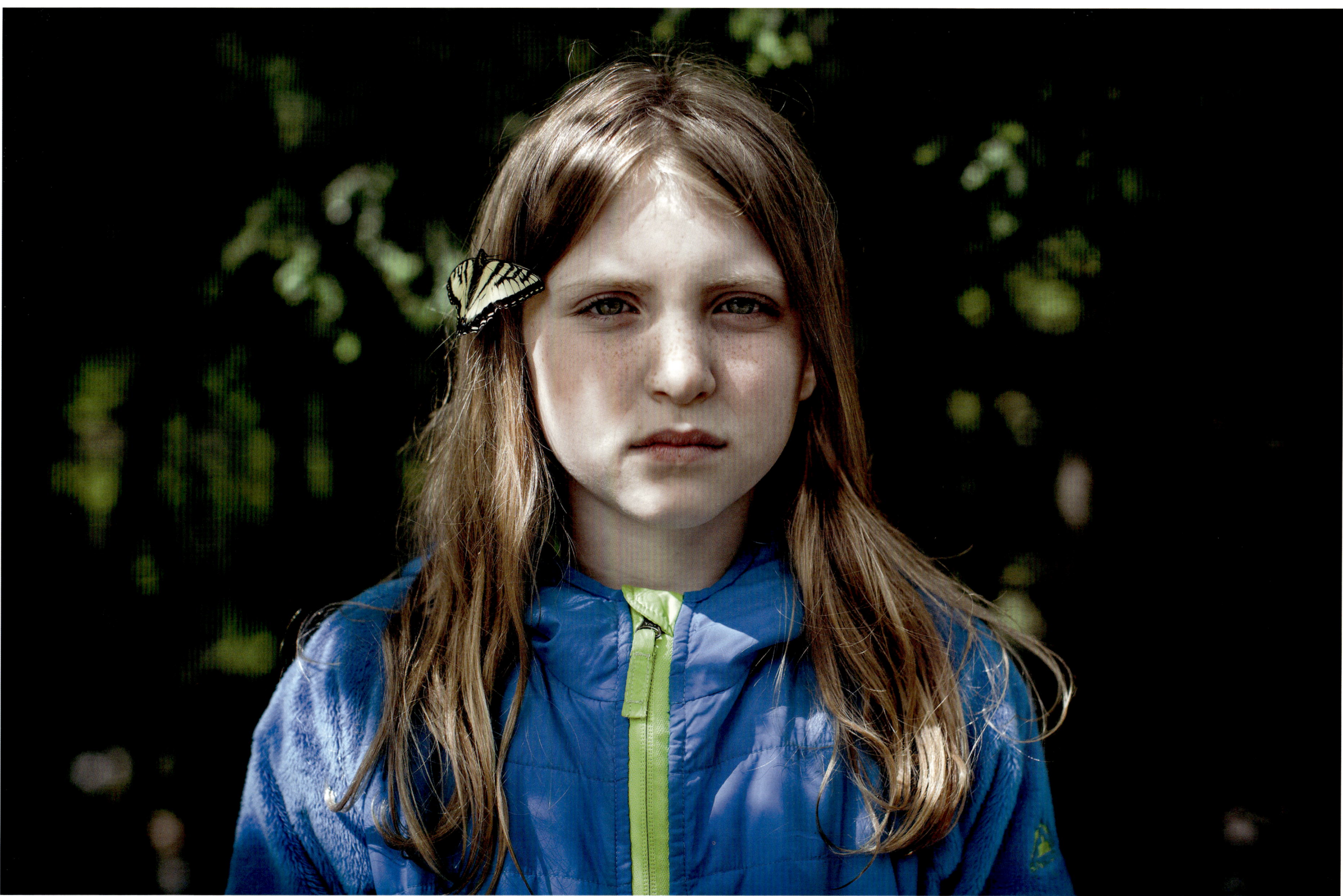

I love our road trips and thinking about all the things we've done together. I remember the time we heard a mountain lion cry like an old man in the woods and the time we heard a bear huffing in Vermont. I felt so nervous, but it was amazing to hear them. There are so many things to listen to out in the world, like woodpeckers, owls, and coyotes. Sometimes I get afraid of the animals in the dark, but you always make me feel safe and I know that you will always protect me. You aren't afraid of anything.

We have spent a lot of time exploring the woods and beaches. We've held animals like birds, bunnies, salamanders, and insects. Normally, I would never get to touch an owl. I remember seeing the dead whale and how bad it smelled. I love the treasures we collect along the way, things like baleen, feathers, shark teeth, fox tails, shells and bones, and jars of water from the rivers. I love animals and being out in nature, it's like my second home.

I think about the time we followed the moose tracks to the top of Cannon Mountain and warmed up with hot chocolate at the hiker's shack. I remember the time we crossed the border to Canada and heard the fishermen speaking French. I was really excited. We have been to so many places together, Daddy. We saw elk in the road in the Hoh Rain Forest. Do you remember that I was able to pet his fur? He was like a deer but bigger. I made a video of them walking and eating grass while you were taking pictures. We were a team.

As we drive along I usually talk with you, sing, and read my books. I look around and watch for animals and new places to explore. I am always so happy to travel with you, Daddy. It makes me feel excited, proud, and brave to have accomplished something with you. I hope we can continue to keep exploring new places together. I can't wait to teach my sisters all that I've learned. Thank you for helping me to build my confidence and teaching me new things. It's fun when I can teach you things, too.

I love you, Nature Buddy.

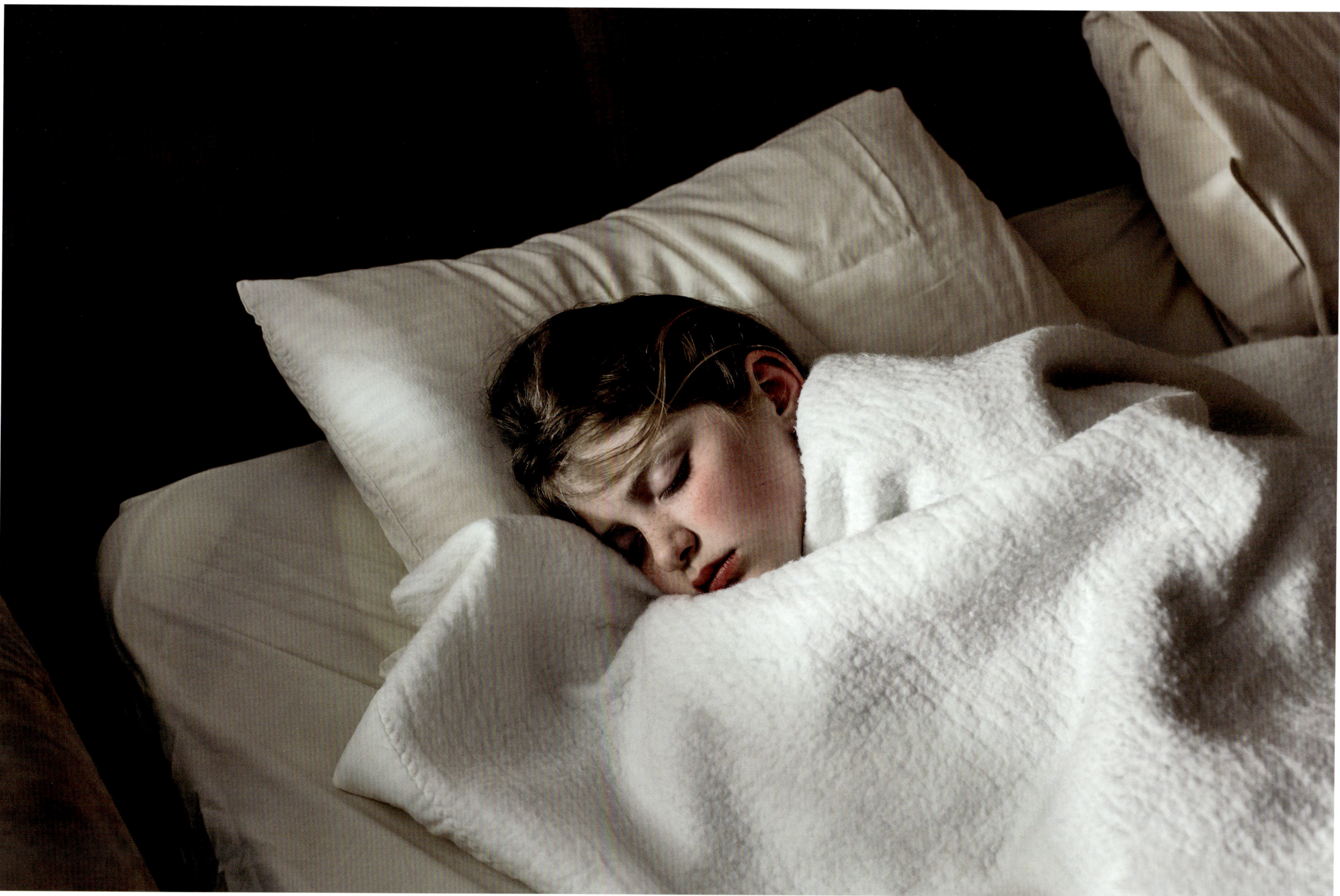

LEAVES, DIRT, AND WOODSMOKE

Yesterday I walked in the woods below our home in northern Vermont. Ostensibly I was hunting mushrooms—it is early August, the heart of chanterelle season—but, of course, the mushrooms were merely an excuse, something tangible I could exploit to justify my wandering. I would bring them home in the pouch of my shirt or in the turned-over hollow of my cap, proof of time well spent.

I had been in the woods for only a dozen minutes or so before I came across a crude shelter. It was one of the first my sons had made, back before they learned to orient the opening to the south to catch the sun's rays, and I was surprised to find it still standing. I remembered when they built it; it must have been four years ago at least. Maybe five. They made the sloped walls of sticks gathered from the forest floor and covered them with a thick layer of leaves to keep the water out. That winter, I slept in the shelter with my younger son. It was just big enough for the two of us. In the middle of the night, I was wakened by snow drifting through the doorway and landing on my face.

My boys are now 12 and 9. They have built more shelters than I can count, more than I even know of. I stumble across them frequently, artifacts of my sons' childhood, and when I do, I like to pause for a minute to think of my boys during the act of construction. What did they talk about? What stories did they imagine, and how did the shelter fit into those stories? I know they often carried their bows, hatchets, and fishing poles with them. I know they built fire rings to cook the brook trout they caught. I know they often spoke of staying in the woods for days on end. I know they were always home by bedtime, their skin smelling of leaves, dirt, and woodsmoke, their hands smelling of fish guts.

Children need nature. Research shows that children who feel connected to the wild do better in school and have increased self-esteem, that they are more sensitive to the needs of others and to nature itself. The list goes on.

But even more than the studies, I believe what I see and feel, and that is why the images in this book are so important. They are important in the same way my sons' rustic shelters and all the imagining they give rise to are so important: they serve as evidence of the eternal link between humankind and nature. You see them and you do not have to stop and think about whether or not this link matters. You do not have to consider the metrics and measurements, that kids who spent *this* much time in the wild do *this* much better in school or have *that* much lower incidence of stress. You just know.

As a writer, I am loath to believe the adage that a photograph is worth a thousand words. But in the case of Jesse Burke's work chronicling his daughter Clover's evolving relationship with the natural world, I'm ready to accept that perhaps some images carry the weight of a thousand words. Maybe even more. They do this not because they convey information—always a flimsy foundation upon which to build a relationship—but because they foment feeling.

My boys don't build as many shelters as they used to. They have moved on to other wilderness pursuits. Like me, they are fond of gathering wild mushrooms and other edibles. They hunt and fish and trap. They spend hours each day in the fields and forest surrounding our home. They talk about Alaska and the northernmost reaches of Quebec, where the lakes are free of motorboats and the woods are full of bear and moose. They're going, is what they say. Just as soon as they can drive.

Will they go? Who knows? So much can change. But when I think of their inevitable departure, be it to Alaska or Los Angeles, I am comforted by the knowledge that I'll still be able to walk down into our woods, to where their simple shelters are slowly returning to the ground, humble artifacts of their childhood. Maybe I'll find more structures that I hadn't even known existed. Maybe I'll stand for a moment, imaging their stories, those simple, timeworn narratives of children at home in the wild.

BEN HEWITT
Author of *Home Grown: Adventures in Parenting off the Beaten Path, Unschooling, and Reconnecting with the Natural World*

AT HOME IN THE WILD

Jesse Burke and his 9-year-old daughter, Clover, have been taking trips into nature for five years, fitting them into their busy lives as best they can. Most often they leave their suburban Rhode Island home and spend four or five days on the road exploring state parks, forest preserves, rivers, and beaches throughout New England. Sometimes the two just pick a heavily green area on the map and drive to it, letting the landscape surprise them. Occasionally they journey farther afield. They usually hike for a few hours a day and sometimes sleep in a tent. Mostly they just hang out, play, and meander, as Burke photographs. He didn't plan for these sojourns into the wilderness to become a regular pastime, but once he saw how much Clover was benefiting from their travels, he made them a priority.

Unlike Clover's usual experience of being a child in the suburbs, when she and her father are in nature she roams freely. Burke admits to harboring a fantasy of the "wild child" as he observes her— existing in nature alone, small and vulnerable but also courageous and, in his words, "not afraid of animals or the dark, but living as one with them."[1] He often sees evidence of Clover's wild side: she holds dead animals, gets dirty, acts rowdy, and relies on instinct—like when a huge elk swam toward her as she stood quietly at a river's edge. As poet Gary Snyder has eloquently written, "Our bodies are wild. The involuntary quick turn of the head at a shout, the vertigo of looking off a precipice, the heart-in-the-throat in a moment of danger, the catch of the breath, the quiet moments of relaxing, staring, reflecting—all universal responses of this mammal body."[2]

Our mammal bodies benefit greatly from being immersed in nature. Numerous studies support the belief that exposure to nature is important to a child's development intellectually, emotionally, socially, and physically. Researchers have concluded that children who attend nature kindergarten, for example, have better corporeal awareness, are more alert, and establish games based less on social hierarchies and skill and more on creativity and imagination.[3] Time spent in nature may also help provide resistance against negative stresses and depression.[4] Yet recent research indicates that children around the globe are spending less and less time in natural environments.[5] This shift away from the outdoors is coupled with an increasing societal perception of nature as unsafe and parents who cite crime and safety concerns as primary reasons for not allowing their children to play outdoors.[6] When children are outside today, it tends to be on playgrounds or asphalt surfaces or through participation in organized sports. Free-range play in nature is a rarity for most of them. As writer Richard Louv has observed, ironically children are increasingly aware of global threats to the environment and issues of conservation, yet their direct contact with nature has been sharply reduced in recent decades.[7] This divide has its consequences.

Although not initially motivated by such concerns, Burke has learned to heed them and to cherish the joy and creativity he sees in Clover when she is outdoors. He has also learned to use the free-spirited character she exhibits there to his artistic advantage—something that was initially at odds with his habit of carefully orchestrating his pictures. Once while in Canada, Burke pulled over at a beautiful beach, excited about the fading light and a swath of fog hanging over the sand. Clover wasn't in the mood to model so instead goofed off, constantly twirling and spinning in some left-behind fishing rope. Burke became annoyed because the light was quickly disappearing and Clover wouldn't stop moving or take his direction. Later that evening, he was surprised by how many of the photographs from the beach had turned out well. He realized that the key to working with Clover was to allow her to feel liberated—to think of the project as a collaboration in which her natural actions and decisions would provide some of the best material for his camera. In his words, "The true power in this project is Clover's ability to take what I show her and to react to it and apply it to the world in her own special way. That's what I document."[8] To this day, a picture of Clover from that shoot, *I Shall Be Free* (2012), is one of Burke's favorites.

To illustrate Clover's synergy with nature, Burke often records her in peaceful, pastoral settings, looking contemplative and wise. Alternately, he juxtaposes Clover with scenes that imply danger and human fragility, such as a heavily leaning tree or even a paper mill ejecting steam from its smokestacks, an image that is included both for its foreboding atmosphere and its backstory—when she first saw it, Clover asked her father, "Is that where clouds are made?"

Over the years, the naïveté and perceived innocence of children have made them good accomplices to photographers who are looking to understand the fraught relationship between humans and the natural world. Some who have had an influence on Burke include Sally Mann, who in the 1990s used her two daughters and son to explore the inherent sensuality of children and received criticism for depicting them as they played naked in the yard outside her rural Virginia home. Emmet Gowin's pictures of his wife, Edith, and her family posing in nature and exhibiting animal-like expressions and poses in the 1960s and '70s are edgy and disturbing. And in the 1950s, Wynn Bullock made classically beautiful images of his daughters in the forest and on beaches to underscore our basic human connection to nature. Bullock's iconic photograph *Lynne, Point Lobos* (1956), for example, deliberately evokes the idea of the wild child, and by placing his daughter Lynne in contrast to the crashing waves and rock outcroppings, Bullock created an image that arguably has less to do with portraiture than with symbolism. Bullock's wise words can perhaps provide the best insight on his intentions: "I disagree with the belief that nature was only made for the use of people. Human beings are not the center of the universe, and, if they are to sustain themselves, it is vitally important for them to be awakened to how closely they are linked with the rest of nature."[9]

Like Bullock, Burke uses his daughter to symbolize our fundamental human connection to the wild and to consider our inherently animal nature. Burke's previous photographic project, *Intertidal* (2004–2010), also has this sort of inquiry at its core. In this work, he investigates what it means to be masculine, depicting the tension between human vulnerability and the prevailing narrative of male gruffness and power. Like *Wild & Precious*, this project probes ideas about identity and seeks to determine what is inherent, or natural, and what is acquired, or learned. Since creating *Intertidal*, Burke has become a father to three girls. So today he is immersed in femininity and the perplexing questions of nature versus nurture that accompany parenthood.

Now that Clover's younger sister Poppy has turned 4, she has begun to accompany Clover and Burke on their outdoor adventures. The final image in the book, in fact, presents the two sisters, one already initiated into the realm of wilderness, one just beginning her education there. And it surely won't be long until their little sister, Honey Bee, age 2, joins her two sisters and their dad in the artful human experience—and portrayal—of nature's inimitable wonders.

KAREN IRVINE
Curator and associate director, Museum of Contemporary Photography at Columbia
College Chicago

NOTES
1. Email correspondence with the author.
2. Gary Snyder, *The Practice of the Wild* (San Francisco: North Point Press, 1990), 16.
3. Richard Louv, *Last Child in the Woods* (Chapel Hill: Algonquin Books, 2008), 88.
4. Louv, *Last Child in the Woods*, 35.
5. See, for example, the results of a global 2014 survey of parental concern about the amount of time their kids spend in nature: http://www.naturerocks.org/international-kids-and-nature-survey-summary-memo.pdf.
6. Cheryl Charles, "The Ecology of Hope: Reconnecting Children and Nature," *Living Green Magazine*, September 28, 2012, http://livinggreenmag.com/2012/09/28/mother-nature/the-ecology-of-hope-reconnecting-children-and-nature/.
7. Michael F. Shaughnessy, "An Interview with Richard Louv: About Nature Deficit Disorder," *Taproot Journal* 15, Fall/Winter 2005, no. 2.
8. Email correspondence with the author.
9. Wynn Bullock, http://www.wynnbullockphotography.com/quotes.html.

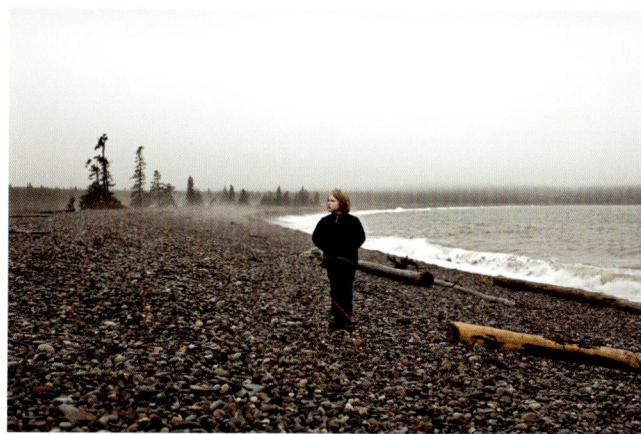

Jesse Burke, *I Shall Be Free* (2012)

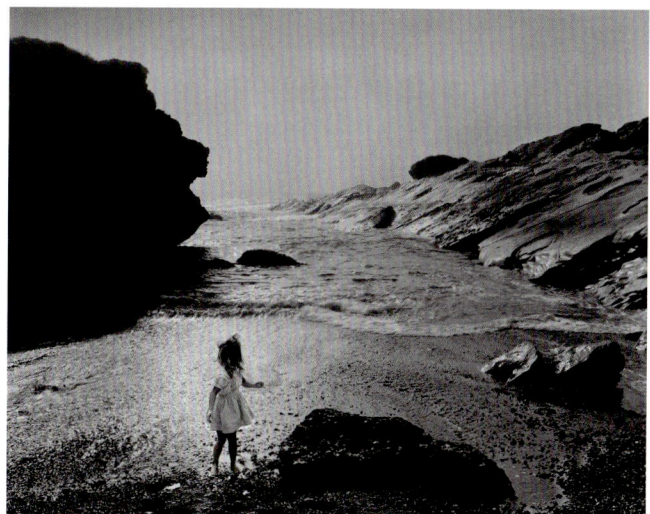

Wynn Bullock, *Lynne, Point Lobos* (1956)

Onward, hand in hand.

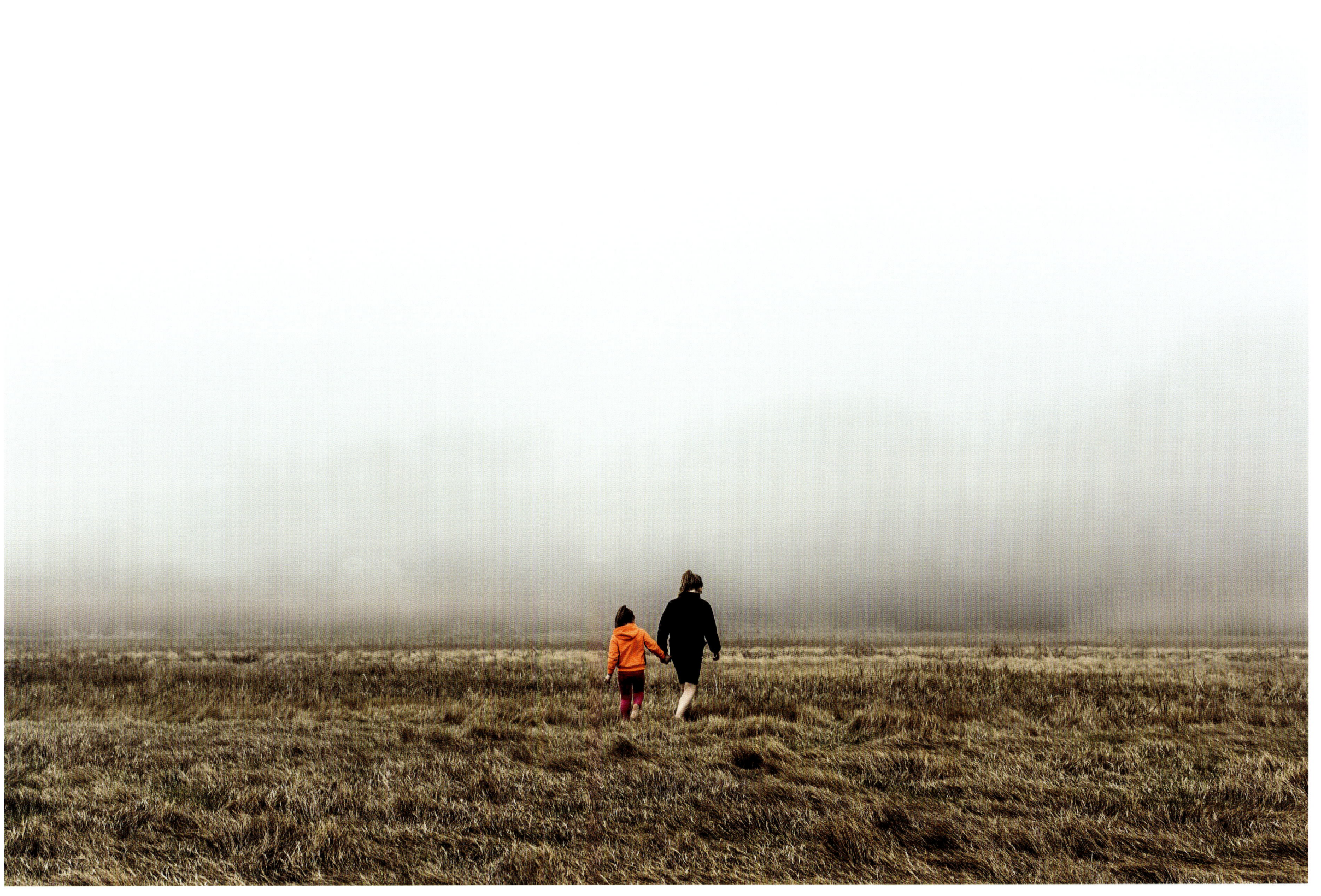

Each image title in *Wild & Precious* is named after a song that Johnny Cash wrote or recorded. His music and lyrics were a big part of our collective experience while on the road.

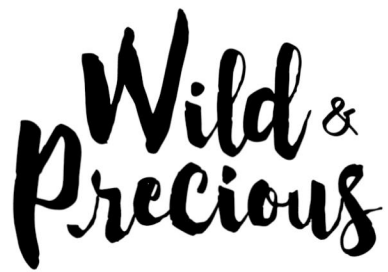

With Gratitude

To Kerry:
The backbone of my being is your love and understanding. You are
the rock upon which I stand, the sea upon which I float.

To my girls:
Your endless patience, inquisitive minds, and unconditional trust
bring me to my knees. This book is dedicated to you.

Many thanks to:
Daylight Books for their belief in my vision; Karen Irvine, Ben Hewitt,
and Dallas Clayton for their beautifully creative minds and words;
Alejandra Carles-Tolra and Nils Ericson for their insightful advice;
Jan Howard, Jo-Ann Conklin, Lizzie Fischbein, ClampArt, and
Platform Gallery for their continual support; Ursula Damm for
her aesthetic prowess; Steve Smith and Mark Doyle for their pixel
mastery; my family for their encouragement and love; John LaRosa
for his sweet soul and unyielding belief in me; and Carol Chernauskas
for her boundless strength and courage.

This book would not be possible without the generous patronage,
advocacy, and friendship of Dr. Joseph Chazan.

Cofounders: Taj Forer and Michael Itkoff
Design: Ursula Damm and Jesse Burke
Copy editor: Laura Fredrickson

ISBN 978-1-942084-11-2

Printed in Turkey, by Ofset Yapimevi

Daylight Books
E-mail: info@daylightbooks.org
www.daylightbooks.org
www.jesseburke.com